Great American Motorcycle Tours

of the West

W9-DIV-314

Gary McKechnie

Contents

Advice from a Road Scholar

The more you ride, the more you learn. A few decades on the road and several thousand miles in the saddle have given me some insights that may improve the quality of your own ride.

Even if you're in a hurry to reach Point B, try not to leave Point A after mid-afternoon. Chances are you'll be racing the sun and you'll miss the moments you're riding for. If you leave in the morning, you'll have a full day to make unscheduled stops and discover points of interest.

Don't run a marathon. While you could ride 600 miles a day, 200 miles max is easy and allows for unexpected discoveries.

If you get off-schedule, don't worry. The purpose of touring isn't to reach as many places as possible, it is to experience as many sensations and places as you can. Don't kill yourself with a self-inflicted plan.

Reward yourself. Every so often, stop at a place you don't think looks very interesting at first. Take a break and meditate.

Watch what's going on around you. A conversation with a general store clerk, a swim in a pond, or the sight of glistening pebbles in a riverbed can be just as pleasing as a good stretch of road.

In general, the best times I've found for riding are May and September. Nowhere is it too hot or too cold, kids are still in or headed back to school, and few places are charging peak season prices.

Have a contingency plan in case your day gets rained out. Write postcards; see a museum or a movie; read, rest, or go to the library; talk to locals. If a day gets screwed up by weather, roll with it.

Carry a few sealable plastic bags. Somehow rain can find wallets and you might want to stow that and any small electronics inside.

If you use a magnetic tank bag, don't toss your wallet in it. The powerful magnets that can withstand 90-mile-an-hour winds can also demagnetize ATM and credit cards in a flash.

It can be maddening when a truck

ahead of you slows you down to its pace. If you pass, often the truck speeds up, and then you've got to worry about a tailgater. Instead, just pull over for a few minutes and take a break. It'll give the truck time to move on and allow you to return to scenic roads unobstructed by Yosemite Sam mud flaps.

It gets mighty cold when the sun goes down. Even if you don't think you'll need it, bring along long underwear.

If you can't avoid the small animal in front of you, grit your teeth and go for it. It's not worth laying down your bike to save a squirrel.

And remember that loose gravel, wet leaves, and oil slicks don't care how long you've been riding. Don't get so swept up in the ride that you neglect safety.

I hate paying banks three bucks to get my money from their ATMs. So I look for a drugstore (CVS, Walgreens, etc.), where I use my debit card for gum or candy or batteries and get cash back. Not only do I avoid a fee, I get something I want.

When I arrive in a town, before I check into a hotel or start walking around, I stop at the local chamber of commerce or visitors center and get maps and advice on hours, admission fees, and what's worth seeing. The staff know what's shakin', and they'll always have current information on back roads.

Don't forget alternative newspapers (usually free) and the Friday edition of most daily newspapers that include listings and reviews of local restaurants, concerts, and special events.

Ask nicely, and some local libraries may allow you to use their computers for free Internet access. Get online to check out upcoming towns, attractions, and seasonal operating hours, and to print out discount coupons if offered.

If you have to ride in peak tourist season, do your best to get up early and wander around the town. Minus the presence of other tourists, it reveals a more natural sense of the community.

A word about the lodging prices listed throughout this book: They are listed for peak seasons, but will vary by day and by month. If they seem to skew high, check their off-season rates and ask for a discount—AAA, AARP, AMA. To secure even better rates, visit websites like www.hotels.com or www.priceline.com. You can deduct approximately 10–15 percent if you're a solo traveler, and even more if you can travel in an off- or shoulder season. The same with admission prices—those are for adults and you can ask for a senior discount if you qualify.

If you plan to visit more than one national park, spring for the $80 America the Beautiful Pass (only $10 for ages 62 and older). It's good for admission to any national park for one year.

It's nice to wear full leathers and clothes that reflect the hard riding you've done, but use common sense and courtesy and dress appropriately when at certain restaurants.

Yes, the boots do make you look like Fonzie, but if you plan on joining any walking tours or beating your feet around a town, you'll appreciate the comfort of a pair of walking shoes.

Take wrong turns. Get lost. Make discoveries.

Wild West Run

Livingston, Montana to Jackson, Wyoming

It's hard to find a tour as good as this. It begins in an authentic Western town before traversing a kaleidoscope of natural wonders and coming to a close in another Western town— one with a nice twist. Although the roads are not exactly challenging, the ride is unforgettable since it gives you access to some of the most magnificent scenery and wildlife in America.

LIVINGSTON PRIMER

Everything was going fine in Clark City until the Northern Pacific Railroad decided to relocate its line. That's when 500 people, six general stores, two hotels, and 30 saloons packed up and headed to nearby Livingston. In 1872, when Congress established Yellowstone, the completion of the park branch of the Northern Pacific brought Livingston new business.

The town profited from the railroad and mining and in the 1880s, cattle, sheep, and grain became the major economic forces. Livingston hasn't grown a whole lot since then, although there's a distinct difference

today. The town's year-round population of about 7,500 swells when part-time residents arrive to take advantage of the spells of good weather. Folks who call Livingston home at least part of the year include celebs like Jeff Bridges, Tom Brokaw, Dennis Quaid, and Margot Kidder. Sure, the veneer here may be Old West, but Livingson has a sophisticated soul.

ON THE ROAD: LIVINGSTON

Start by swinging by the well-stocked **Visitor Center** (303 East Park St., 406/222-0850, www.livingston-chamber.com), where there's a surplus of local maps and guidebooks and folks to point out numerous great loop roads outside of town. Considering there's a ride ahead, though, you may want to spend some time around the anachronism that is Livingston. Because the town seems tied to a time warp of Eisenhower-era America, your senses won't be assaulted by the familiar and redundant sight of franchises and chain stores. It's their absence, I think, that makes

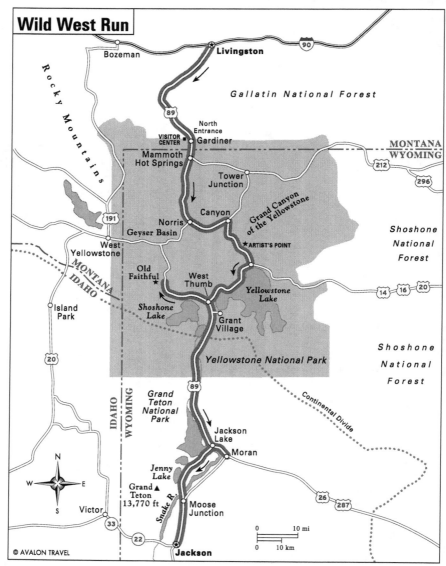

Wild West Run

Route: Livingston to Jackson via Yellowstone National Park, Grand Teton National Park

Distance: Approximately 210 miles

First Leg: Livingston, Montana to South Yellowstone, Wyoming (125 miles)

Second Leg: Yellowstone to Jackson, Wyoming (82 miles)

Helmet Laws: Montana and Wyoming do not require helmets.

wandering around downtown as satisfying as any ride.

On the surface, Livingston may seem to be an ordinary Western town. But when you dig a little deeper, you'll detect a level of sophistication that's revealed in more than a dozen art galleries, eclectic restaurants, and encounters with ranchers who probably carry more money than the Federal Reserve.

So, for now, park your bike and look around. The road will be waiting for you.

PULL IT OVER: LIVINGSTON HIGHLIGHTS
Attractions and Adventures

The great outdoors is big around Livingston, and several outfitters can take you to it. While it certainly doesn't sound like a name that would pump up the testosterone, the objective of **Rubber Ducky River Rentals** (15 Mount Baldy Dr., 406/222-3746, www.riverservices.com) is to get you out on the Yellowstone River for hair-raising whitewater rafting trips as well as scenic floats, fishing excursions, rowing instruction, overnight kayak tours, canoe floats, fishing, and raft and gear rentals.

The Zen experience of fly-fishing is one of Livingston's greatest attractions, and to help novices and professionals experience the serenity and challenge of the sport is **Dan Bailey's Fly Shop** (209 W. Park St., 406/222-1673 or 800/356-4052, www.dan-bailey.com). One of the most famous names in the sport, Dan Bailey's has been a town presence since 1938, and the store is packed to the gills with everything you need and hundreds of things you don't. How many hours of sleep have you lost wondering where you could find strung schlappen, hackle capes, and bumblebee popper foam? You'll rest easy after a visit here, open 7:30 A.M.–6 P.M. Monday–Saturday, and 7:30 A.M.–3 P.M. on Sunday. A word of warning: It'll cost. Bailey's organizes daylong fishing excursions that start at $425 per person (three bucks bought me a four-minute session); but if you can swing it, this may be the best place to get hooked on the sport.

In town, the **Livingston Depot** (200 W. Park St., 406/222-2300, www.livingstondepot.org, $3) is a museum built within a beautiful restoration of the Northern Pacific passenger depot. Open May–September, it features exhibits on Western life and art, and hosts annual events such as railroad swap meets. Check out the building's ornate brickwork and lion's-head accents, and in the basement of the baggage room there's a model railroad exhibit. Call for hours.

Just down the road is Yellowstone, but right here in town is where you can learn about its incredible history. The **Yellowstone Gateway Museum** (118 W. Chinook St., 406/222-4184) has an extensive collection of artifacts, exhibits, photos, and oral histories that cover the area's natural history and geology as well as the stories of pioneers, prospectors, lawmen, the railroad, the park itself, and the Old West. If your ancestors came from these parts, the museum maintains birth, death, and cemetery records and the staff can help you conduct genealogical searches.

Shopping

Gil's Got It (207 W. Park St., 406/222-0112), open 9 A.M.–5 P.M. daily, carries everything you used to crave when your parents were lugging you around the country in the backseat of the Buick. Here since 1914, it's approaching the century mark by giving the people what they want: things like straw cowboy hats, popguns, and wallets with cowboys on them.

Pardner, if you collect Old West memorabilia, then mosey on by the

Cowboy Connection (110 1/2 N. Main St., 406/222-0272, www.thecowboy-connection.com). Stocked items include gambling mementoes, antique Colts and Winchesters, saddles, chaps, spurs and bits, Stetsons, artwork, bronzes, boots, frock coats, knives, and shotguns.

Blue-Plate Specials

At the corner of 8th and Park streets, **Mark's In and Out** is a drive-in where you can fuel up on the four food groups: burgers, hot dogs, onion rings, and milkshakes. Clean as a whistle, Mark's service and prices are straight out of the 1950s—fitting, considering it opened in 1954. Burgers and cheeseburgers are easily affordable and if you don't mind bypass surgery, order a mess of Cadillac fries with gravy, chili, or cheese sauce.

Filled with local characters who hang out at the bar (open 'til 2 A.M.), **The Stockman** (118 N. Main St., 406/222-8455) also serves lunch and dinner to folks who believe that this small restaurant's got the best steaks in town. Weekends are packed, so try to go on a weeknight for a hand-cut top sirloin, New York strip, or rib eye. Bring cash—credit cards aren't accepted.

The best thing about **The Sport and Spaghetti Western** (114 S. Main St., 406/222-3800) is that it's not a sports restaurant. The original opened in 1909, when the popular sports were hunting and fishing; women weren't allowed in until the late 1940s. This must-see restaurant has an authentic Old West atmosphere with mounted heads, worn wooden floors, and tin ceilings. While the menu continues the Western flavor with steaks, the accent is now Italian.

Northern Pacific Beanery (108 W. Park St., 406/222-7288, www.thenpbeanery.com) was once filled with ranchers, cowboys, and working folks sitting at well-worn countertops. Located at the old railroad depot, the century-old eatery has been jazzed up to cater to a new clientele, although they bow to tradition by serving old favorites like chicken fried steaks and homemade corned beef hash. The Beanery serves breakfast and lunch 'til 2 P.M., and dinners Thursday through Saturday 'til 9 P.M.

For the big Western food you'd expect in these parts, drop by **Montana's Rib & Chop House** (305 E. Park St., 406/222-9200), which serves lunch and dinner in a bustling atmosphere. Featured on the menu are half-pound burgers, cedar plank salmon, coconut shrimp, pulled pork sandwiches, rack of ribs, baseball cut sirloin, and lamb ribs.

Not much to argue with at the **49er Diner** (404 E. Park St., 406/222-4414), where you can settle in for good home-cooked breakfasts and lunches. Nothing fancy, but simple, hearty, and affordable.

Watering Holes

I only drink to excess, so I had a hard time staying out of Livingston's bars. Each has the feel of a Western roadhouse, bartenders who can be sassy or sympathetic, and enough smoke to trigger the oxygen masks. They're all over downtown Livingston, but there are a few standouts. The bar at the Murray Hotel is the logically-named **Murray Bar** (201 W. Park St., 406/222-9816), which features two pool tables, seven beers on tap, a full liquor bar, live bands, and lots of energy. If you stepped into a time machine and were transported back to the '40s, you'd see just what you missed at **The Mint** (102 N. Main St., 406/222-0361). Break out the booze and have a ball.

There used to be a brothel upstairs at the **Whiskey Creek Saloon and Casino** (110 N. Main St., 406/222-0665), but no more—if there were, the ladies on call would be pushing 100. The bar still attracts locals who come early and stay late. **The Office Lounge** (128 S. Main St., 406/222-7480) has drinks and eats and has won local polls for being the best bar, having the best happy hour and staff, and being the best place to play pool and watch sports. Why the "Office?" It offers free Wi-fi and complimentary computers, copies, and faxing.

Shut-Eye

Not a motel, but a legend, **The Murray Hotel** (201 W. Park St., 406/222-1350, www.murrayhotel.com, rooms $89 and up, suites $119 and up) premiered in 1904 and has since greatly enlarged its pleasant rooms while retaining the touches of an old-fashioned hotel. Check out the washbasins in the rooms, rocking chairs in hallway alcoves, and desk clerks who double as elevator operators. But be prepared—noise from the bar and nearby trains may keep you up at night.

Chain Drive

These chain hotels are in town, or within 10 miles of the city center:

Best Western, Comfort Inn, Econo Lodge, Quality Inn, Rodeway, Travelodge

For more information, including phone numbers and websites, see page 151.

ON THE ROAD: LIVINGSTON TO YELLOWSTONE

The interesting thing about the 55-mile straight shot to Yellowstone National Park is that even though the ride doesn't compare to the park itself, south of Livingston the landscape of Paradise Valley starts to look larger and actually becomes a portent of things to come. The country ride introduces mountains on your left and hills to your right, but it takes a while to

notice that there *is nothing out here.* You are so swept up with the emptiness that you forget to notice the absence of homes, stores, and billboards. At some point the Yellowstone River shows up and brushes against the road and then retreats toward the mountains. As for you, you have only to enjoy the sun and the mountains, pausing if you wish at a roadside chapel and rest stop about 30 miles south of Livingston. Later, as the river starts picking up steam, rolling and boiling and churning as it flows north, the road tries to match its energy by adding some curves and descents. This all builds up to your farewell to mighty Montana—a state that God must have designed for motorcycling.

The town of Gardiner is just north of the Wyoming state line and it's where you'll find restaurants, motels, and service stations. If you don't need them, just roll around the corner and you'll find a perfect photo op for you and your machine. The Roosevelt Arch says more than the words inscribed on it: "Yellowstone National Park. For the Benefit and Enjoyment of the People. Created by Act of Congress March 1, 1872." Well, you are the people, and you're about to enjoy something spectacular.

Unless you have an America the Beautiful Pass (available from the National Park Service, it's an $80 investment that gets you into every national park for one year), motorcyclists pay $20 to enter Yellowstone (www.nps.gov/yell). The Yellowstone pass is valid for the Grand Tetons as well. Even though you may have seen the park in elementary school filmstrips, you've never seen anything like the real thing.

YELLOWSTONE PRIMER

Instead of its history, consider what makes up Yellowstone National Park: steaming geysers, crystalline lakes, thundering

Animal Sense

Riding a bike through Yellowstone poses an element of danger. Seriously. People in cars can shield themselves from bears and bison, but you can't. Here are some tips that may save your life:

- Give animals plenty of space when they are crossing the road.
- If one animal crosses the road, wait to see if another is following before proceeding.
- Don't try to entice any animal with food.
- If you see an animal and wish to stop, try to park in an established turnout, not in the middle of the road.
- If you're shooting photographs, don't try to get closer to the animals. For a good shot, use a telephoto lens.

waterfalls, and panoramic vistas sprawled across two million acres of volcanic plateaus. This was the world's first national park and accounts for 60 percent of the world's active geysers. The Lower Falls on the Yellowstone River are nearly twice as high as Niagara's. The land rises in elevation from 5,282 feet at Reese Creek to 11,358 feet at Eagle Peaks Summit. Yellowstone is home to 10 tree species, more than 80 types of wildflowers, 67 mammal species, and 322 species of birds.

Yellowstone contains five "countries." Mammoth Country, a thermal area in the northwest, is home to elk, bison, hot springs, and limestone terraces. Geyser Country, in the southwest, encompasses Old Faithful, fumaroles, mud pots, and hot pools. Lake Country, in the southeast, is habitat to native cutthroat trout, osprey, and bald eagles, as well as moose, bison, and bears, which wander the 140-mile shoreline of Yellowstone Lake. Roosevelt Country, in the northeast, recaptures the Old West. And Canyon Country comprises the Lower Falls, Hayden Valley, and the Grand Canyon of the Yellowstone. Free ranger-led programs, sightseeing tours, fishing, boating, horseback riding, and more than 1,210 miles of marked hiking trails all conspire to help you explore the park.

Believe it or not, all of this takes up less than 4 percent of the park itself. The rest is wilderness.

ON THE ROAD: YELLOWSTONE

Why do I love Yellowstone? Let me count the ways…Commercial trucks are prohibited; it has more wildlife than a hundred zoos; it fulfills every image I had formed about it; and it delivers what the government intended when it protected these lands in 1872.

The road from Tower Junction to Canyon Junction over Dunraven Pass in the northeast corner is the first to close and last to open when snow hits, so there's a good chance you won't be able to ride it. If it's open, terrific; if not, start at the park's north entrance section at Gardiner and head south, soaking in the views as you climb a quick 1,000 feet to blow past a mile as you ascend to 6,200 feet. Dealing with the campers who clog the road is discouraging at first, but within about two miles you'll have the satisfaction of crossing the 45th parallel—the midway point between the equator and the North Pole.

Your first stop should be the **Albright Visitors Center** at Mammoth Hot Springs to talk to a park ranger, get maps, and check on programs. You'll see it as you arrive through the main entrance on the north. From 1896 to 1916, this was the site of Fort Yellowstone, where the U.S. Army protected the park from poachers, vandals, robbers, and anyone or anything that threatened the preserve and its early tourists. Today a ranger's job is much easier. They can help you decide how and where to allot your time, and you'll find that time is precious since there's much to see and you'll be moving slow. Even though the speed limit's usually 45 mph, chances are you'll be riding closer to 30. Be selective on what you see if you're on a schedule.

Follow the road south to the Mammoth Terraces, which constantly builds tier upon tier of cascading terraced stone. These are interesting not only for their beauty but also because, despite clearly visible warning signs, some idiots have scalded or burned themselves to death by stepping out on them before falling through the fragile layer of minerals.

Soon you'll smell a familiar aroma. This is no kitchen cleanser, though—it's just the trees emanating the original pine-fresh scent. Around you the geological wreckage of mountains is omnipresent, and when you approach Swan Lake Flat it feels like you're on top of the world. If you ride in the late spring, you may share my good fortune and see a grizzly and her cubs— an experience that made me appreciate nature and wish my bike had automatic door locks. Moments like this remind you that, despite the string of roads here, this is actually wilderness and it doesn't belong to you, it belongs to the animals. Respect them.

Riding on, you'll spot the glacial green waters of North Twin Lakes, and past the Gibbon River there could be buffaloes grazing. It should go without saying that you should steer clear of these brutes. They're big enough to wreck a Humvee and could easily demolish a bike.

Near the Norris to Canyon road (in the middle of the figure 8 formed by roads), the Norris and Firehole River Geyser Basins feature the largest display of geysers. Steamboat Geyser, at Norris, is the world's tallest, with infrequent, unpredictable eruptions that reach an astounding 400 feet. Next, head east on the middle road toward Canyon Village. The landscape isn't quite as impressive here, but if you head straight until you reach the Grand Canyon of Yellowstone you won't mind the break. The 24-mile-long canyon sneaks up on you, and, once in full view, is majestic. At 800–1,200 feet deep and 1,500–4,000 feet wide, it is marked by rainbow-hued cliffs of orange, yellow, pink, white, and tan. It is also marked by another natural wonder.

At first, you can only hear the steady roar of the 308-foot-high Lower Falls, and then when it appears through the trees it'll take your breath away. You've reached a geological crossroads, where hot springs have weakened the rock and spout into the river to create an unusual confluence of waterfalls, cliffs, canyon, and geysers.

Down the road, a bridge crosses to Artist's Point on the opposite side of the canyon. When you get back on the road, the ride improves as the road follows the river's winding course. While the frostbite on your fingers tells you you're reaching higher elevations, there's something else in the air...bubbling, churning, sulfurous mud boils that smell worse than the awards ceremony at a baked bean festival.

Depending on where you're staying, you could wrap up a long day by resting at the Lake Lodge or the Lake Yellowstone Hotel or by continuing the journey to Old Faithful. Either way, monumental Yellowstone Lake opens up on your left. Big enough to create its own weather, the lake is actually a large crater formed by a volcano and then filled in by glaciers about 12,000 years ago. It'll follow you for miles and miles and while you would swear this lake should come to a close, it has a lot of stamina. Even after miles of lush forests block the view, you round the corner... and the lake's still there. Eventually, you'll adopt the lake as your riding buddy and hope it continues.

After about 45 minutes, less than half of its 140 miles of shoreline finally come to a close and you're alone again as you ride to the West Thumb Geyser Basin. This is where you'll find the quirky Fishing Cone, so named because anglers catching trout from the frigid lake cooked them still on the hook in the cone's boiling waters.

Between here and Old Faithful, a long but enjoyable 17 miles away, the thrill of the road may depend on the weather. When the snow is packed up high on the sides, it's like being in a bobsled race as the road rises and falls like the Roman Empire. Even though there's not a lot to see, the flow of the road may make this the best stretch for motorcycle travelers.

If you've timed it right, when you reach the exit to Old Faithful you shouldn't have long to wait before the geyser blows. Approximately every 92 minutes, thousands of gallons of thundering, hissing, steaming water blast into the sky. An American icon, it's worth seeing and the benches close to the Old Faithful Inn may afford the best view.

From here, you can double back and commence your trip south, or check into whichever lodge you were smart enough to book in advance.

PULL IT OVER: YELLOWSTONE HIGHLIGHTS
Attractions and Adventures

Yellowstone is less like a park and more like a nation. Seven full-service gas stations and four auto repair shops function within the park. *Yellowstone Today,* a free newspaper available at visitors centers and at the entrance, carries seasonal news and current information about park facilities and programs. The powers that be have also developed a complete retinue of tours and adventures that, depending on your budget, will be a natural or an extravagance. Check the park's website (www.nps.gov/yell) for non-fee activities; although the places and excursions you'll have to pay for can be found through a concessionaire at 307/344-7311 or 866/439-7375, and at www.travelyellowstone.com. Check with them for complete details and to reserve choices such as a horseback ride to the **Roosevelt Cookout** ($66–80); the **Stagecoach Adventure** ($10); various guided tours ($9–52); horseback trail rides (one hour, $37; two hours, $56); guided fishing trips (from $152 for two hours, with longer excursions available); power-boat rental ($47 per hour); and photo safaris ($15–81, offered June–September). There are also several all-day bus tours (about $65) that roam across the park and deliver information on the park's history, geology, and botany. If you'd like to do things on the cheap, rely on the NPS rangers who can tell you what's worthwhile and who also lead free tours that can help you understand this most incredible park.

Blue-Plate Specials

With the number of snack bars, delis,

cafeterias, fast food joints, and grocery stores you'll find, sometimes you'd suspect you were in New York and not Yellowstone. Since roads are supernaturally dark after sunset, for dinner try to stick around the **Mammoth Hot Springs Hotel, Old Faithful Inn, Grant Village, Canyon Lodge,** or **Lake Yellowstone Hotel**—each of which features dining rooms (which also serve breakfast and lunch). Dinner menus include prime ribs, steak, seafood, and chicken; reservations are strongly recommended at all restaurants, and required at the Lake Yellowstone Hotel and Old Faithful Inn. Grant Village and Roosevelt Lodge feature family-style restaurants. If you've got a hankering for cowboy cuisine, an Old West Dinner Cookout leaves from Roosevelt Lodge. You won't need your bike, instead you ride on horseback through Pleasant Valley to reach a clearing where there's a hearty dinner of steak, corn, coleslaw, cornbread muffins, homemade Roosevelt beans, watermelon, and apple crisp. For dining or cookout reservations, call 307/344-7311 or contact any lodging front desk, dining room, or activities desk.

Shut-Eye

I have to underscore that the best riding will be just before or after the peak summer tourist season. But if you do ride when the park is packed and the roads filled, definitely make reservations well in advance by calling **Xanterra** (307/344-7311 or 866/439-7375, www.travelyellowstone. com) the concessionaire that takes reservations for this and other national parks. Lodging options range from rustic cabins to fine hotels, but because of the park's remoteness, few rooms have phones, and none have televisions. Request a private bath if that's important to you and also be aware that prices tend to rise each year.

An iconic classic, the **Old Faithful Inn** ($98 shared bath, $213 upscale room) is your best bet. Built in the winter of 1903–1904 with local logs and stones, it features a towering lobby with a 500-ton stone fireplace and a handcrafted clock made of copper, wood, and wrought iron. This stunningly beautiful hotel offers a nice dining room, fast food restaurant, gift shop, and the Bear Pit Lounge. The inn shares a general store and service station with the **Old Faithful Snow Lodge and Cabins,** which opened in 1998 and charges around $99–201, while the **Old Faithful Lodge Cabins** fetch from $69–113. Completed in the 1930s, **Mammoth Hot Springs Hotel and Cabins** ($79–121) offers hotel rooms and cabins with and without private baths.

A classic historic hotel, **Lake Yellowstone Hotel and Cabins** opened in 1891 and has been restored to the grandeur it enjoyed during the 1920s. Even the original wicker furniture has been returned to service. The sun room, a sitting area designed for relaxation and conversation, affords wonderful views of the lake and is also a good place to relax with a cocktail and listen to piano-playing or chamber music in the evening. Choices range from deluxe historically renovated hotel rooms to more moderately priced annex rooms. Rooms are the most luxurious (and expensive) at $216–227; annex rooms are more affordable at $151; and cabins even more so at around $135. The motel-like **Grant Village** ($145) sits at the west thumb of Yellowstone.

You'll also find lodges and cabins (with and without baths) at the **Lake Lodge** ($70–157), **Canyon Lodge** ($74–173), and **Roosevelt Lodge** ($68–113), as well as more than 2,100 campsites (about $18 per night), and you'll need to call for reservations (advance reservations 307/344-7311 or 866/439-7375, same-day reservations 307/344-7901).

ON THE ROAD: YELLOWSTONE TO JACKSON

After you slip out of Yellowstone via U.S. 89 heading south, you'll notice little to distinguish Yellowstone from the neighboring **Grand Teton National Park** (307/739-3399 or 307/739-3300, www. nps.gov/grte). Between the pristine wilderness of Yellowstone and the Grand Tetons you'll enjoy what's a very quiet ride, interrupted only by the **Flagg Ranch Resort** (307/543-2861 or 800/443-2311, www. flaggranch.com). If you do stop here, it's likely because you want to savor every minute of the overpowering scenery or it could be because this gives you a chance to get some food and fuel. You can also rest easy here with Flagg's camping and lodges.

Just past Flagg Ranch, the vistas have received a booster shot of spectacular scenery thanks to efforts made in 1929 when more than 500 square miles were set aside to preserve and protect the land around the Teton Range. In 1950, that area was expanded when John D. Rockefeller Jr. donated adjacent lands. You can also thank the Rockefellers (I'm sure they'd enjoy a lovely bundt cake) for purchasing the land needed for Acadia National Park as well the area around Woodstock, Vermont.

One fantastic way to experience this park on your bike is by checking out the Jenny Lake Loop. Actually, the first body of water you'll see is Jackson Lake, which deserves a few hundred photos and its own miniseries. The water of the broad lake mirrors the mountains beyond and the result is a surreal, colorful blend of green waters, white mountain peaks, and blue sky. Even as the mountain chain recedes in the distance, the peaks appear uniform in height and shape, which offers a clue to why French trappers called them Les Trois Tetons (The Three Breasts).

Four miles later, the road has risen in elevation to place you midway between the lake and the towering peaks. At Colter Village there is a museum, store, and gas station. But by now you may be so inspired by the visuals that you'll just stick with the road. Not a bad choice since the mountain chain stays with you as you rocket toward Grand Teton, which, at 13,770 feet, is the largest mountain in the chain.

In addition to seeing these most incredible peaks, you get to ride Alpine runs, then pine-bordered roads and quick drops when the valley floor opens and the road dives right into it. Seemingly custom-designed for bikes, after riding it I felt like I needed a cigarette—and I don't even smoke.

At some point well south of here, the road Ts and you turn right to head into another stretch of vast emptiness. You are in Jackson Hole, the 48-mile-long valley that actually began just south of the Yellowstone entrance. Although it all seems like a lonely, deserted land, just wait, cowboy. A few miles later and you'll reach one of the nicest towns in the West.

JACKSON PRIMER

Trailblazers were the ones who made their mark on this town. The territory was named Jackson's Hole (later Jackson Hole) after trapper David E. Jackson. Prior to Jackson's arrival, however, there were summer residents: the Shoshone, Crow, Blackfoot, and Gros Ventre tribes.

What made this town stick was that with six trapping trails converging at Jackson Hole, it became a popular fur trading area. Around 1845, the trade—not to mention the animals—was in decline and for about the next 30 years, the isolated area lay dormant until the Hayden

Expeditions of 1871 and 1878 introduced the region to the rest of the country. After Yellowstone was formed, big game hunters, foreign royalty, and East Coast "dudes" started showing up.

The town itself was founded in 1921 and soon after cattle ranching took hold. Nearly a century later, this mix of hard-working locals and affluent outsiders still typifies the town, though tourism and skiing have long since supplanted ranching. One thing that'll likely remain the same is the landscape: Only about 3 percent of Teton County is privately owned, with the rest contained within Grand Teton National Park, the Bridger-Teton National Forest, and the National Elk Refuge.

It's hard to imagine a more perfect town.

ON THE ROAD: JACKSON

You can't disguise it. Jackson is a cowboy Carmel. There's lots of money here, generated by tourism and movie executives who invest part of their time and much of their fortunes here.

As in Montana, great rides await you on the outskirts of town, but wandering around Jackson is damned fun. Everything here centers around the Town Square which is marked by the famed Antler Arches. Each year, Boy Scouts have exclusive permission to scour the nearby National Elk Refuge and collect the horns that had been shed. The horns that aren't used to create arches in the park are auctioned off, purchased by western export houses, regional craftspeople, and Asian druggists who believe that powdered elk horn works faster than Viagra. It doesn't. *Trust me.*

Around the square, wooden sidewalks lead you through numerous shops, bars, restaurants, and art galleries. Take an afternoon, find some places on your own, check out a few listed here, and enjoy a pocket of civility in an otherwise harsh world.

PULL IT OVER: JACKSON HIGHLIGHTS
Attractions and Adventures

Whitewater rafting is the warm-weather equivalent of Jackson's winter ski season. Most excursions run the same rapids and charge about the same rate (from around the mid-$50s). Some trips combine whitewater and scenic float trips with the majestic Grand Tetons as a backdrop. Ask if trips include breakfast and/or lunch. If you have time, for around $150 or so, you may be able to find ones that offer overnight rafting/camping trips.

I can't attest to all of these, so you'll have to make the call on selecting the best whitewater rafting outfitters. I would recommend avoiding those that advertise high casualty rates. Try **Charlie Sands Wild Water River Trips** (307/733-4410 or 800/358-8184, www.sandswhitewater.com); **Dave Hansen Whitewater** (307/733-6295 or 800/732-6295, www.davehansenwhitewater.com); **Jackson Hole Whitewater** (307/733-1007 or 800/700-7238, www.jhww.com); **Lewis & Clark Expeditions** (307/733-4022 or 800/824-5375, www.lewisandclarkexpeds.com); and **Mad River Boat Trips** (307/733-6203 or 800/458-7238, www.mad-river.com).

The beauty you'll see in the American West is so inspiring that you may be motivated to ride a few miles north of Jackson on U.S. 89 to the **National Museum of Wildlife Art** (307/733-5771 or 800/313-9553, www.wildlifeart.org, $10). This is the premier collection of wildlife art in America, from prehistoric carvings to art created by mound dwellers to the sculptures and paintings of historic and contemporary Western American artists like W. R. Leigh, C. M. Russell, Robert Bateman, and Andy Warhol. In all, the museum showcases more than 2,000 paintings, sculptures, photographs, and works on paper by more than 100 wildlife artists. No unicorns and rainbows here—this is fine art that could turn a condo into a lodge.

Shopping

Sure, you can buy a hat off the rack, but you'd end up looking like a dude. For a custom-made beaver felt hat, walk over to the nationally-known **Jackson Hole Hat Company** (245 N. Glenwood Ave., 307/733-7687, www.jhhatco.com). I agree that a custom hat may not be cheap, but just think: *You will own an American original.* If you like leather (and I imagine you do), **Hideout Leather** (40 Center St., 307/733-2422) has a dynamite collection of hand-painted custom clothing, moccasins, boots, chaps, Native American headdresses, flying helmets, and leather jackets with fringe and studs and buckles and zipout linings and body armor…. Having a nicotine fit? Head to **Tobacco Row** (120 N. Cache Dr., 307/733-4385) and check out the cigars, pipe tobacco, and hand-carved pipes.

Blue-Plate Specials

Whether they're cowboys or corporate execs, locals fuel up on breakfast and lunch at **Jedediah's House of Sourdough** (135 E. Broadway, 307/733-5671). Breakfasts are big, with inexpensive sourjack pancakes, Teton taters, eggs, waffles, and bacon. You may have to waddle out, but you'll have no regrets.

Bubba's BBQ Restaurant (515 W. Broadway, 307/733-2288) serves breakfast, lunch, and dinner for folks that love meat. It's basic and inexpensive grub that includes ribs, chicken, pork, sandwiches, baked beans, coleslaw, and corn on the cob. On the high end of the spectrum, **Snake River Grill** (84 E. Broadway, 307/733-0557, www.snakerivergrill.com) was named Jackson's best restaurant by *Wine Spectator.* That said, don't expect the place to be diner cheap. For some, though, the premium has a payoff. The Grill serves only fresh fish and free-range veal and chicken, as well as more than 200 wines, plus ports and single-malt scotches. In this casual Western setting, you can order Chilean sea bass, venison chops, double-center-cut pork chops, and a bunch of other stuff I love to eat when somebody else is buying.

Watering Holes

Images of the **Million Dollar Cowboy Bar** (25 N. Cache Dr., 307/733-2207, www.milliondollarcowboybar.com) still stick with me. This is one of the absolute coolest bars you'll ever see, from the cutout stagecoach in the chandelier diorama to the saddle seats at the bar, from the chiseled faces of the patrons to the Western swing bands who lure the wallflowers out on the dance floor, this place has got it all. And the patrons aren't just drugstore cowboys. On weekends, ranchers who sowed their wild oats here 50 years ago return, their faces filled with more character than you'd find in a dozen Louis L'Amour novels.

Attached to one of the nation's Top 10 historic hotels, the Wort Hotel, is the **Silverdollar Saloon** (50 N. Glenwood Ave., 307/733-2190 or 800/322-2727, www. worthotel.com). Although it doesn't have the character of the Million Dollar, it's accented with saws, saddles, antlers, and a few thousands dollars worth of silver dollars embedded in the bar. The saloon serves wines, microbrews, and bar food. It's open 11:30 A.M.–11 P.M. daily.

Sidewinders American Grill (945 W.

Broadway, 307/734-5766, www.sidewinderstavern.com) has a classic Western look which is a perfect backdrop for their full slate of regional microbrews, wines, and whiskeys; all of which tend to overshadow the fact that it's a restaurant.

Shut-Eye

For such a small town, Jackson offers many options for bunking down. A central number for the **Town Square Inns** (800/483-8667, www.townsquareinns.com) puts you in touch with four reasonably priced, generic, and clean motels.

Motels and Motor Courts

The **Cowboy Village Log Cabin Resort** (120 S. Flat Creek Dr., 307/733-3121 or 800/483-8667, www.townsquareinns.com, $122 and up) rents great little air-conditioned cabins equipped with combinations of queen beds, sofa sleepers, kitchenettes, TVs, tub/showers, covered decks, and barbecue grills. It also throws in a continental breakfast.

Inn-dependence

The **Parkway Inn & Spa** (125 N. Jackson St., 307/733-3143 or 800/247-8390, www.parkwayinn.com) borders on a motel, but the rooms are large and clean; it sits a few blocks outside the rush of Town Square; it feeds you a good breakfast; and the pool and hot tub are just right after a day on the road. If you arrive preseason (April–May), you'll pay around $109—in the summer, it'll more than double. Ka-ching!

Chain Drive

These chain hotels are in town, or within 10 miles of the city center: **Best Western, Holiday Inn, Motel 6** For more information, including phone numbers and websites, see page 151.

Saddle Up

Read this only if you think you may want to park your bike for a week and rough it on the saddle of a real horse. Within 20 miles of here, dude ranches and trail rides are a cottage industry (actually, a bunkhouse industry). While I can't attest to any of these, check 'em out if you'd like to live the life of Hoss.

Among them are **Triangle X Guest Ranch** (307/733-2183 or 800/860-0005 www.trianglex.com); **Gros Ventre River Ranch** (307/733-4138, www.grosventreriverranch.com); **Lost Creek Ranch** (307/733-3435, www.lostcreek.com); and the **Red Rock Ranch** (307/733-6288, www.theredrockranch.com). Most dude ranches include one or a variety of activities, including trail rides, fly-fishing, swimming, horseback riding, float trips, pack trips, cookouts, hunting, square dancing, hiking, scenic tours, photography, breaking stock, and shoeing horses. Lodging will usually be in log cabins. Prices aren't inexpensive, but they may be a bargain for what you get and how many people you can crowd into a group rate. Plus, at most ranches, you get your own horse and a chance to ride like the Lone Ranger. Hi-yo!

Resources for Riders

Wild West Run

Montana Travel Information
Montana Bed & Breakfast Association—www.mtbba.com
Montana Camping Reservations—877/444-6777, www.recreation.gov
Montana Fish, Wildlife, and Parks—404/444-2535, www.fwp.mt.gov
Montana Road Conditions—800/226-7623, www.mdt.mt.gov/travinfo
Travel Montana—800/847-4868, www.visitmt.com

Wyoming Travel Information
Wyoming Game and Fish—307/777-4600, gf.state.wy.us
Wyoming Inn and Ranch Adventures—307/359-1289,
   www.wyomingbnb-ranchrec.com
Wyoming Road Conditions—888/996-7623, www.wyoroad.info
Wyoming State Parks and Historic Sites—307/777-6323,
   www.artsparkshistory.com
Wyoming State Parks Camping Reservations—877/996-7275,
   wyoparks.state.wy.us
Wyoming Tourism—307/777-7777 or 800/225-5996, www.wyomingtourism.org
Wyoming Weather—307/635-9901 or 307/857-3827

Local and Regional Information
Jackson Hole Area Chamber of Commerce—307/733-3316,
   www.jacksonholechamber.com
Jackson Hole Central Reservations—888/838-6606, www.jacksonholewy.com
Livingston Chamber of Commerce—406/222-0850,
   www.livingston-chamber.com
Yellowstone Activities and Reservations—307/344-7311, or 866/439-7375,
   www.travelyellowstone.com
Yellowstone National Park Visitors Services—307/344-2107 or 307/344-7381,
   www.nps.gov/yell

Montana Motorcycle Shops
Alpine Yamaha—301 N. Main St., Livingston, 406/222-1211
Yellowstone Harley-Davidson—540 Alaska Frontage Rd., Belgrade,
   406/388-7684, www.yellowstoneharley.com

Wyoming Motorcycle Shops
Jackson Hole Harley Davidson—40 S. Millward St., Jackson, 307/739-1500,
   www.tetonharley.com

Mighty Montana Run

Missoula, Montana to Bozeman, Montana

Montana shines with mountains, rivers, ghost towns, and saloons, while its residents project a refreshing self-reliance and strength of character. The essence of the state is palpable on this journey since this is a grand ride: large in scope, large in scenery, and large in memories.

MISSOULA PRIMER

Geographically, this is the perfect setting for a town. The Flathead Indians called the area Nemissodatakoo, meaning "by or near the cold, chilling waters." It's an apt moniker, considering that four trout-rich rivers—Rock Creek, Blackfoot, Lower Clark Fork, and Bitterroot—converge here. Lewis and Clark passed through this way in the early 1800s. But the first permanent settlement, Hellgate Village, wasn't established until 1860. Four miles from Missoula's current location, the town limits encompassed the flour and sawmills; but when the railroad came to town, folks painted over the Hellgate sign and changed the name to the more welcoming Missoula.

Missoula offers a great starting point and a great way to get used to Montana. The third-largest city in Montana, Missoula is easy to tour. It also reveals reasons to love this state: there's no sales tax; saloons and roadhouses still have character; and the citizenry is comprised of a pleasing mix of university students, artists, and regular folks.

ON THE ROAD: MISSOULA

Don't expect to ride into Missoula and stay indoors. The town is surrounded by some of the most pristine country and abundant waters in America, which is why fly-fishing is as popular here as jai alai is in Miami and purse-snatching is in Central Park.

The road south is a fine ride—and you'll see it soon—but first spend a few hours wandering around downtown through the heart of the city where independent merchants, junk shops, and watering holes haven't changed much in half a century. Reserve Street is one of the

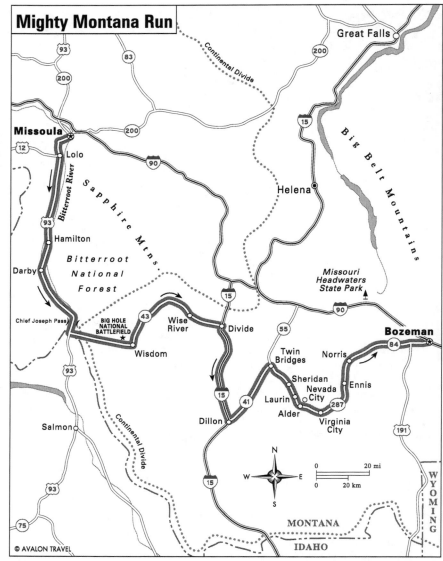

Route: Missoula to Bozeman via Lolo, Hamilton, Big Hole National Battlefield, Divide, Dillon, Sheridan, Nevada City, Virginia City, Ennis, Norris

Distance: Approximately 335 miles

First Leg: Missoula to Dillon (210 miles)

Second Leg: Dillon to Bozeman (123 miles)

Helmet Laws: Montana does not require helmets.

busiest thoroughfares, and the arrival of box stores has made it a hassle. That said, look for Higgins Avenue, a great road for reminiscing and tripping into a 1950s time warp. On Saturday morning, local farmers and craftspeople set up shop on side streets to sell their plants, handcrafted rugs, jewelry, and weavings. The University of Montana is also near downtown, as are bookstores, cool, dark saloons, and the historic and eye-popping art deco **Wilma Theatre** (131 S. Higgins Ave., 406/728-2521, www.thewilma.com), which hosts concerts and shows current and classic flicks.

PULL IT OVER: MISSOULA HIGHLIGHTS
Attractions and Adventures

At the **Smokejumpers Center** (5765 W. Broadway/U.S. 10, 406/329-4934, www. smokejumpers.com) trainees learn how to skydive behind fire lines in the remote wilderness and fight forest fires. It's open 8:30 A.M.–5 P.M. daily in season. The center features free tours, videos, a lookout tower, and exhibits showing the history and training requirements for these brave bastards. If riding across the country isn't exciting enough for you, they're always looking to recruit new members…

Montana rivers and streams teem with trout: rainbows, cutthroats, browns, and brook. Guides can take you to where the fish are; most head out about 60 miles to find a favorite fishing spot. Some gear can be rented, licenses and other items must be purchased, and a tip is never included in prices. This is admittedly an expensive proposition, since an angling adventure can start at around $400 for a day's outing for you and a buddy. Fishing trips are offered by **Missoulian Angler** (401 S. Orange St., 406/728-7766 or 800/824-2450, www.missoulianangler.com) and **Grizzly**

Hackle (215 W. Front St., 406/721-8996 or 800/297-8996, www.grizzlyhackle.com).

To those of us who live in towns and cities, Montana's stretches of wilderness are so vast it looks like a foreign world. In addition to exploring this relatively pristine frontier on your bike, you may want to see it from other angles by walking in the footsteps of America's greatest explorers. **Lewis and Clark Trail Adventures** (912 E. Broadway, 406/728-7609 or 800/366-6246, www.trailadventures.com) offers biking, hiking, and whitewater trips, including overnights, where all meals, tents, camping, and rafting gear are provided and where there are no roads, no cities, no phones…Paradise.

If you'd rather climb every mountain, **The Trailhead** (221 E. Front St., 406/543-6966, www.trailheadmontana. net) rents gear for camping, climbing, kayak, and canoe excursions. Not a bad start for novices.

The fastest-growing wildlife conservation center in the country, **Rocky Mountain Elk Foundation** (5705 Grant Creek, 406/523-4500 or 800/225-5355, www. rmef.org) works to preserve more than 2.4 million acres of elk country (depleting by an estimated 5,000 acres a day, they claim) by hosting exhibits, talks, and displaying stuffed dead elk. This is an inspirational stop for outdoors enthusiasts. Summer hours are 8 A.M.–6 P.M. Monday–Friday, 9 A.M.–6 P.M. weekends.

Blue-Plate Specials

A Northwestern-style downtown restaurant, **Iron Horse** (501 N. Higgins Ave., 406/728-8866, www.ironhorsebrewpub. com) has a good vibe with college students and mature people. Lunch and dinner fare includes steaks, quesadillas, hamburgers, and pub food. A pitcher of cold beer here is particularly enjoyable at the sidewalk café. It's a good place to hang out, with nightly drink specials and a bar that's open 'til 2 A.M.

It was at the **Double Front Cafe** (122 W. Alder St., 406/543-6264) where I ordered a chicken and an egg just to see which would come first. It sold its first chicken in the 1930s, and the current owners have been plucking and frying here since 1961. You can order burgers and seafood in the restaurant, but the big deal is the $8 chicken dinner, chased by a glass of pop. Check out the full bar in the basement, and then go back upstairs and get some more chicken. A Missoula legend.

Absolutely appetizing is **Doc's Gourmet Sandwich Shop** (214 N. Higgins Ave., 406/542-7414, www.docsgourmet.com). This nice retro diner in the heart of town serves an impressive range of big sandwiches and homemade soups. The menu also features a concoction known as "hangover stew," a potato corn chowder with an active ingredient of green chiles.

Watering Holes

Drop in at any bar along Higgins Avenue, and you'll find a hole in the wall filled with cowboys and mountain folk and a distinct personality. Here are a few to try.

Enter the **Oxford** (337 N. Higgins Ave., 406/549-0117), and you fall into a Steinbeck novel. It's been here since the 1880s and in its present location since the 1940s. It's open 24 hours a day. Step inside to a full liquor bar, an interior unchanged since World War II, gun displays, a card room in back, pool tables, and a revolving lineup of local characters. **Charlie B's** (428 N. Higgins Ave., 406/549-3589) stays open 'til 2 A.M. As you enter, notice the wall of photos of regular patrons and, when your eyes get accustomed to the dark, check out the elk heads, pool tables, and mountain folk. Charlie B's is regularly a leading contender

in *Esquire's* "Best Bars" poll in which a voter suggests that it's "Without question the best place in the country to find a beautiful woman who can gut her own trout."

The Rhino (158 Ryman St., 406/721-6061) has a slightly less impressive lineage (it's been around only since 1988), but it compensates by having 50 beers on tap. What's more, the beer flows through a beer engine, which uses air instead of $CO2$ to make the cask-kegged beer smoother and creamier—exactly the way they poured it in the Old West (before cowboys would go in the street and kill each other).

Shut-Eye

Most of Missoula's best lodging choices are chain hotels.

Chain Drive

These chain hotels are in town, or within 10 miles of the city center: **Best Western, Clarion, Comfort Inn, Courtyard by Marriott, Days Inn, Doubletree, Econo Lodge, Hampton Inn, Hilton, Holiday Inn, La Quinta, Motel 6, Quality Inn, Sleep Inn, Super 8, Travelodge**

For more information, including phone numbers and websites, see page 151.

ON THE ROAD: MISSOULA TO DILLON

As you leave Missoula, Montana doesn't assault your senses. It just grows on you until you realize there is no other state quite so attractive and no great outdoors quite so great. As Missoula recedes in your mirrors, the sky ahead opens up and draws you forward.

U.S. 93, a wide four-lane road, sweeps you up and over Missoula toward Lolo, then south through the Bitterroot Valley toward Hamilton. The road opens into a straightaway and, spotting mountains far on the horizon, you get your first inkling of how large this trip will be. Ahead, the stretches of emptiness are long. When they are interrupted, it's usually by Montana businesses, such as **Gulli Totem Poles** (964 U.S. 93, 406/961-4853, www.gullitotempoles.com) in Victor. The wood carver here can carve you a nice made-to-order totem pole of any size, with any configurations of totems. I ordered one that includes the entire Brady Bunch.

Hamilton appears after you cross the Bitterroot River, offering several opportunities for gas and food, like at the **Coffee Cup Cafe** (500 S. 1st St./U.S. 93, 406/363-3822). Try to make this your lunch stop since there's great home cooking, homemade soups, and mighty tasty pies and cakes that'll push you back into husky pants.

After Hamilton, the road is effortless. The slow curves don't ask much, and thus begins a perfect combination of scenery and landscape. Fires in 2000 took out thousands of acres of forest, but nature has done what it can to replace the loss. The road widens and does something special—it gives you room to simply breathe and to think and enjoy the ride. Sheep graze in the fields, and as you roll past small towns like Darby, you're witness to the American West without the pretense. Only about 970,000 people live in America's fourth-largest state, which is an average of six people per square mile. All around you the land reflects this pioneering spirit.

About 25 miles south of Hamilton, the road narrows and the riding becomes more challenging. As you enter the backcountry and head toward the Bitterroot River, the road leads through the valley and to the **Sula Country Store** (7060 U.S. 93 S., 406/821-3364, www.bitterroot-montana. com), which, according to the owners, is "one of the cleanest and friendliest stops

you'll make." Although I suggest riding miles ahead, if you'd like to stay awhile and explore the expansive backcountry of the **Bitterroot National Forest** (Sula Ranger District, 7338 U.S. 93 S., 406/821-3201, www.fs.fed.us/r1/bitterroot), they offer lodging here as well. There are cabins, cottages, a campground, gas, a diner, fishing licenses, and a nice front porch to kick back on, and every reason to stop and do absolutely nothing.

Civilization lies behind you and for the next 13 miles, you'll see every vision the name Montana brings to mind. The road wraps around mountains, swings into 25-mph curves, and propels you into snow-capped elevations. Keep one eye on the gravel and the other on the vistas that appear as you top this mountain chain. Pine trees puncture the snow cover, and when you reach the Lost Trail Pass at 7,014 feet, you're on top of the world.

This is only the beginning. On Highway 43 at the Montana/Idaho border, turn left to reach Chief Joseph Pass (7,241 feet) and cross the Continental Divide. Great descents, pristine woodlands, and the first of hundreds of miles of split-rail fencing follow. You're not riding through some puny East Coast farm country now. You're into something far greater. This is big.

Although the entrance to **Big Hole National Battlefield** (17 miles from the turnoff at U.S. 93 on Hwy. 43, 406/689-3155, www.nps.gov/biho, free) isn't well marked, it's the only detour for miles, so you should be able to spot it on your left. It's as sad a place as I've seen, and here's why: In the summer of 1877, five bands of Nez Perce had fled Oregon and Idaho to escape the U.S. Army and General Oliver Howard, who were trying to round them up and put them on a reservation. They outmaneuvered the army in nearly a dozen battles across 1,200 miles as they tried to reach safety in Canada. But when they made it here, Colonel John Gibbon's Seventh U.S. Infantry attacked their sleeping camp on August 9 and 10, 1877, killing men, women, and children. Despite the surprise attack, the Nez Perce managed to kill or wound nearly 70 soldiers and drive them back.

The Nez Perce beat the army again at Canyon Creek but surrendered in October 1877, at Bear Paw Battlefield, just 40 miles from Canada. Nez Perce civil leader Chief Joseph had had enough. He told Colonel Nelson Miles, "Hear me, chiefs. I am tired; my heart is sick and sad. From where the sun now stands, I will fight no more forever."

In my opinion, this reflects the very worst of American history. And while I shouldn't feel personally responsible for what happened here, I sure felt bad.

When you leave the center, the breadth of the land you see becomes phenomenal. There is enough earth here to build new planets. You're in the Big Hole Valley, riding at an average elevation of 1.2 miles. Even though the horizons are empty, the view is more inspiring and far more beautiful than you can comprehend.

A few miles later, when you ride into Wisdom (pop. 100-plus), you'll encounter something else to file in your growing collection of "on the road" stories. Pull into the **Big Hole Crossing Restaurant** (105 Park St., 406/689-3800, www.bigholecrossing.com) and you've entered an anomaly. The restaurant is no Montana greasy spoon. They serve up damn good food here (breakfast, lunch, and dinner) and have as a backdrop a toasty fireplace, an art gallery, and a clothing store where handcrafted dresses sell for as much as $250 and cool leather jackets for $1,000. If you're on a liquid diet, next door is **Antlers Saloon** (100 Main St., 406/689-

9393), where cowboys shoot stick and locals work out with 16-ounce weights. The decorative touches, antlers, and guns recall an early roadhouse. I expect that by now the sights have tempted you to become a part-time Montanan. Don't. A local told me that if you're not ready to "earn your spurs," leave the state to the people who belong here, those who endure its hardships and deserve its rewards.

If your mind can handle it, the road and landscape following Wisdom improve exponentially. The Great Plains lay themselves out beneath your wheels, sunlight falls in large shafts on the valleys below, and the landscape grows so large that even grazing horses look as insignificant as Shetland ponies. You're in the "Land of 10,000 Haystacks." By the time you're through riding, only reconstructive surgery will be able to erase the smile from your face.

Amid the straights and curves and low sloping hills, something is missing: This great land is uncluttered by houses, billboards, factories, gas stations, and strip malls. There is nothing but land and the road, which, when you get down to it, is really all you need.

The ride's grandeur sustains itself as you cruise alongside the Wise River, taking 40-mph turns as the water churns and boils on your left. In the town of Wise River you'll be seduced by the Wise River–Polaris Road (NF-73), a scenic byway that slices south through the 3.3-million acre Beaverhead Deerlodge National Forest. The bad news is that the road's seldom open because of impassable snows and even when it is it's not all paved and you'll have to contend with sections of gravel. That said, if it *is* open and you have time and a taste for adventure, go off on a tear and enjoy what one local says is the most beautiful scenery in the region, filled with coniferous forests of lodgepole pine and Douglas fir.

Odds are, though, that you'll keep plowing along on Highway 43 toward Divide, where you'll find **Blue Moon** (406/267-3339), a mile off I-15 in Divide. The gas station and saloon are filled with friendly locals, and odds are you'll want to stop and have one for the road. From here it's tempting to jump on the lonesome interstate and head south, which is not as bad as urban highways since you can ride without hardly seeing any other car, truck, or bike. Odds are that for the last 40-some miles you'll want to continue that lonely country riding you've enjoyed. Old Highway 10 (aka SR 361) leads you south, eventually switching identities and becoming Highway 91 as it rolls into Dillon.

I can't claim that there's a lot to do here, but in lonely Montana, lonely Dillon's a fine place to rest up and prepare for the next day's ride.

DILLON PRIMER

Dillon had an impressive start. It was born when the Utah and Northern Railroad headed toward Butte in 1880, but the railroad stopped when it reached rancher Richard Deacon's spread. He wouldn't let the line continue until a group of businessmen promised to raise enough cash to buy him out. While the railroad stalled here during the winter of 1880–1881, the site where they stopped was named after railroad president Sidney Dillon.

That's really about all you need to know. Dillon also enjoyed a gold boom that went bust, and today the town relies on agriculture. There's not much else shaking here. Not much at all.

ON THE ROAD: DILLON

Thumb through this book, and you won't find another town like Dillon. Usually even if there's nothing to see in a town, there's something to talk about. Not so much here. I won't belabor the point. There are a few chain motels, a grain silo, a quiet downtown, the University of Montana-Western, and, most important, a Dairy Queen. There's a popular rodeo here each Labor Day, but overall it's a pretty remote town in a pretty remote area.

About 25 miles southwest of Dillon is the ghost town of Bannack, which was Montana's first territorial capital and where the first major gold strike struck. It was also here in the self-proclaimed "Toughest Town in the West" that a renegade sheriff, Henry Plummer, created a terrorist network credited for killing and robbing more than 102 victims, which was about 102 too many for the town's law-abiding citizens. Forming a vigilante squad, the good guys tracked down the sheriff and 28 of his gang, and gave them a serious going away party by letting them hang on the same gallows Plummer had built. Today the town is the site of **Bannack State Park** (Bannack Bench Rd., 406/834-3413, www.bannack.org), which, if you have time for a ride, is a nice and nearby destination.

If you want to know more about local history and nearby sites that include mountain lakes and reservoirs and forests, mountains and kilns, stop by **Dillon Visitors Information Services** (10 W. Reeder St., 406/683-5511) and the folks on duty will tell you why they're here and why you should stick around.

Shut-Eye
Chain Drive

These chain hotels are in town, or within 10 miles of the city center:

Best Western, Comfort Inn, Super 8

For more information, including phone numbers and websites, see page 151.

ON THE ROAD: DILLON TO BOZEMAN

Leaving Dillon on Route 41 North takes you right back to the prairie and photo ops with a Rocky Mountain backdrop. The landscape varies little, so just let your mind wander until you've gone about 25 miles to Twin Bridges which is as close to not being a town as any town I've seen. The road forks here; turn onto Highway 287 toward Virginia City.

About now, you'll notice a few things: The fierce wind smacks your body as it pours over the plains; every pickup you've passed since Missoula has a dog in back (I believe they come standard with Montana trucks); and there is so much of nothing around you that it's really something.

Sheridan will come and go, too, fizzling to a close and merging with the prairie as you head out of town. About five miles later, you'll pass Robber's Roost on your right, the place where desperadoes, rustlers, and Wall Street execs came to plan their heists. Beyond that, random towns crop up when nothing else is around, such as Laurin, Ruby Valley, and Alder, each of which grows progressively dirtier and more lonesome.

The landscape beside the road is rapidly changing into mining country. The ground is gritty with sagebrush and the mean brown creeks that penetrate the deadwood. This is the perfect setting for **Nevada City** (Hwy. 287, www.virginiacitymt.com), a strange shambles of a place that's half ghost town, half museum. Restored by the Bovey family between 1945 and 1978, there's a hotel here worthy of *Gunsmoke,* a saloon where you can bring your own drinks, and a complete town hidden beyond the streetfront buildings. Check out the darkened music hall and find nickelodeons, fortune telling machines, and the "famous and obnoxious horn machine" stashed inside. In the village, they've saved everything from a two-story outhouse (lookout below!) to stores stocked with unopened merchandise.

Your decision to ride will be repaid in full on the wide-open roads of Montana.

© NANCY HOWELL

A hundred years ago and a few miles southeast of Nevada City, six discouraged prospectors stopped to pan for enough gold to buy tobacco. Within three years, the Alder Gulch gave up $30 million in gold and **Virginia City** (Hwy. 287, 406/843-5555 or 800/829-2969, www.virginiacity.com) was born. It's a more modern town than Nevada City, but the term is relative since Virginia City is still a frontier town as well—although it does have a few great shops, saloons, and restaurants.

Without embellishing, I can say the road from here to Ennis is about as magnificent a road as you'll ever ride. As you climb into the hills, the glorious country is at your feet, and soon you'll reach an overlook hundreds of feet above the Madison Valley. *This* is a sight that will dazzle and humble you with mountains, rounded hills, broad beams of sunlight, and far more beauty than your mind can take in. Now's a good time to thank whatever gods you believe in for their handiwork.

Descending from the promontory is a kick. If you're traveling with others, take time to stage a few photographs on this wide open road. I did, and it's the one I treasure most. When you reach Ennis, turn left on Highway 287 toward Norris. Ride toward the brink of a cliff and look down the shaft of a long, empty valley where shadows of clouds smudge the ground. When you reach Norris and the junction of Highway 84, turn right, and the terrain takes you back into hill country where the low, flat road gives you instant twists beside the fantastic Madison River.

Anglers wade in the waters here, and the canyon turnouts are perfect for resting your bike, peeling off your boots, and cooling yourself with a walk into the river. Try this, and when you shut off your bike and listen to the silence, I defy you to imagine a more beautiful country.

As you continue into Bozeman, the land turns into farmland. Hear the wind pouring over your helmet and the engine's low-pitched, pulsing hum.

Combined with Montana, it is a symphony.

BOZEMAN PRIMER

Others arrived here before Lewis and Clark, but in 1805 and 1806 those two were the first to generate a written description of the valley. Decades later when gold was discovered, Bozeman Trail became the chosen path west—and then east, when the prospectors returned here to create the town in 1864.

By 1883, the Northern Pacific Railroad had completed its line through the town, and Montana Agricultural College held its first classes in 1893. With settlers arriving from around the country, Bozeman developed a unique local heritage. Today, the town has eight historical districts, more than 40 properties listed on the National Register of Historic Sites, and is the home to Montana State University (which explains the abundance of students you'll see in the saloons).

While the outskirts of town look suspiciously like everyplace else, the heart of downtown still has a 1940s flavor, with 10-gallon hats, pointy-toed boots, drugstore cowboys, and antiquated signage at stores like Western Drug at 44 East Main Street.

Mosey on down and check it out.

ON THE ROAD: BOZEMAN

As in Missoula, the road has been so generous that it's satisfying to stay in town and see what's shakin'. Main Street is the main part of town, more compact than Missoula's. Just a few hours up and down the street will acquaint you with the more interesting shops. Beyond that, see some local attractions, head out into the wilderness on a fly-fishing excursion, or just savor the opportunity to take it easy in the Old West.

PULL IT OVER: BOZEMAN HIGHLIGHTS
Attractions and Adventures

If you've never been fly-fishing, there's no better place to start than right here. What does it take to take up this sport? Money, mostly. Guides charge $300–450 for a half to a full day of fishing, but as you learned in Missoula, that doesn't include gratuities, a license, or equipment. In most shops, you can rent a rod, reel, and waders, but you have to buy gear and flies— unless you've got some plastered on your visor. Most excursions depart at 8:30 A.M. and return about nine hours later. Bear in mind that this is catch and release— you're fishing for the fun of it (if you think spending 450 bucks is fun). The shops below also arrange trips and guides.

Opened in 1944, **Powder Horn** (35 E. Main St., 406/587-7373) is sacred ground for sports enthusiasts, featuring books, rods, reels, clothing, boots, rifles, shotguns, shells, and cooking supplies. It also represents 20–30 local guides—not college students—who know where to go. Working with novice to serious fly fishers, **Bozeman Angler** (23 E. Main St., 406/587-9111 or 800/886-9111, www.bozemanangler.com) offers walk/wade or float trips on the Yellowstone, Beaverhead, Gallatin, Madison, and Missouri rivers. A few miles outside of Bozeman in the town of Belgrade, Dave Warwood at **Bridger Outfitters** (15100 Rocky Mountain Rd., Belgrade, 406/388-4463, www.bridgeroutfitters.com) can arrange a half-day horseback ride, a full day with sack lunch, or a full-on adventure that

lasts four days and three nights and features overnight camps, cattle drives, horseback rides, and fishing in backcountry lakes and streams. Does he know his stuff? He grew up in the business his great-granddad started almost 100 years ago.

The biggest draw in Bozeman, the **Museum of the Rockies** (600 W. Kagy Blvd., 406/994-3466, www.museumoftherockies.org, $10 museum and planetarium) is a great source of intelligence that centers around dinosaur fossils unearthed by local legend Jack Horner. I'm glad I came here. I was investing my money in coprolite until I learned that it's just fossilized dinosaur crap. You'll get a kick out of knowing that when you're riding in Montana, you're riding atop what was once the stomping grounds of the stegosaurus and T-Rex. On display are fake dinosaurs, CAT-scanned dinosaur eggs that reveal embryos, skulls of a triceratops and tyrannosaurus, and thoughtful exhibits on Native Americans and Lewis and Clark. It presents a massive amount of information in intriguing displays, so pace yourself and concentrate only on the exhibits that catch your interest. The museum is open daily 8 A.M.–8 P.M. in the summer; 9 A.M.–5 P.M. in fall and winter.

The free **Gallatin County Pioneer Museum** (317 W. Main St., 406/522-8122, www.pioneermuseum.org) pays tribute to the history of Bozeman and the pioneers who settled in the Gallatin Valley. Take a look at the travels of your spiritual ancestors, Lewis and Clark, who are honored in this old jail at the L&C library. Other exhibits include an 1870s log cabin, American Indian exhibits, a sheriff's room with a hanging gallows, a whiskey still, and more than 11,000 archival photos from the early days of the town.

Blue-Plate Specials

A downtown explosion in 2009 destroyed

three of Bozeman's finest restaurants and one of its legendary bars. Until they're resurrected, try the **Western Cafe** (443 E. Main St., 406/587-0436) which opens at 5 A.M.—just in time to serve early rising regulars tins of fresh-baked cinnamon rolls and pies. When lunch rolls around, it rolls out the T-bone steaks, chicken-fried steaks, homemade soups and stews, and dinner rolls. The only drawback? There's just not enough time to eat it all—closing time's 2 P.M.

Even if you've never been to Bozeman, you probably know the proprietor of **Ted's Montana Grill** (105 W. Main St., 406/587-6000, www.tedsmontanagrill. com): media magnate and philanthropist Ted Turner. The first Montana link in a nationwide chain, this destination is where you can dine inside or on an outdoor patio, relaxed by its turn-of-the-century Arts and Crafts design and the architectural touches of the 1929 hotel in which it resides. The classic American grill focuses on affordable made-from-scratch comfort foods, fresh vegetables, and hand-cut premium beef or bison steaks, chicken and seafood.

Watering Holes

If you wear boots even when you aren't riding, you may feel at home at **Crystal Bar** (123 E. Main St., 406/587-2888), open 8 A.M.–2 A.M. daily. This country cowboy bar attracts its fair share of college students, and it opens a second-floor rooftop beer garden in the summertime. Year-round, you'll find a few pool tables and lots of beer.

The clientele changes throughout the day at **The Cannery** (43 W. Main St., 406/586-0270), from doctors and lawyers after work, to college students after class, to regular folks later at night. Open 11 A.M.–2 A.M. daily, this joint features sassy bartenders and a pool table attached to the ceiling.

A bit removed from downtown is a collection of three taverns which comprise the "Bar-muda Triangle." Beer, mixed drinks, live music and more can be found at **The Haufbrau** (22 S. 8th Ave., 406/587-4931), **Scoops** (712 W. Main St., 406/522-9141), and **The Molly Brown** (703 West Babcock, www.mollybrownbozeman.com).

Shut-Eye

Motels and Motor Courts

The **Lewis and Clark** (824 W. Main St., 406/586-3341 or 800/332-7666, www. lewisandclarkmotel.net, $79 and up) is a best bet for riders, with sheltered parking or a space in front of your room, rags to clean your machine, and fresh coffee and banana bread when you return from the ride. Its retro look goes along with its dining room, coffee shop, and lounge as well as 50 clean and large rooms with a king or two queen beds. Plus, it all comes with a heated indoor pool, fitness room, and three taverns right next door.

Chain Drive

These chain hotels are in town, or within 10 miles of the city center: **Best Western, Comfort Inn, Days Inn, Fairfield Inn, Hampton Inn, Hilton, Holiday Inn, Ramada, Residence Inn, Rodeway, Super 8**

For more information, including phone numbers and websites, see page 151.

Resources for Riders

Mighty Montana Run

Montana Travel Information
Montana Bed & Breakfast Association—www.mtbba.com
Montana Camping Reservations—877/444-6777, www.reserveusa.com
Montana Fish, Wildlife, and Parks—404/444-2535, www.fwp.m.t.gov
Montana Road Conditions—800/226-7623, www.mdt.mt.gov/travinfo
Travel Montana—800/847-4868, www.visitmt.com

Local and Regional Information
Beaverhead Chamber (Dillon)—406/683-5511,
   www.beaverheadchamber.org
Bozeman Chamber of Commerce—406/586-5421, www.bozemanchamber.com
Bozeman Visitors Bureau—406/586-5421 or 800/228-4224,
   www.bozemancvb.com
Missoula Chamber of Commerce—406/543-6623, www.missoulachamber.com
Missoula Convention and Visitors Bureau—800/526-3465,
   www.missoulacvb.org
Missoula Weather—406/329-4840

Montana Motorcycle Shops
Adventure Cycle—201 E. Helena St., Dillon, 406/683-2205,
   www.adventurecycleandsled.com
Al's Cycle—619 U.S 93 S., Hamilton, 406/363-3433, www.alscycleyamaha.com
Big Sky BMW Kawasaki—2315 South Ave. W., Missoula, 406/728-5341,
   www.bigskybmwkawasaki.com
Five Valley Honda-Yamaha—5900 U.S. Hwy. 93 S., Missoula, 406/251-5900,
   www.fivevalleyhondayamaha.com
Mike Tingley Suzuki Yamaha—2150 South Ave., Missoula, 406/549-4260
Mountain Motorsports and Marine—620 U.S. 93 S., Hamilton, 406/363-4493,
   www.mms-motorsports.com
Team Bozeman Polaris/Kawasaki/Yamaha—2595 Simmental Way, Bozeman,
   406/587-4671, www.team-bozeman.com
Yellowstone Harley-Davidson—18 W. Main St., Bozeman, 406/586-3139; and
   540 Alaska Frontage Rd., Belgrade, 406/388-7684 or 877/388-7684,
   www.yellowstoneharley.com

Colorado Rockies Run

Durango, Colorado to Mesa Verde National Park, Colorado

This ride won't take very long, but the memories it generates could last a lifetime. Every image of a standard Colorado beer commercial is evoked here. There are repeated images of waterfalls, mountain switchbacks with sheer drops, frontier towns in no hurry to leave the 19th century, and a mysterious village frozen in time. You'll ride across mountain passes at 11,000 feet, and have the option of renting a Jeep to climb beyond 13,000 feet...if you don't mind a collapsed lung.

DURANGO PRIMER

After the Ancestral Puebloans had vanished from the land and the Utes, Navajo, and Spanish had come and gone, what is today's Durango was born by way of the rails.

With the San Juan Mountains overflowing with gold and silver, the folks at the Denver and Rio Grande Railroad had a brainstorm. In 1880, they established the town of Durango as the base point for their railway. By 1882 the tracks had been completed and by the time the line stopped in the 1960s, miners had removed about $300 million worth of gold and silver from the hills.

Durango was a wealthy town at the turn of the 20th century and, judging by the architecture, it still looks well-off today. But it's not just money that makes this town rich. Its natural setting on the free-flowing Animas River and the town's proximity to cool, lush forests and broad, powerful mountains both play a role. And its greatest asset is arguably its people, whose hospitality and lack of pretense would make Tibetan monks look like schoolyard bullies.

ON THE ROAD: DURANGO

Trust me that the upcoming ride north will more than satisfy your thirst for adventure, so while you're here you might as well just hang out in downtown Durango. And if you have an extra day to invest, consider boarding a steam train for a real cliffhanger of a ride.

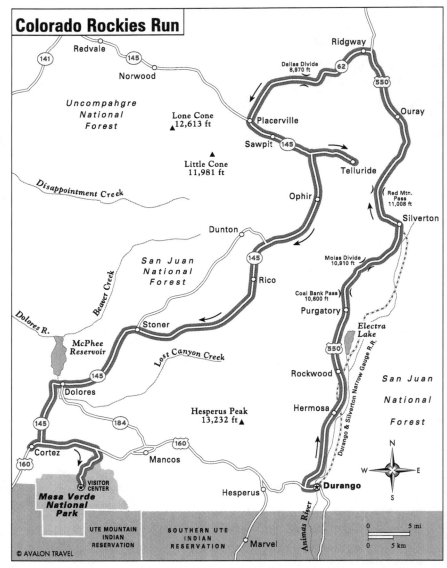

Colorado Rockies Run

Route: Durango to Mesa Verde via Silverton, Million Dollar Highway, Ouray, Telluride

Distance: Approximately 200 miles

First Leg: Durango to Telluride (120 miles)

Second Leg: Telluride to Mesa Verde (80 miles)

Helmet Laws: Colorado does not require helmets.

The epicenter of downtown activity is along Main Avenue, stretching between 5th and 12th streets. On most days, there's a showroom's worth of motorcycles angled along the curb, and they're all here because this happens to be an Old West walking town that hasn't lost its flavor. When mall developers were flashing their cash and looking for tenants, the independent merchants, local saloons, and historic buildings here gave the folks in Durango every reason to stay put and stick with downtown.

Along Main Avenue and spreading out on the cross streets, you'll find leather and saddle shops, newsstands, old photo shops, and a one-of-a-kind hatmaker. After strolling Main Avenue, don't leave town by bike. Not yet. Seriously consider a run on the **Durango-Silverton Narrow Gauge Railway** (479 Main Ave., 970/247-2733 or 888/872-4607, www.durangotrain. com). Back in the 1880s, about the same time the Rolling Stones released their first wax cylinder, mining up in Silverton was going full steam and the best way to get the goods back down to Durango was via this narrow gauge railway.

If you think the San Juan Skyway is gonna be tricky on a four-cylinder bike, surrender the job to the engineer of a 50-ton, circa 1923 coal-fired steam train as he creeps it along the cliffs of the Animas River Gorge. When you enter the mountainous terrain and peer 400 feet straight down, you'll understand why cruising at 10 mph makes sense.

The locomotive chuffs along the canyon for more than three hours, rising from 6,512 feet in Durango to 9,288 feet in Silverton (a town you'll see later on your bike, even if you don't take the rail). The round trip lasts about nine hours, with the layover in Silverton lasting only two hours—just enough time to eat, down a

beer, and buy some cheap souvenirs. If you get a kick out of historic modes of transportation and have never ridden a steam train, then it could be worth the price (about $80, and closer to $150 to reserve a parlor car). Reservations are recommended for the ride. If you skip the trip, you can still tour the museum and railyard for five bucks.

Back in Durango, rest up and get ready for an old-fashioned evening listening to a honky-tonk pianist at the Diamond Belle Saloon or watching live entertainment at the Henry Strater Theatre. When you're in Durango, this sure as shootin' beats a night at a sports bar.

PULL IT OVER: DURANGO HIGHLIGHTS
Attractions and Adventures

With a river like the mighty Animas sitting in your backyard, you'd be a dope not to use it. Outfitters here wring maximum use out of the Animas with river runs that range from serene to extreme. **Outlaw Rivers and Jeep Tours** (690 Main Ave., 970/259-1800, www.outlawtours.com) offers excursions on the rapids lasting from two hours ($25) to a full day ($65), as well as Jeep rentals ($135 daily) and Jeep and Hummer tours that travel to ghost towns and mining districts. **Durango Rivertrippers** (720 Main Ave., 970/259-0289 or 800/292-2885, www.durangorivertrippers.com) provides whitewater rafting from $25 for two hours to $39 for a half day plus lunch. You can also do it yourself in an inflatable kayak.

Trimble Hot Springs (6475 CR 203, 970/247-0111, www.trimblehotsprings. com) doesn't exactly qualify as a water adventure, since whitewater only appears when someone does a cannonball. You can ease your saddle-sore muscles at this natural spa that features Olympic pools, massages, herbal wraps, and mineral-rich waters ranging from a tepid 85°F to a muscle-melting 108°F. The springs are open 8 A.M.–11 P.M. daily.

When you see the sublime setting of the airstrip at the **Durango Soaring Club** (27290 U.S. 550, three miles north of Durango, 970/247-9037, www.soardurango.com), you may never want to leave. But the lure of the sky is undeniable and when you soar from ground level (which is already at 6,500 feet) you'll be towed to as high as 10,000 feet before popping off from the tow plane and soaking up tremendous views of the San Juan Mountains, as far away as 100 miles, and seeing the Animas River snake through the valley. If you're in a pack, your friends will be nearly as content sunning themselves on the observation deck. The weight limit is 300 pounds and reservations are suggested. Flights start at $100 for 15 minutes in the air.

Shopping

Long before trendsetters beatified cigars, **Hall's Brothers Smoke Shop** (113 W. College Dr., 970/247-9115 or 800/742-7606, www.durangosmokeshop.com) was smoking. Claiming to be the "tobacconist to the Four Corners," Hall's stocks many cigars, Zippo lighters, Indian peace pipes, and risqué postcards.

Thomas and Melissa Barnes are experts at making custom hats and saddles, which they do with great skill and care at the accurately named **Durango Custom Hats and Saddles** (723 E. 2nd Ave., 970/385-8486). After you've had your head examined, it'll take Thomas a few months to create a hat that you'll own for a lifetime. Motorcycle seats, too, are a specialty and for about $650, he'll measure your seat, get your input, and go to work to create a custom saddle displaying anything that

can be carved, tooled, or stamped on it. Avoid unicorns and rainbows.

Blue-Plate Specials

Francisco's Restaurante y Cantina (619 Main Ave., 970/247-4098) is a local favorite for its homemade soups, great Mexican food, impressive wine list, and full bar, where margaritas are a specialty and locals gather to watch the big game. Expect a long wait if you travel in peak season. It's open for lunch and dinner.

The **Ore House** (147 E. College Dr., 970/247-5707, www.orehouserestaurant.com) looks like it's placed in a rustic miner's shed, which sets the stage for a great evening retreat. The chefs start with pan-fried steaks and work their way up to chateaubriand; in between, they whip up center-cut bacon-wrapped filets stuffed with king crabmeat, steak ranchero, and the Ore House grub steak. Eat dinner here and annoy a vegetarian.

Inside a renovated Ford tractor showroom, the **Steamworks Brewing Company** (801 E. 2nd Ave., 970/259-9200, www.steamworksbrewing.com) draws local college students and a smattering of tourists for lunch and dinner and for five regular and three seasonal microbrews. The style is basic, with corrugated tin walls, copper vats, and smooth concrete floors. Oh yeah, the food: Mexican, chicken, pastas, sandwiches, and pizza. The patio deck is great for all of this plus a cold one and conversation.

The **Durango Diner** (957 Main Ave., 970/247-9889, www.durangodiner.com) is a local landmark, and it keeps going thanks to its no-frills meals. Beyond serving breakfast all day, it spices up the menu with its trademark green chili, Southwest salsa, and enchilada sauces—sold here and across the country. If you're afraid you'll run out of gas on the San Juan Skyway, stop here first.

Watering Holes

You cannot *not* have a good time at the **Diamond Belle Saloon** (in the Strater Hotel, 699 Main Ave., 970/247-4431 or 800/247-4431, www.strater.com). This corner bar, locked in the 1880s, boasts a full line of drinks, from beer to bourbon. From the flocked wallpaper to the honky-tonk piano player to the nude painting to the sign that suggests "work is the curse of the drinking classes," this is one of the best bets for bikers I've seen. Chances are you'll meet people from around the world. The only thing missing here is Festus. It's open 11 A.M.–midnight daily.

If you're driven by thirst, check out **Lady Falconburgs** (640 Main Ave., 970/382-9664), open 11 A.M.–2 A.M. daily. The rathskeller-style interior isn't that impressive (the basement of a shopping mall), but the establishment pours 100 types of bottled beer, 38 beers on tap, and serves a five buck sampler. There are two dollar pints all day on Mondays and Thursdays. Bottoms up.

If your nights aren't fueled by beer, the **Henry Strater Theatre** (at the Strater Hotel, 699 Main Ave., 970/375-7160, www.henrystratertheatre.com) is a venue where live performances include comedians, bluegrass, blues, Western swing, and stage shows.

Shut-Eye

The city operates a central reservations line (800/525-8855, www.durango.org) for lodging, activities, and the Durango-Silverton train. Most chain hotels are north of downtown on Main Avenue.

Inn-dependence

A block off the main drag, Kirk Komick and his mom, Diane Wildfang(!), run both the **Leland House** and **Rochester Hotel** (721 E. 2nd Ave., 970/385-1920 or 800/664-1920, www.rochesterhotel.com, $169 and up high season). Both offer superb rooms. I liked the Rochester for its Western film–themed rooms (some with kitchens), the mighty rugged decor, huge breakfast, fresh coffee and tea, and the fact that it used to be a bordello. Yowsah! Then again, both give you the comfort of an inn with the conveniences of a hotel.

The magnificent **Strater Hotel** (699 Main Ave., 970/247-4431 or 800/247-4431, www.strater.com, $169 and up in summer) was built in 1887 and is one of the nicest restored hotels you'll have the pleasure of finding. The antiques are real, the restoration flawless, and the saloon will add flavor to your tour. Not only are the 93 rooms large and quiet, the elegant Gilded Age accoutrements throughout the lobby will turn you into a frontier high roller. Western novelist Louis L'Amour loved room 222—he said the ragtime music from the bar below gave him inspiration for the plots and characters of his Sackett Series novels.

Chain Drive

These chain hotels are in town, or within 10 miles of the city center:
Best Western, Comfort Inn, Days Inn, Doubletree, Econo Lodge, Hampton Inn, Holiday Inn, Quality Inn, Ramada, Residence Inn, Super 8, Travelodge
For more information, including phone numbers and websites, see page 151.

ON THE ROAD: DURANGO TO TELLURIDE

Before you saddle up for the San Juan Skyway, heed the advice offered by local riders: Plan to stay longer than you expect; be aware that at night, it gets supernaturally dark; be careful of gravel on mountain corners; and watch for wildlife that includes bighorn sheep, elk, mountain goats,

Riding at High Elevations

If you're not accustomed to riding in the high mountains, the first few nights may find you experiencing symptoms that accompany reduced amounts of oxygen: insomnia and headaches. If you're in good physical condition, you'll have better reserves to cope with the change in altitude, but it's smart to gradually adapt to physical activities over several days—especially if you'll be residing or riding at elevations over 6,000 feet.

black bears, and mule deer. Although I suggest Telluride as the first overnight, you'll ride through other intriguing towns where you can stay the night without disappointment.

You're going to love what's coming. The 236-mile-long loop road known as San Juan Skyway is designated as an All-American Road, a National Forest Scenic Byway, and a Colorado Scenic & Historical Byway. It's recognized as one of the most beautiful drives in America and noted as the place "where the road touches the sky."

When you leave via U.S. 550 North, the road rises slightly as you enter the San Juan National Forest. Soon you are surrounded by nothing but Colorado, where the purple mountains' majesty will elicit enough *Oh, my God!*s to start a new religion. After Cascade Creek, it gets trickier, but you will fear no mountain, even as you ride over 10,000 feet into thin air. If you parked your bike and trotted 50 feet, you'd be panting like a dog.

When you reach the Coalbank Pass Summit at 10,640 feet, you may think you've hit the highest height—but you haven't. There's much more to come, but for now observe the waterfalls, great timber, Alpine meadows, and switchbacks that open the trapdoor into valleys below and then rise again to 10,910 feet at Molas

Pass. If you wanted to go underground, you wouldn't need the FBI's help. You'd just camp out here.

Ride with caution: What follows are miles of steep grade, yet only a two-foot-high guardrail stands between you and eternity. When you reach the overlook outside of Silverton, make sure your seat-back's in its upright position for the final approach.

Silverton (elevation 9,318 feet), the terminus for the narrow gauge steam train, is a Victorian mining town that dates to 1874. As you cruise into town, the information center lies on the right (open 9 A.M.–5 P.M. daily), followed by a small village of gift shops, bakeries, small hotels, and markets. The same is found on notorious Blair Street, where bordellos once thrived. If you never rode the Durango train, listen for its cacophonous grand arrival, and then roam around town. If you're an early riser as well as an early rider, the **Brown Bear Cafe** (1129 Greene St., 970/387-5630) has the best breakfast in town with thick cut bacon and great hash browns to power you over the pass. The owner, Fred, is a rider. If it's later, drop by **Handlebars** (117 13th St., 970/387-5395, www.handlebarsco.com), a combination bar and paraphernalia-cluttered restaurant, where you can order up big food for lunch or dinner, or a big brew.

Succeeding Silverton is a fantastic ride on Russian immigrant Otto Mears's Million-Dollar Highway, where roadside creeks flow outside rainbow-wide curves. Be careful here, since both the air and the road are thin and there's no margin for error in the mountains, especially when you approach Red Mountain Pass, which, at 11,075 feet, is the highest pass on your journey.

From here, it's back to Monaco riding, with more twists than a Hitchcock film. Some of the sharpest banked curves are right here, and the road becomes confused, not knowing which way it's supposed to turn. The repetitive corners give way to high canyon walls and valley overlooks that will remain with you for years, especially as you approach the town of Ouray (elevation 7,706), an optional overnight. For lodging information, check with the **Ouray Chamber of Commerce** (970/325-4746 or 800/228-1876, www.ouraycolorado.com).

Like Silverton, Ouray (you-RAY) made and lost its fortunes through mining. It recovered and remade itself as the "Switzerland of America." Jah, they did. Whether you stay overnight or not, don't miss **Box Canyon Falls** (970/325-7080). If you venture across the steel grating ($3 fee) to get close to the falls within this narrow gorge, the spring runoff thunders and throws the full weight of its freezing waters on you.

If your body's aching after the long ride, head to Ouray's main attraction, the **Hot Springs Pool** (970/325-7073), right on Main Street. You'll pay $10 to soak in waters ranging from pleasantly warm to a muscle-melting 106°F.

Ouray also has Jeep tours and rentals that peel you off your bike and thrust you into the country and up to the stratosphere, with trails climbing past 13,000 feet. **Colorado West Jeep Rentals** (701 Main St., 970/325-4014 or 800/648-5337, www.coloradowestjeeps.com) and **Switzerland of America Jeep Rentals** (226 7th Ave., 970/325-4484 or 866/990-5337, www.soajeep.com) rent Wranglers and Cherokees for half- and full-day excursions. Most riders, though, seem to prefer to leave the driving to guides who know area history and the right roads to reach fields of wildflowers, mining districts, waterfalls, and Alpine meadows. Either way, with a Jeep, you can explore ghost towns, old mining camps, and gold mines in and around Ouray. Bring warm clothes, food, a camera, and around $60 per person (for tours) to $149 (on your own).

One must-see is the **Bachelor-Syracuse Mine Tour** (970/325-0220, www.bachelorsyracusemine.com). Take U.S. 550 North to County Road 14, and then turn right and follow a gravel road to the mine entrance. Save room for food since the cowboys here cook killer breakfasts and lunches. After boarding a rickety mine car ($17), you'll head 3,350 feet through a cool (55°F), CAT scan–style tunnel eight feet wide by eight feet tall. It's eerie as hell riding along the veins of gold and silver, and it's even worse when the guide turns out the lights. Guides will provide a historical perspective to give you an in-depth and painless education on the hazards faced by Western miners. Don't miss it.

The second leg down to Telluride is easier than the first, starting atop a plateau that gives way to a valley floor. When you reach Ridgway, before you turn left at Highway 62 you may want to take a lunch break at the rustic, rider-preferred **True Grit Café** (123 N Lena St., 970/626-5739). Located on the west side of the park in town, it pays tribute to the classic John Wayne film that was shot around here.

The landscape grows larger and more impressive, and the consistently nice road affords several photo ops. This is not a road to be hurried through. This is slow-paced cowboy country and chances are you'll be tempted to unscrew the footpegs and string up some stirrups instead. The curves, neither dangerous nor demanding, lead easily to Route 145, which turns south on the western side of the San Juan Skyway.

The road rides through Placerville, into a canyon, and then beside red rock cliffs and into the Uncompahgre National Forest. Sixteen miles after you reach Route 145, Telluride comes into view and you'll stare in awe at staggering Bear Mountain Pass, a zigzag, motorcycle-destroying road that scales the mountainside beside a gushing river.

A great introduction, and the follow-up will not disappoint.

TELLURIDE PRIMER

Telluride has a mighty strange history, friend. The nomadic Utes arrived in the Telluride Valley searching for elk, deer, and mountain sheep, and then they split. The Spanish arrived in the 1700s searching for an overland route to the Pacific Coast, but they didn't stay either. The settler who decided to stick it out was a man who had a reason to stay: prospector John Fallon.

Fallon staked his claim above the town in 1875, registered the Sheridan Mine, and then struck it rich with zinc, lead, copper, iron, silver, and gold. This was the Silicon Valley of the 1870s, drawing fortune-seekers from around the world: Finns, Swedes, Irish, French, Italians, Germans, and Chinese. But unlike today's California technogeeks, the boys here had gambling halls, saloons, brothels, and friends like Butch Cassidy, who arrived to plan his first heist at the San Miguel Valley Bank in June 1889.

When the mining boom collapsed, the town suffered a slow decline until the 1960s when it approached ghost-town status. That's when a few resolute citizens realized that "white gold" (aka snow) could save their town. With a few shakes of entrepreneurial spirit, they transformed Telluride into a ski resort.

The result will keep you satisfied. There are hippies trying to re-create the halcyon days of Haight-Ashbury; there are art galleries; there's a surplus of natural beauty; and attractive young ski bums (who make life worth living for some middle-aged women and comparably depressing for some middle-aged men). And then there is money, lots of it, imported by recent transplants and celebrity residents.

Beneath it all, however, this is an ordinary mountain town. There are small markets, a hardware store, the Free Box with donations for the needy, and a calendar of events from Telluride Blues & Brews to the Bluegrass Festival to the legendary Telluride Film Festival.

It's a great little town. Have fun.

ON THE ROAD: TELLURIDE

You entered through the valley's one-way entrance when you arrived in Telluride, so a pleasure ride isn't worth the effort—at least, not on a bike. There are ways to get around and experience the town, most of which you can do fairly easily.

I'd suggest starting before 9 A.M., when the morning light bathes the mountains in a rich gold and the streets are perfectly deserted for photos. After grabbing a breakfast with the locals at **Maggie's Cafe** (110 E. Colorado Ave., 970/728-4882), walk over to the gondola on the south end of Oak Street. When it's not hauling skiers in winter, it hauls sightseers and mountain bikes in summer. And it's free.

Wait for an empty car and start your

13-minute trip to the summit. From this vantage point, the aerial views of the town and mountains grow increasingly more majestic—but hold off on photos until the return trip so ski or bike racks won't block your view. There are two stops along the way, the first at Sophia Station (just under 11,000 feet) and the second at Mountain Village (9,545 feet), a picturesque and affluent—yet oddly artificial—neighborhood. Return for a nighttime ride and you can soak in equally magical views.

When you return to town, it's small enough to do on foot. Don't pressure yourself. Just savor the mountain air and views and the fact that you're not in an office.

PULL IT OVER: TELLURIDE HIGHLIGHTS
Attractions and Adventures

You can wander around searching for individual outfitters and rental companies, or you can save some shoe leather by stopping at **Telluride Sports** (150 W. Colorado Ave., 970/728-4477 or 800/828-7547, www.telluridesports. com). Since 1972, it's been a one-stop shop for all things outdoors: fly-fishing, whitewater rafting, horseback riding, and kayaking. Prices range from $26–51 for a mountain bike day rental, although prices for guided excursions and adventures are much higher.

It'd be a shame to be way out West without saddling up at least once. A professional wrangler and full-time character named Roudy offers "gentle horses for gentle people, fast horses for fast people, and for people who don't like to ride, horses that don't like to be rode." Choices at **Riding with Roudy** (off Hwy. 145—call for directions, 970/728-9611, www.ridewithroudy.com) include a variety of trail rides starting at roughly $30 an hour, as well as dinner rides ($60) and custom pack trips.

If you ride, ride with Roudy—he's good company.

Telluride Outside (121 W. Colorado Ave., 970/728-3895 or 800/831-6230, www.tellurideoutside.com) is a full-service provider of fly-fishing and float trips, whitewater rafting, ballooning, and Jeep tours.

Shopping

If you haven't already invested in a custom hat from Thomas Barnes in Durango, I'm sure Ann McClelland, proprietor of the **Bounty Hunter** (226 Colorado St., 970/728-0256, www.shopbountyhunter. com), would like to take a crack at your skull. She and her family of hatmakers have created custom hats for Ted Nugent, Madeleine Albright, and the Clintons and can easily make a classic customized beaver-skin hat for you in a variety of styles (Rodeo, Rio Grande, Explorer, Rancher, etc.). They also craft custom-made python or alligator boots, belts, straps, and Western art.

A cool little neighborhood spirits shop, **Telluride Liquors & Wine Shop** (123 E. Colorado Ave., 970/728-3380) features about 450 wines—100 in the wine cellar—and 250 bottled beers, as well as a small humidor with a good selection of cee-gars. Its counterpart and competition is **Telluride Bottle Works** (129 W. San Juan Ave., 970/728-5553, www.telluridebottleworks.com), which has delivery service, a wider selection, and lower prices.

Now that most antiques shops claim that *Flintstones* jars are collectibles, it's great to find a place like **Telluride Antique Market** (324 W. Colorado Ave., 970/728-4323), which sells quality antiques, such as silver-plated Indian prints, cheesecake calendars, art deco items, and old travel posters and prints.

Blue-Plate Specials

Perhaps the best place to grab an early breakfast, **Maggie's Cafe** (110 E. Colorado Ave., 970/728-4882) is the hometown gathering spot. A favorite with locals, they gather for mean breakfast burritos, French toast, and fresh baked goods. Also on the menu are a variety of sandwiches and salads.

Noticing a dearth of affordable dining options, **Smugglers Brewpub and Grille** (225 S. Pine St., 970/728-0919, www.smugglersbrew.com) opened in 1998 and gained an instant following for its 10 onsite microbrews, ribs steeped in barbecue sauce, drunken chicken breasts, Philly cheesesteak sandwiches, and an interior created from an old miner's warehouse. Open for lunch and dinner, this casual, laid-back joint is a great place to grab a brew on the patio.

If you're on a writer's budget, you'll be pleased with **Baked in Telluride** (127 S. Fir St., 970/728-4775), serving breakfast, lunch, and dinner. You can grab a baked breakfast, slice of pizza, deli sandwich, soda pop, or big salad. Nothing fancy, but the food's real groovy.

Watering Holes

There are two authentic hangouts in Telluride. And the **Last Dollar Saloon** (100 E. Colorado Ave., 970/728-4800, www.lastdollarsaloon.com) is one of them. "The Buck" (as locals call it) comes complete with hardwood floors, brick walls, tin ceiling, jukebox, full liquor bar, bottled beers, and a few on tap. Can't do much better when you want a main-street view and a place to meet real people.

O'Bannon's Irish Pub (121 S. Fir St., 970/728-6139) is the other authentic hangout. This one's a small and loud basement bar with $4.50 pints of Harp, Bass, and Guinness; a pool table; a jukebox; a well-worn bar; and a ceiling draped with flags of Ireland.

One of the town's original drinking establishments, **Sheridan Bar** (231 W. Colorado Ave., 970/728-3911) is open 3 P.M.–2 A.M. daily. The oldest bar in town is topped out by a tin ceiling and features an old upright piano, long bar, and mighty cool pool hall in back. You'll feel like a cowboy.

Shut-Eye

There are no chain hotels in town, but lodging options abound in Telluride. Rates peak during winter and are higher in summer than in spring and fall. The town offers a booking service: **Telluride Central Reservations** (970/728-3041 or 888/355-8743, www.visittelluride.com) handles lodging as well as air service, performance tickets, and activities. Keep in mind that some accommodations require two-night minimum weekend stays, and prices rise during special event weekends like the film and Bluegrass festivals.

Inn-dependence

The **New Sheridan Hotel** (231 W. Colorado Ave., 970/728-4351 or 800/200-1891, www.newsheridan.com, $169–289 high season) is one of the town's best bets. It was built in 1891 and has since gotten itself gussied up with 26 spacious, tasteful rooms and suites with nice furniture and spa tubs. There are also a few condo-style suites. The full breakfast, library, and fitness room are impressive, but what puts it over the top are the two rooftop hot tubs with spectacular mountain views.

ON THE ROAD: TELLURIDE TO MESA VERDE

The overwhelming beauty of this run will either inspire you or cause cardiac arrhythmia. Leave Telluride via West Colorado and turn left after the service station on Route 145. You're back on the San Juan Skyway now, gearing up for scenery you cannot imagine.

Within minutes, you're riding into the mountains for a view of wildflowers, lakes, cliffs, and valleys slung between jagged mountain peaks. The road curves, drops, dives, and twists, taking your bike down into portions of these valleys like an elevator falling down a shaft. This section of highway is where all your Colorado visions come together. The curves are not difficult, but the overwhelming combination of colors and textures is hard to fathom. Drink in multiple shades of green from the rail-straight pines, fields of brilliant wildflowers, black-and-white mountains, and surreal blue skies.

The road is reluctant to become routine, and the surge of energy it triggers may spark you to goose it—but watch your speed, since some curves can be deceptively tight. You'll cross the 10,000-foot plateau once again and see tundra and meadows before descending to 8,827 feet into the little town of Rico.

After Rico, the road transforms into an ordinary ride through the country. It may not be as inspiring as the earlier run, but when you consider the alternative—bending paperclips in an office or sitting in city traffic—you should have no complaints.

Ride past red rocks and, before you know it, you've reached the Colorado Plateau between the San Juan Mountains and Sonoran Desert. When you reach the end of Route 145, turn left onto U.S. 160 East toward Durango. As you ride toward Mesa Verde, look to your left; about 40 miles away, you'll see the mountains you conquered a few hours earlier.

From here, it's only seven miles to **Mesa Verde National Park** (970/529-4465 or 970/529-4465, www.nps.gov/meve).

Although if you opt to stay the night at Far View Lodge (the park's only indoor lodging option), you'll have another 15 miles to go as you head deep into the park.

Whether or not you stay inside the park or in nearby Cortez, get ready for the grand finale of your nearly circular run. After springing for the $5 fee (free if you carry an annual $80 America the Beautiful Pass), you'll ride a road that rises like a phoenix, with fantastically sharp ascents that open up to endless views of the desert plains.

Four miles later, the Morefield Campground has a launderette and café, as well as the park's only option for gas. The road continues with curves similar to those of the Pacific Coast Highway, with each corner opening up to an ocean of earth. Once you've risen to the top of the mesa, take everything you recognize—and then erase it from your databank. That is what you'll see—absolutely nothing. The emptiness lasts for mile after mile, with the only constant being the shifting, braking, and cornering you'll undertake to reach the visitors center.

Now the mystery begins.

MESA VERDE PRIMER

Mesa Verde is a strange and mysterious place. Take the tales of ghost ships and the Lost Colony, multiply them by a hundred, and you still won't even begin to understand Mesa Verde.

The Ancestral Puebloans (the term now preferred over the previously common Anasazi) settled here, carving homes into the cliffs. They were hunters, traders, artisans, and farmers, and this area was the heart of their civilization for nearly 800 years.

They built stone villages on mesa tops and cliff dwellings within canyon walls, and they created elaborate stoneworks,

The Mesa Verde Mystery

You'll soon recognize Mesa Verde as one of the most mysterious places you'll visit. Someone else who was intrigued by this abandoned region was novelist Willa Cather who, in 1925, wrote:

I saw a little city of stone asleep...that village sat looking down into the canyon with the calmness of eternity, preserved with the dry air and almost perpetual sunlight, like a fly in amber, guarded by the cliffs and the river and the desert.

ceremonial kivas, intricately designed pottery, and four-story housing structures. Then, around 1300 A.D., the inhabitants of Mesa Verde packed it up. No one knows what they left with, but they left behind crops and personal belongings. Since they had no written records, to this day no one knows for sure why they left. Some archaeologists believe they moved to New Mexico and Arizona where their descendants still live today.

Their very existence remained a mystery until 1888, when ranchers Richard Wetherill and Charles Mason rode through the area to round up stray cattle. That's when Wetherill saw Cliff Palace hidden within the canyon. A few years later, amateur archaeologist Gustaf Nordenskiold arrived from Sweden to document the dwellings and sites.

What's intriguing is that there are mysteries that remain to this day. Even though the park and services aren't on the level of Yellowstone or Yosemite, Mesa Verde was still selected the world's number one historic monument by readers of *Condé Nast Traveler*—even ranking ahead of the Vatican. In 1978, UNESCO, a United Nations organization, named the park a World Heritage Cultural Site, and Mesa Verde was also the first park dedicated to the preservation of cultural resources. While it doesn't feature the multitude of services you can find in Durango and Telluride, it's a logical and fascinating archaeological find that'll wrap up your San Juan Skyway run.

ON THE ROAD: MESA VERDE

Unless you're an anthropologist or Indiana Jones, there's a smart way to see—and really understand—Mesa Verde: Take one of the half-day tours departing from the Far View Lodge. I admit that the ride around the park's juniper- and piñon-dotted landscape is fantastic, but I'd argue that it's just not worth traveling solo—at least not yet. You can always ride later, but for now borrow some insights from trained guides and let them share what happened here or you'll simply be looking at your free map and at structures and struggling to comprehend close to 5,000 identified sites. By the way, according to the modern Pueblo people, these are *sites* and not ruins since they believe their ancestors spirits still inhabit the place, and after time the structures will return to nature.

So start deep in the park at the **Far View Visitor Center** (15 miles from park entrance, open mid-April–mid-October, 8 A.M.–5 P.M.) and arrange a special ranger-led tour ($3) to either Cliff Palace, Balcony House, or Long House, since demand restricts guests to one site per day. Hold off on touring the park's museum—it will make more sense once you've taken the tour.

On just the half-day bus/walking excursion, I learned more in three hours than I did in three years of high school. The first sites you see are ordinary, but the stories and structures become increasingly more fascinating as you move on. Starting with a simple kiva (a ceremonial room), you'll eventually reach Spruce Tree House, an elaborate structure of 130 rooms and eight kivas that you can walk to and, in some sections, through. Keep in mind that with ingenious hand and toe-holds carved directly into the cliffs, many of these structures were accessible only by scaling cliff walls. You also have to walk a half-mile down to reach it, although it seems like two miles coming back up. Wear comfortable shoes and carry your own drinking water—none is available at any site.

I can't even begin to explain what you'll see and learn here so, as I've stressed, just swing by the Far View Visitor Center, sign up for a tour, and talk to the rangers who are more than ready to share what they know. When you're done, plan to return to some of the places you missed, such as the visitor center and **Chapin Mesa Archaeological Museum** (20 miles from park entrance, open 8 A.M.–6:30 P.M. daily), where dioramas and exhibits on pottery, jewelry, tools, weapons, and beadwork will fill in some of the blanks. The park also has well-stocked bookstores as well as inexpensive and informative pamphlets on specific sites. And now that you're armed with a history of the place, it's time to hit the road and see it on your own.

Hard to explain how cool this is. You have to see it for yourself.

PULL IT OVER:
MESA VERDE HIGHLIGHTS
Attractions and Adventures

The entire park is a historic site, with guided bus tours departing from **Far View Lodge** (800/449-2288). Half-day tours ($42) leave at 8 A.M. and 1 P.M. from early April to late October. Make reservations, especially in peak season.

Adjacent to the Chapin Mesa Archaeological Museum, **Spruce Tree Terrace** sells silver jewelry, etched and painted pottery, and sand paintings and there's also a shop at the Far View Terrace.

Blue-Plate Specials

There are few places to eat at Mesa Verde. Snack bars and cafeteria-style restaurants at Far View and Spruce Tree are adequate if you're not agile enough to kill and skin a rabbit with an *atlatl*. If you can swing it, the **Metate Room** at Far View Motor Lodge is the park's signature restaurant. No corn dogs here—load up on dishes such as Rocky Mountain Elk Tenderloin, Mesquite Smoked Buffalo, Blue Corn and Pine Nut-Dusted Trout, and Foxfire Farms Lamb Shank. The Southwestern-style dining room has a huge wall of windows that reveals the mesas and finger canyons, so the views are as good as the cuisine.

Shut-Eye

If you don't stay in the park, the town of Cortez, 10 miles west, has loads of chain hotels. Durango is 36 miles east of the park entrance station on U.S. 160. The park offers two options. The exterior of the top-of-the-line **Far View Lodge** ($118–132) is 1970s ugly, and the interior is generic hotel, but you get a balcony with stunning views from a 2,000-foot plateau.

The **Morefield Campground** ($20 tent, $30 full hookups), a popular spot if you don't mind roughing it, has 435 campsites with picnic tables, grills, and benches, as well as a grocery store, showers, and a laundry. Reservations for either can be made by calling 800/449-2288 or 888/896-3831 or visiting www.visitmesaverde.com.

Chain Drive

These chain hotels are in the nearby town of Cortez:

Days Inn, Econo Lodge, Holiday Inn, Rodeway, Super 8, Travelodge

For more information, including phone numbers and websites, see page 151.

Resources for Riders

Colorado Rockies Run

Colorado Travel Information
Bed & Breakfast Innkeepers of Colorado—800/265-7696,
www.innsofcolorado.org
Colorado Division of Wildlife—303/297-1192 or 303/291-7534,
www.wildlife.state.co.us
Colorado Road and Weather Conditions—303/639-1111 or instate 877/315-7623,
www.cotrip.org
Colorado State Parks Reservations—303/470-1144 or 800/678-2267,
www.parks.state.co.us
Colorado Travel and Tourism—800/265-6723, www.colorado.com

Local and Regional Information
Durango Area Chamber Resort Association—970/247-0312 or 800/525-8855,
www.durango.org
Mesa Verde National Park—970/529-4465, www.nps.gov/meve
Mesa Verde National Park Reservations—602/331-5210 or 800/449-2288,
www.visitmesaverde.com
Silverton Chamber of Commerce—970/387-5654 or 800/752-4494,
www.silvertoncolorado.com
Telluride Chamber of Commerce—970/728-3041 or 888/605-2578,
www.visittelluride.com
Telluride Visitor Services—888/353-5473, www.telluride.com

Colorado Motorcycle Shops
Basin Motorcycle Works—200 U.S. 160 Frontage Road, 970/259-9489,
www.basinmotorcycleworks.biz
Durango Harley-Davidson—750 S Camino Del Rio, Durango, 970/259-0778,
www.durangoharley.com
Fun Center Suzuki-Kawasaki—29603 U.S. 160 East, Durango, 970/259-1070,
www.funcentercycles.com
Handlebar Motorsports—346 S. Camino Del Rio, Durango, 970/247-0845,
www.handlebarmotorsports.com
Mesa Verde Motorsports—2120 S. Broadway, Cortez, 970/565-9322
Ridgway Motorsports—566 Hwy. 62, Ridgway, 970/626-5112

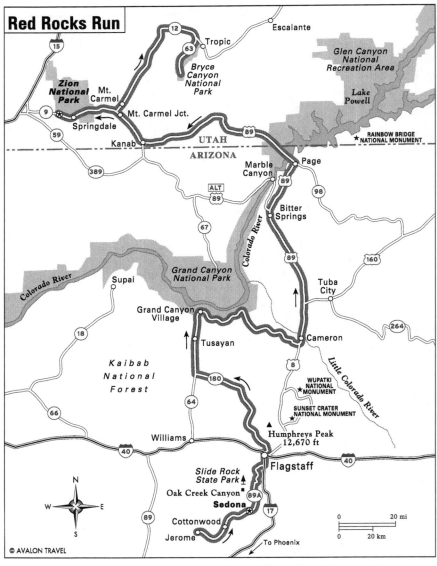

Red Rocks Run

Route: Sedona to Zion National Park via Oak Creek Canyon, Tusayan, Grand Canyon, Page, Lake Powell, Bryce Canyon

Distance: Approximately 365 miles

First Leg: Sedona to Grand Canyon, Arizona (110 miles)

Second Leg: Grand Canyon to Page, Arizona (143 miles)

Third Leg: Page, Arizona to Zion, Utah (112 miles)

Helmet Laws: Arizona and Utah do not require helmets.

Red Rocks Run

Sedona, Arizona to Zion National Park, Utah

Over the next several days, you'll find that just as the Calistoga–Sausalito–Carmel run is a perfect showcase for California towns and roads, Sedona–Grand Canyon–Zion is the right blend for Arizona and Utah. With the exception of the wild landscape and canyons around Sedona, the roads are not very challenging. Still, you may not mind too much. The vast openness of this part of the country is intriguing in its own way.

SEDONA PRIMER

Sedona. It's a beautiful name for a beautiful place. But would you feel the same way if you were riding into Schnebly Station? That was the first name proposed by settler T. Carl Schnebly when he wanted to establish a post office here in the early 1900s. When the postmaster decided the name was too long for a cancellation stamp, the honor went to Schnebly's Pennsylvania Dutch wife, Sedona.

Turn back the clock a little further, and you'll see that it's taken nature about 350 million years to make Sedona what it is today. No standard-issue brown and gray rocks here. Sedona's fire-red buttes and mesas, spires, and pinnacles are the result of a prehistoric sea washing over and receding from the area several times. The cyclic sea coverings left behind a patina of iron oxide that colors these hills.

First settled around A.D. 700, the area was home to the Sinaguans, who stuck around until 1066, when a volcano blew. They left, and the Ancestral Puebloans (also known as the Anasazi) arrived to take advantage of the recently fertilized soil and introduce modern amenities like multistoried pueblos and burglar-proof homes. Low doorways forced intruders to crouch upon entering, so the vigilant homeowner could bash their brains out.

No one knows why the Ancestral Puebloans left in the 1300s. Spanish explorers came looking for gold in the 1500s, but when they didn't find any they left, too. Prospectors, pioneers, and trappers began to arrive in the early 1800s and got along fine with the new tribes who were living here until the white man began fencing off the hunting grounds of Native Americans who rightfully argued that the land was theirs. The U.S. Army didn't want to argue, so in 1872 they shoved the Native Americans off their land.

Despite the injustice, Native Americans are well represented throughout Sedona. Today, this is a major cultural center with dozens of artists, actors, writers, and musicians gaining their inspiration from the beauty outside their doors. New Age disciples also congregate here, claiming Cathedral Rock is Sedona's most powerful female "vortex"—an electromagnetic energy force rising from within the earth. If you believe, you may find balance in health, relationships, work, and money.

Chances are you'll spend the majority of your time in Uptown Sedona, the older commercial district, or take a quick run down Oak Creek Canyon, the path that'll later lead you towards the Grand Canyon. There's nearly nothing you'd want to do indoors except sleep and eat, which makes this a natural for motorcycle travelers.

Wherever you ride, the roads will be right.

ON THE ROAD: SEDONA

It's been said that God created the Grand Canyon, but he resides in Sedona.

Sedona *is* divine. When you arrive, you'll see that the physical beauty combines the mountains of Vermont, the rocks of California, and the clay of Georgia's back roads. If it looks at all familiar, you may recall seeing a similar landscape from Pathfinder's mission to Mars.

There's a lot to see on surrounding roads, and perhaps the most popular stop for motorcycle travelers is about 30 miles away in Jerome, an old mining town that's become a strangely popular destination.

The ride's not that spectacular, but if you didn't go there your friends might beat you with sticks.

From Uptown Sedona, South Highway/West Highway 89A is a wide four-lane road that passes franchise restaurants and rides away from the red rocks which look outstanding in your mirrors. The road remains the same until you near Cottonwood, where you turn left at the gas station in Clarkdale and begin your steep ascent. It's another four miles up the mountain, where it seems that the landscape was left behind from a Saturday-morning cowboy matinee.

Next to Taos, it seems that the town of Jerome has done the best job of creating something out of nothing. In its heyday as a copper mining community, it was the third-largest city in Arizona. After copper bottomed out, residents headed out and today the town can't even rustle up a gas station, grocery, doctor, or pharmacy. None of this will matter after you park your bike with all the others outside the **Spirit Room** (144 Main St., 928/634-8809, www.spiritroom.com) and consider yourself at home.

This joint has become the base for local riders making their way across high mountain country, low desert, red rocks, and canyons in easy one-day rides. No fighting, no country music, no pointy boots here, just a watering hole for riders who appreciate the lack of a cover, live music, cold brews, and Bloody Marys that can hurt you. You can add to the bar's collection of graffiti or donate a bra (if you wear one).

Farther down on Main Street, **Paul and Jerry's** (206 Main St., 928/634-2603) has been a saloon since 1887. Today, it serves beer and has a full bar and three pool tables in back. **Mile High Grill & Inn** (309 Main St., 928/634-5094, www.jeromemilehighinn.com), built in 1899, is one of a few restaurants here, with an upscale appearance that runs counter to a fairly basic menu of hamburgers, enchiladas, soups, and appetizers.

Unless you've got a mighty deep hankering for a drink, Jerome should take only a few hours. When you return to Sedona, you'll be tempted to examine the red rock monoliths that contrast beautifully with the green of piñon, juniper, and cypress trees. Pick up a Sedona map that identifies the monoliths, which are named for their appearance: Cathedral, Courthouse, Snoopy, Elephant...You'll have to find the local off-color favorite on your own.

Since you'll be running down Oak Creek Canyon on your way north, head down Highway 179 to Chapel Road and turn left to reach the **Chapel of the Holy Cross** (780 Chapel Rd., 928/282-4069, www.chapeloftheholycross.com). A labor of love, the chapel was purposely designed to appear like part of the rock formation, with a magnificent cross seeming to project from the mountainside. From its summit, you have an unobstructed view of Courthouse Butte, Bell Rock, and the Two Nuns. Time this for late afternoon and you'll be here to witness one of the most spectacular sunsets in the country.

Afterward, the town is yours to explore. Wander around uptown or go deeper into the desert on a Jeep tour. Sedona is a great town—you shouldn't cheat yourself.

PULL IT OVER:
SEDONA HIGHLIGHTS
Attractions and Adventures

The term "great outdoors" doesn't do justice to Sedona. It's actually much greater than that here, but largely inaccessible to touring bikes. Other modes of transportation—rental Jeeps, guided tours, and hot air balloons—can be almost as much fun if you can afford it. Most ground-based tours take you on rugged and historic trails leading to off-the-beaten-path canyons and mountains.

Ride with a guide on **Sedona Red Rock Jeep Tours** (270 N. Hwy. 89A, 520/282-6826 or 800/848-7728, www.redrockjeep.com). Choose from an introductory vortex tour to a horseback ride. Everyone needs a gimmick, and **Pink Jeep Tours** (204 N. Hwy./W. Hwy. 89A, 928/282-5000 or 800/873-3662, www.pinkjeep.com) has chosen color. These folks offer tours ranging from a $45 90-minute Coyote Canyons ride to the $72 Ancient Ruin ride. The 2.5-hour trip heads to a Sinaguan Indian cliff dwelling, where a guide points out and explains the rock art. Roughriders can try the Broken Arrow run, which offers two hours of heavy-duty 4x4-ing.

A Day in the West (252 N. Hwy. 89A, 928/282-4320 or 800/973-3662, www.adayinthewest.com) has an array of tours. Photo tours, Jeep tours, horseback rides, and chuckwagon trips are planned by guides "who've been riding these trails so long, there's red dust in their veins." Prices range from $45 for the pioneer trail ride to $170 for a Jeep/horseback/Western dinner.

Although it's mighty 'spensive and you won't see the rocks up close, **Northern Light Balloon Expeditions** (928/282-2274 or 800/230-6222, www.northernlightballoon.com) offers the most peaceful way to see the hills—provided you can shake yourself awake for the sunrise flight. These folks will pick you up at your place and get you worked up for an hour flight (nearing $200), but the entire experience lasts up to four hours when you consider there's the inflation and post-flight champagne picnic. The payoff for the early day is that you'll feast on a brilliant palette of colors found only in nature. And Sedona.

If you're looking for a concentration of Southwestern art, you'll find it in Uptown or at **Tlaquepaque** (tah-lah-ca-POK-ee, Hwy. 179, 928/282-4838, www.tlaq.com) at the bridge, open 10 A.M.–5 P.M. daily. Modeled after a Mexican village, the shopping district spreads out and rambles through shaded courtyards and ivy-covered walls.

Blue-Plate Specials

It looks like a hole in the wall, but at **Cowboy Club Grille & Spirits** (241 N. Hwy. 89A, 928/282-4200, www.cowboyclub. com), "high desert cuisine" goes hand in hand with Old West tradition and hospitality. Try the rattlesnake(!), pistachio-crusted halibut, buttermilk fried chicken, or buffalo(!) sirloin, low in fat, high in protein. There are other dining choices here, too—Redstone Cabin and the Silver Saddle Room—and the bar is great, too, with legendary margaritas. The prices seem fair and the service excellent. Cowboy is open for lunch and dinner. Oh, and the Cowboy Artists of America was founded here.

I usually wake up before breakfast, so it was a boon to find the **Coffee Pot Restaurant** (2050 W. Hwy. 89A, 928/282-6626), which can create—upon request and with no help from confederates—101 types of omelettes. I ordered one with pencil shavings, string, and gravel and got the bejeezus beat out of me. Here since the 1950s, the Coffee Pot is the place for locals, celebs, and any traveler who wants a hearty breakfast or lunch.

Shut-Eye

For a complete listing of nearly 20 bed-and-breakfast inns that are inspected and approved by the Sedona Bed & Breakfast Guild, check 800/915-4442 or www. bbsedona.net. The **Sedona Chamber of Commerce** (928/282-7722, www.sedonachamber.com) is a good source of information on the many cabins of Oak Creek Canyon.

Motels and Motor Courts

The **Sedona Motel** (218 Hwy. 179, 928/282-7187, www.thesedonamotel. com, $90–100) is an old-fashioned motel just over a half mile from the town center. Clean and neat, it offers 16 ground level rooms with microwaves, coffee makers, and mini fridges.

La Vista Motel (500 N. Hwy. 89A, 928/282-7301 or 800/896-7301, www. lavistamotel.com, $69 and up) is one of the most economical choices. Don't expect luxury from this family-owned motel, but for a clean room close to everything, it's a fine place to bunk down.

Inn-dependence

The highly ranked **Creekside Inn** (99 Copper Cliffs Dr., 928/282-4992 or 800/390-8621, www.creeksideinn.net, $199 and up) rests—coincidentally—right beside Oak Creek. Although the setting is wild, the inn is not—it's Victorian, with swank guestrooms featuring jetted tubs and a furnished garden patio. This is the place for grown-ups who've paid off the mortgage.

If you're traveling in a pack or need room to spread out, **Junipine** (8351 N. Hwy. 89A, 928/282-3375 or 800/742-7463, www.junipine.com, $190–320) features one-bedroom, two-bedroom, and creekside cottages—all in the heart of Oak Creek Canyon. The cottages (ranging from 900 to 1,400 square feet) contain a fully equipped kitchen, private deck, living room, and two fireplaces. The secluded, wooded setting may make it hard to break away.

Chain Drive

These chain hotels are in town, or within 10 miles of the city center:
Best Western, Comfort Inn, Days Inn, Fairfield Inn, Hampton Inn, Hilton, Hyatt, Radisson, Super 8

For more information, including phone numbers and websites, see page 151.

ON THE ROAD: SEDONA TO THE GRAND CANYON

If you weren't able to resist temptation, you may have already ridden up this road. Not a bad idea, because this route is definitely worth a second look.

The beginning of this run is a perfect goodbye to Sedona since it is just as beautiful, albeit in a lush, more verdant way. You'll notice the topography changing as North Highway 89A slides into Oak Creek Canyon and from the seat of your bike, you command a vantage point not enjoyed by motorists. The canyon appears on your right, clinging so close to the guardrail that it seems much deeper than it actually is.

For several miles this gentle ride doesn't demand a lot, except that you pay attention to nature and the guardrail barely high enough to keep you out of the canyon. Just when you didn't think it could get better, it does, with red rocks on one side and a canopy road on the other. You're descending into the canyon now and approaching **Slide Rock State Park** (6871 N. Hwy. 89A, 928/282-3034, http://az-stateparks.com/parks/slro), a slippery run down the rocks that's worth a stop if you have a bathing suit in your bags. Admission is $10 per vehicle in the summer, $8 off-season, with visitors crowding the park and parking lots in summer.

Continuing north, you'll pass small motels and creekside cabins before, gradually, the red rocks give way to white granite formations that look like El Capitan in miniature. Soon you begin your ascent into hearty pine forests, riding up to 6,000 feet and facing some exciting 20-mph twisties. As the ride continues it gets even more thrilling when you look straight up and see the Babel-esque–road winding overhead. While it can be tricky riding, it's quite a bit safer thanks to a sprawling chain-link fence that keeps the mountain from falling on top of you.

At 7,000 feet, pull off at Oak Creek Vista, often where a contingent of Native American merchants are selling silver and turquoise jewelry and other handcrafted artwork. This is a great place for a break and a picture—look over the side and see Oak Creek rushing past 1,500 feet below you.

Just about the time you've gotten used to the curves, the road levels out in a pine forest before Oak Creek Canyon Road surrenders to I-17. A few miles ahead is I-40, but bypass it and veer to the west of Flagstaff to find U.S. 180, a two-lane that forks to the left and takes you on a roughly 30-mile tour of pine forests and mountains. You are riding in proximity to Humphrey's Peak which, at 12,633 feet, is the highest point in Arizona. As the road skims along its base, you have the privilege of continuing the same pine forest run that's become a part of your life. You won't face the challenge of switchbacks, nor will you suffer from the hypnotizing effects of straights either. Instead, the road is marked by slow, meandering curves that glide across a fairly level landscape. As soon as you've grown accustomed to the richness and verdant green of the forest, nature decides to change the scene. You start dropping slowly and imperceptibly as you cruise into the high desert. As you ride steadily along U.S. 180, you'll cross another 20 miles of desert and sagebrush before reaching the junction of Highway 64, with U.S. 180 taking a sharp turn to the north.

Even though the road is flat, you may have the same gut feeling I did, namely that you're riding atop the crest of an abnormally massive mountain. In reality, you are. This is the Kaibab Plateau and you're cruising across the wide, flat peak of a low, rounded mountain. While you still have about 30 miles to ride before hitting Grand Canyon, the ease and solitude of the landscape around you grant abundant time to just relax and think, especially near mile marker 196 when the land rises slightly and an incredible vista of the plains spreads out before you. It's moments like this that enhance a ride—creating memories that'll follow you back home and find you planning future road trips. On a clear day, look to the horizon and you can see the Grand Canyon, just a black streak from here.

There's little to note between here and there, just straight riding until you reach the growing village of Tusayan—and your destination.

GRAND CANYON PRIMER

Each time a magazine or TV program does a "Best of America" piece, you can bet you'll see an image of the Grand Canyon—and for good reason. It's large, it's beautiful in an empty sort of way, and, as a national park, it belongs to you.

Back in 1530, though, it belonged to Don Lopez de Cardenas, a captain in Coronado's expedition. It was de Cardenas who discovered the Grand Canyon—which was news to the Indians who were already here.

Fast forward to the 20th century. The Grand Canyon was named a national monument in 1908 and a national park in 1919 and it was obvious why it deserved the honor. If you've never seen it, every image you can picture in your mind pales in comparison to the real thing because it is far larger than anything you can imagine. Even when you're actually there and standing at the rim, you're seeing only a

fraction of the entire canyon. Measured by river course, the dimensions are staggering. The chasm is 277 miles long and up to 18 miles wide, and has an average depth of one mile. It took six million years (give or take a few hours) to cut the Grand Canyon, and nature is not finished yet. Rain, snow, heat, frost, and wind are constantly sculpting new shapes, bluffs, and buttes. The reed-thin creek at the bottom is the Colorado River, which averages 300 feet wide and up to 100 feet deep. It is this relative sliver of water that is the erosive force that carved the canyon.

If your schedule permits, try to avoid a summer tour. Naturally, when the kids are out of school they're all here with their parents and the Grand Canyon Village is packed. Summer's also the season when vehicles—even your faithful mount—are restricted from riding Hermit Road to clear the way for a fleet of more practical shuttle buses. Overall, the combined crowds and dense traffic can detract from the experience. Whenever you arrive the colors of the canyon seem to change throughout the year, from the crisp frosts in winter to the cool autumn hues. Try to arrive in the morning before the high sun washes out its colors. If you have the wherewithal, see it via mule train, helicopter, or raft.

ON THE ROAD: THE GRAND CANYON

You'll pay $12 to enter the park (free with the $80 America the Beautiful Pass) and unless you've already invested in an aerial tour or have some sense of the canyon's history, your first stop should be the park's visitors center. Here you can get a map of the park that shows the best overlooks, watch an introductory film, and see a very large-scale model of the canyon that, in proportion, would make you as thin as a paper match.

When you reach the canyon rim what you'll see is Sedona in reverse. Every red rock is sucked down into the earth until the heroic hole loses all sense of dimension. Whether you look at the canyon from a helicopter, airplane, mule, or just standing at its edge, it looks as if the Colorado River far below is just a squirt-gun stream, and an 8,000-square-foot boulder on its banks appears no larger than a pebble. I've said it before: The canyon's architecture is far larger than anything you can comprehend. You can take pictures until you pass out, but unless you blow them up to actual size they won't begin to reflect the breadth, width, depth, and grandeur of this place.

What you *can* appreciate is that the view is different from each overlook, although one thing that remains the same is the sight of tourists who seem to flock to the same point at each protective barricade. Be bold. Walk about 30 feet to either side and you'll likely find a secluded spot where the view is just as nice and you can find a secluded promontory to call your own, a place where you can relax uninterrupted and contemplate the scene before you. If you have time—and you should allow some—arrive near dusk and head down Hermit Road to watch the canyon moon rise and the shadows fall like the sweep of a watch's second hand.

Perhaps the most spectacular view is several miles east in Desert View. Climbing the 70-foot Watch Tower, built in 1932 as an observation station, places you a total of 7,522 feet above sea level. Of all the vista points at the Grand Canyon, this is definitely worth a stop, and the pictures are priceless.

PULL IT OVER: GRAND CANYON HIGHLIGHTS
Attractions and Adventures
Grand Canyon: The Hidden Secrets

is a must-see. Catch it at the National Geographic Visitor Center's **IMAX Theater** (Hwy. 64, Tusayan, 928/638-2203, www.explorethecanyon.com, about $13). The film captures great views of the canyon, offers a historical perspective, and earns your undying respect for the one-armed stuntman who portrays explorer William Powell shooting the rapids on the Colorado. How he didn't paddle in circles, I'll never know. Some scenes in this film are so scary, you'd swear you're in the raft yourself. Outside, the tourist information center and gift shops are a convenient stop.

There are abundant fun and freakishly expensive opportunities to kick up your adrenaline. Helicopter and airplane tours are the most popular, but if you can swing it (because it *is* pricey), invest in a helicopter tour. Flying lower and slower than an airplane (although no one can fly beneath the rim), you'll cross the 18-mile-wide canyon twice at about 100 mph and receive the benefit of the pilot's narrative along the way. Among the stories guides tell is the tale of Louis Boucher, a man who obviously didn't like company. When a settler encroached on Boucher by establishing a homestead two miles away, the silver miner retreated into the Grand Canyon for a little privacy.

The easiest way to make reservations for area helicopter, airplane tours, and Jeep tours is to contact the **Grand Canyon CVB** (928/638-2901, www.grandcanyonchamber.com) and let them do it for you. They can also explain the advantages of each tour and steer you in the direction you need. If you'd prefer to make arrangements yourself, here are a few helicopter services to contact, each are open from about 8 A.M.–6 P.M. daily during summer, 9 A.M.–5 P.M. in the winter, and charge approximately $130 for 30 minutes, and about $200 for a 50-minute tour. Choose from **Grand Canyon Helicopters** (928/638-2764 or 800/541-4537, www.grandcanyonhelicoptersaz.com); **Papillon Grand Canyon Helicopters** (928/638-2419 or 800/528-2418, www.papillon.com); or **Maverick Helicopters** (702/261-0007 or 888/261-4414, www.maverickhelicopters.com).

If you don't trust helicopters, opt for an airplane tour, which starts at around $75 for a 30-minute flight, and around $95 for 50 minutes. **Grand Canyon Airlines** (928/638-2359 or 866/235-9422, www.grandcanyonairlines.com) takes you up in a twin-engine Otter for one of the longest (45–50 minutes) and most complete air routes permitted over the canyon. Operating since 1927, the Otters fly more slowly than other planes, and their high wings and panoramic windows are designed for aerial sightseeing. Flights cost around $95. **Air Grand Canyon** (928/638-2686 or 800/247-4726, www.airgrandcanyon.com) offers flights from 30 minutes long, with extended trips flying over the western canyon so you can see waterfalls and the Native American village.

If you'd rather be on the river than up in the air, choose from nearly 20 Colorado River outfitters, who take either gentle cruises down the river or hair-raising, coronary-busting, life-threatening (or life-affirming) races through the rapids. Some are one-day affairs, most go overnight or longer. The best source for information on these companies is the **Grand Canyon River Trip Information Center** (928/638-7843 or 800/959-9164, www.nps.gov/grca). The center also provides updates on which launch dates have been cancelled. Rafting is popular enough to recommend reservations up to six months in advance.

Less thrilling than a raft ride, **Grand Canyon Mule Trips** (303/297-2757, www.xanterra.com) nevertheless can be fun and save your feet. On one-day trips to Plateau Point (around $160), you'll spend about six hours in the saddle. Another pricier proposition is taking an overnight to Phantom Ranch, located at the bottom of the canyon. Although the ranch is not luxurious, you get a sack lunch on the way down, a stew or steak dinner that evening, and breakfast the following morning. Cabins include bunk beds and showers, and prices vary based on the number of people in your party. The more you bring, the less you'll pay. As a guideline, this'll cost about $430 each for two people. Both are physically rigorous trips and there's a weight limit of 200 pounds.

Outside the park, the center of Grand Canyon commerce lies in the **Tusayan General Store** (Hwy. 64, Tusayan, 928/638-2854). This grocery store serves double duty as a post office and gift shop. While it's certainly not an adventure, the general store is a convenience place to gather supplies.

Blue-Plate Specials

Choices inside the park are limited, but you can find meals at the Maswic Cafeteria, Yavapai Cafeteria, the Arizona Room, the Bright Angel Restaurant, and at other park service hotels. The only one that requires reservations is the fine dining restaurant **El Tovar Dining Room** (inside El Tovar Hotel, www.grandcanyonlodges.com). You can get the full rundown on this and other Grand Canyon choices by calling 928/638-2631. In Tusayan, the **Canyon Star** (inside Grand Hotel, 928/638-3333, www.grandcanyongrandhotel.com) serves big food, such as hand-carved steaks and turkey, and features a large salad bar. The entertainment (folk singers or Native American dancers) doesn't cost you a dime.

Shut-Eye

For general information on lodging within the park itself, call the park at 928/638-7888 and they can detail some of your options. Bear in mind that if you do stay inside the park, prices are pretty steep (illustrating the lesson of supply and demand).

All told, more than 2,000 rooms are available in adjacent Tusayan and the Grand Canyon Village, and the park has several campgrounds including **Mather Campground** (800/365-2267, www.recreation.gov, $18) which features full amenities, a store, and showers, and takes reservations. Sites at **Desert View** (928/638-7851, $12), are available on a first-come, first-served basis, but organized groups of 9–40 people may make reservations ($2 per person, plus $2.50 per campsite). Facilities include restrooms and picnic tables, but no showers.

Grand Canyon National Park Lodges (303/297-2757 or 888/297-2757, www.grandcanyonlodges.com or www.xanterra.com) features the most prized lodging options, and reservations can be made up to two years in advance; same-day reservations are taken at 928/638-2631. The 78-room **El Tovar Hotel** ($174–250) is the most expensive and most beautiful lodge, although only four suites have a view of the canyon. Opened in 1905, the precursor to Yosemite's Ahwahnee features a stone-and-timber design, concierge and room service, and fine dining at the on-site restaurant. Less than 40 steps from the rim, it also includes a gift shop and small general store. Other less attractive options include **Maswik Lodge,** which is a quarter mile from the canyon's edge and features cabins as well as motel-style rooms with two queen beds and a full bath ($90–170). Other choices that lack the traditional Western look the park calls for include the **Bright Angel** ($79 and up for a basic room with a shared bath, $90 with a private bath; around $140 for a rim cabin). The ugly-ass **Thunderbird and Kachina Lodges** range from $170–180.

Less expensive options are the chain hotels and suites that line Highway 64 in Tusayan. The **Grand Hotel** (928/638-3333 or 888/634-7263, www.grandcanyongrandhotel.com, $85 and up) styles itself after an Old West national park resort, but is housed in an attractive and relatively new building. The rooms are large and comfortable, and at night they feature Western entertainment and Native American dancers.

Chain Drive

These chain hotels are in town, or within 10 miles of the city center: **Best Western, Holiday Inn, Quality Inn** For more information, including phone numbers and websites, see page 151.

ON THE ROAD: GRAND CANYON TO PAGE

When you head east on Highway 64 cruising along the South Rim, you'll start to see a little more of the Grand Canyon. The ride starts out gently, with pine forests on both sides and, occasionally, a turnout where you can pull over for one last, less crowded look. After Navajo Point, you'll pass the Watch Tower, which is definitely worth a stop, and then depart the park by the East Rim.

The road is nice and wide, and the way it's laid out you can cruise into curves low and slow. The landscape can be deceptive: When you leave the Grand Canyon, you assume the views are behind you, but now you are granted just enough elevation to afford glimpses into the canyon's tributaries. Unfortunately, the near seamless natural beauty is often interrupted by the self-derogating signs of roadside Navajo trinket stands: "Nice Indian behind you! Chief sez turn back now! Chief love you!" Kind of sad, really.

Like the highway through Death Valley, Highway 64 is breathtaking in its desolation and that emptiness is only broken when you reach U.S. 89 at Cameron. Turn left (north) and ride a few hundred yards to a good fuel and food stop. The **Cameron Trading Post** (928/679-2231 or 800/338-7385, www.camerontradingpost.com) is a mini-empire with a motel, artwork, fudge, gas, moccasins, cowboy hats, ponchos, rugs, replica weapons, jackets, and Indian headdresses priced at hundreds of bucks. Other than that economic anomaly, prices are fair here and the merchandise is of surprisingly good quality. Get gas here—the next leg across the Navajo reservation is relatively empty. Speaking of empties, if you need evidence of the alcohol problem on reservations, just look at the roadside, where beer bottles bloom like sagebrush.

There's scant scenery as it's typically defined, but you may be satisfied that you can observe a different way of life here. No suburbs or neighborhood beautification programs, just a scattered collection of old trailers that come complete with horse and truck.

Things pick up about 34 miles south of Page, where great red cliffs rise on the horizon. About 10 miles later, near Bitter Springs, you'll start to ride right into those red cliffs. They are majestic and overpowering, and as you ride directly down the throat of one of these giants, the road turns and you ascend to one of the most amazing vistas on the trip. Stop here and take a long look. A gorgeous gorge opens up far below and the plains spread out for hundreds of miles. I stopped here for quite awhile, pleased to be away from phones, desks, and computers and focused on nothing but the pleasure of riding a motorcycle and making chance discoveries like this. Nature's not finished yet.

After you saddle up, around the corner is yet another fantastic sight: You're riding through a red cavern created where a road was laid between a mountain. Although the sensation only lasts for a few hundred yards, when the walls dwarf you it creates another memorable moment.

After twisting your bike through canyon walls, you'll encounter mile after mile of nothing but plains at 6,000 feet with nearby cliffs rising higher. The desert floor is red and white and brown and yellow and speckled with sagebrush. At sunset the light reaches out to the farthest points on the horizon and over the wonderful buttes that dwarf actual smokestacks. It sounds strange, but seeing this endless vista makes you feel as if you're part of infinity.

Let this scene fix itself in your mind. After that, you can turn to Page.

PAGE PRIMER

Back before Page was Page, the Navajos thought that this barren land was a bewitched place where the trees had died of fear. They didn't care too much after 1956, when they swapped about 20 square miles of this land with the government for a larger tract in Utah.

Back then, Page was just a construction camp for workers building the nearby Glen Canyon Dam. When they weren't busy, workers applied their engineering skills to the sand and rock and turned this into a frontier town of metal structures.

Page was incorporated in 1975, and in the last quarter century or so, this slow-paced town of about 8,000 has become a base for water sports on Lake Powell, which now fingers its way up into Utah. There's not much to see here unless you plan on fishing, skiing, or sitting on a houseboat. Page is the hub of the "Grand Circle," though, and from here you can opt to continue the final 115 miles to Zion or 133 miles to Bryce Canyon, or go off script and ride the 235 miles to Mesa Verde National Park.

ON THE ROAD: PAGE

Page still feels a little too new to be of too much interest, but the people are nice and if you stay over, just ride down to the visitors center at the **Glen Canyon Dam** (928/608-6404 for visitors, 928/608-6072 for tour information) for a look at the dam and displays on geology, water, turbines, and dams. By any measure, this is a damn big dam. At 1,560 feet across, 710 feet high, and 300 feet thick at the bottom, it holds back the force of a 186-mile-long lake. Bear in mind that the dam only scratches the surface of the 1.25 million-acre **Glen Canyon National Recreation Area** (928/608-6200, www.nps.gov/glca).

Since the roads here are relatively ordinary, you may be better off cruising on Lake Powell. With its sinuous stretch across the desert, to see every nook and inlet on the lake you'd sail nearly 2,000 miles—nearly the width of America—to see blue waters lapping at cliffs, buttes, and gentle sands where the color of the canyon changes as evening shadows fall. The easiest way to get on the water is through the **Lake Powell Resorts & Marinas** (928/645-2433 or 800/528-6154, www.lakepowell.com), which has cornered the market on water sports. The recreation area's largest marina and lodging facility, five miles north of Glen Canyon Dam on U.S. 89, has gift shops, campgrounds, RV park, laundry, showers, and a service station. From here, you can rent houseboats,

powerboats, personal watercraft, and assorted water toys, or arrange a fishing excursion for bass, catfish, bluegill, crappie, trout, and walleye. Float down below the dam, where the cold waters are a favorite spot for trophy trout.

Remember: Dam. Good fishing.

PULL IT OVER:
PAGE HIGHLIGHTS
Attractions and Adventures

Page is at the front door to the Navajo Nation and if you want an introduction to the Navajo culture and their way of life, visit the **Navajo Village Heritage Center** (Coppermine Rd. and Hwy. 98, 928/660-0304, www.navajovillage.com). They offer an evening tour ($50, 2.5 hours) that touches on the Navajo Creation Story and progression through its four worlds. You learn about silversmithing, rug weaving, living on Mother Earth, and appreciating all things under Father Sky. The tour includes a traditional dinner and entertainment by the Red Moccasin dancers. Reservations are required.

Although early settlers did their best to crush the Indian culture, the Navajos retained some of the nation's most amazing landscapes. Near Page it is **Antelope Canyon** (928/698-2808, www.navajonation-parks.org), a fantastically deep, narrow, and extraordinarily colorful slot canyon carved into the layers of sandstone by water and wind. The Navajo Nation parks system operates the upper and lower canyons. Check the website for a list of guides who can lead you to one of the most beautiful places on earth.

It's not an adventure per se, but **Stix Bait and Tackle** (5 Lake Powell Blvd., 928/645-2891, www.stixbaitandtackle.com) is Page's favorite fishing spot. Locals congregate here before dawn to swap fish stories and plan their fishing strategies.

The store has everything: licenses, tackle, sporting goods, rod and reel rental, guide referral, groceries, snacks, pop, beer, liquor, coolers, ice, bait (live, plastic, or frozen), fresh anchovies, coffee, and doughnuts.

Colorado River Discovery (130 6th Ave., 928/645-9175 or 888/522-6644, www.raftthecanyon.com) offers a calming half-day cruise ($75) into historical canyons first navigated by Major John Wesley Powell. Guides are part pilot, part historian as they explain ancient petroglyphs left by Ancestral Puebloans. Bring a wide-brimmed hat, tennis shoes, a bathing suit, and a camera. A bus will drive you to the base of Glen Canyon Dam for the cruise, and then pick you up at Lee's Ferry for the one-hour trip back to Page. Water and soft drinks are provided on the rafts, and box lunches are available from the River's End Café at the outfitter's.

For a full list of activities or to make reservations for water sports on Lake Powell, call the **Wahweap Reservations Service** (800/528-6154, www.lakepowell.com).

Blue-Plate Specials

Serving big food for lunch and dinner, **Ken's Old West** (718 Vista, 928/645-5160) is appropriately accented with miner's lamps, sturdy wooden beams, and an old upright piano. Entrées include thick meat—steaks and barbecue ribs. The backroom bar and dance floor make it one of Page's few nightspots.

Finding an authentic, unpretentious '50s diner is a rarity, so don't miss **R. D.'s Drive-In** (143 Lake Powell Blvd., 928/645-2791). Settle in a booth and pretend you're Fonzie. Open for breakfast, lunch, and dinner, R. D.'s serves all the good and occasionally greasy foods your parents fed you on road trips (before you heard about cholesterol), including flavor-burst cones, chili, burritos, shakes, fries,

and the "famous" R. D. burger. Good food, cheap.

Whiners, crybabies, penny pinchers, and complainers are barred from the **Dam Bar & Grille** (644 N. Navajo Dr., 928/645-2161, www.damplaza.com), a restaurant/saloon serving dinner and the self-proclaimed "best bar by a dam site." The huge dining room serves all the basic food groups, including porterhouse steak, king crab, ribs, dirty Sonoran chicken, and pastas.

Also part of the Dam Bar is the **Blue Buddha Sushi Lounge** (644 N. Navajo Dr.). Exotic dishes include hip presentations of traditional sushi created with southwest flair, like the Lake Powell Roll created with salmon, mango, jalapeno, avocado, and a sweet chili sauce topping. Save room for the deep-fried Oreos.

Watering Holes

Next door to the Dam Bar, the **Gunsmoke Saloon** (644 N. Navajo Dr., 928/645-2161, www.damplaza.com) features a large rectangular bar, numerous widescreen TVs, several beers on tap, a fireplace, dance floor, billiards, and darts. **Slackers** (635 Elm St., 928/645-5267) serves beer and "burgers that will change your life," all in a casual setting with flat screen televisions tuned to sports. Another joint for billiards and dancing is the **Windy Mesa** (800 N. Navajo Dr., 928/645-2186), a popular local hangout with live entertainment and a variety of beer and stronger beverages.

Shut-Eye

Page has several chain hotels, so take your pick. The **Lake Powell Resort** (100 Lake Shore Dr., 928/645-2433 or 888/896-3829, www.visitlakepowell.com, $165–225) features 250 hotel-like rooms—some that overlook the lake—a restaurant, a convenience store, and a gift shop, along with boat rentals, boat tours, and marina services.

Chain Drive

These chain hotels are in town, or within 10 miles of the city center:

Best Western, Courtyard by Marriott, Days Inn, Holiday Inn, Motel 6, Quality Inn, Rodeway, Super 8

For more information, including phone numbers and websites, see page 151.

ON THE ROAD: PAGE TO ZION

As you rode north from the Grand Canyon you may have noticed colorful examples of geological rioting. That trend continues as you leave Page. During the last 10 million years innumerable rock compressions, deformations, and uplifts created Grand, Zion, and Bryce canyons as well as cliffs that change color from chocolate to vermilion, white, gray, and pink.

You'll be cruising through the Vermilion Cliffs on your ride to Zion, which begins with views of scattered sagebrush and grazing cattle. Less than 10 miles out of Page you arrive in Utah where the rocks begin to take on new shapes with the forces of wind, water, and erosion applying a whitish finish to these cliffs.

After awhile the scenery dissipates and the long, straight roads change little in elevation until about 18 miles into Utah when you reach a section of the Grande Escalante (Grand Staircase). Arches striped red, brown, and white monitor the landscape, and you'll spot numerous caves that'll tempt you to park your bike and go look for Injun Joe.

After that, the lull in scenery returns and the ensuing lack of visual activity can tend to make you less alert, but the roadside monuments for dead motorists who suffered the same malady may rouse you. After covering about 50 miles, you'll see a town in the distance. This is Kanab. Although folks in Page speak of Kanab with a reverence usually reserved for the Holy Trinity, I didn't find much here.

Now you're not so far from Zion National Park, and U.S. 89 continues winding across the plains. Foreshadowing what's to come, as if created from a watercolor painting, the cliffs add more swirls and colors to their composition. Embedded in the coral pink rocks are designs suggesting knotted rope, tire marks, and the fluid pattern of whipped cake batter.

When you reach Mount Carmel Junction, where U.S. 89 veers sharply north, you'll likely be tempted to detour 60 miles to Bryce Canyon. If so, you'll find an ordinary road, a few valleys, and a town called Orderville, where there's a rock shop, then another rock shop, and across the street— a rock shop. A little farther along on the left, there's a rock shop. The road and the riding is easy. When you reach Bryce itself, by following Highway 12 East toward Tropic, at first glance you'll know it was worth the ride. The landscape is not so much red as orange, and it beckons you with short rock tunnels and arches followed by a ride on a wide-open plain with mesas.

At Highway 12, turn right and you'll see **Ruby's Inn** (435/834-5341 or 866/866-6616, www.rubysinn.com), a small town disguised as a gas station/hotel/restaurant/rodeo arena/store. Here since 1916, this may not be a bad place to bunk down if you're tired of riding and you'd like to rest up and appreciate what's ahead. It's only a few miles more until you've arrived at **Bryce Canyon National Park** (435/834-5322, www.nps.gov/brca). Twelve bucks takes you and your bike to overlooks where you'll see the fabled "hoodoos," pillars of red rock created about 60 million years ago in a prehistoric lake. If time is short, the first five pullouts should give you a sense of the park fairly quickly.

If you forsake Bryce, stick with Highway 9 into Zion National Park. For roughly four miles, you get a few twists and curves, and the speed limit drops to 30 mph—slowing not for curves, but for cows. A few miles later, you'll reach the east gate of Zion National Park. Although you may have booked a room at Zion Lodge in the park, more likely your night's rest awaits in the town of Springdale, a few miles beyond the southern exit. Either way, right now you'll get a small taste of Zion—enough to inspire you to feast on the park once you've settled down.

ZION PRIMER

It's no small praise that, even when compared to Yosemite and the Grand Canyon, Zion exudes a stronger sense of nature. Zion National Park contains less than one-tenth of 1 percent of Utah's land area, but it contains more than 70 percent of the state's native plant species. Within its 229 square miles are plateaus, canyons, waterfalls, creeks, and narrows. Differences in elevation, sunlight, water, and temperature have created microenvironments that nurture hanging gardens, forested side canyons, and isolated mesas. It is altogether a beautiful place.

If you're wondering where "Zion" came from, credit the Mormons, who borrowed the Hebrew word for "a place of safety or refuge" to name the area in the 1860s. Today, Zion is a refuge for 2.7 million visitors a year, a figure that suggests that you should ride well before or after the summer peak. Another reason is that from Easter weekend to October, shuttles—and not cars or motorcycles—are the only transportation for park guests traveling from Springdale to the Temple of Sinawava at the far reaches of the park. Only hikers, bicyclists, shuttle vehicles, and overnight lodge guests are allowed on the Zion Canyon Scenic Drive, although the rest of the park is open for riding.

With that in mind, accept this advice: Cash in your 401(k), build a log cabin, live here, and be happy.

ON THE ROAD: ZION

What can I say about the perfect blend of road and land? Once you enter Zion ($12), you have nearly free rein to ride and gorge yourself on the impressive and endless views. From the east gate, the Checkerboard Mesa appears just as its name implies. Unlike at other national parks, you have the freedom to park your bike and stride up rippled, textured rocks.

Around each copper-colored curve are rocks with fantastic shapes and variegated swirls ranging from dark red to light orange to pink and white. This wonderful ride connects 15-mph switchbacks with the magnificent motorcycle-friendly Zion-Mount Carmel Tunnel. Too small for large motor homes, this tunnel offers one of the best biking experiences you'll ever have. As if a cosmic drill punched through the mile-long mountain, the passage loses daylight on both ends before you're halfway through. The adrenaline rush continues when you exit and see another mile or two of switchbacks ahead, the first of which propels you into the presence of a natural amphitheater created inside a cliff at least a quarter mile wide. On these curves, beware the low retaining wall that's just high enough to snag a footpeg and toss you over the side.

You can't help but gun it past the 35-mph limit when you realize that the best Le Mans roads aren't in Monte Carlo, but right here. Again, the seven-mile Zion Park Scenic Drive is great if you can ride through, but, again, it's open only to shuttle buses Easter weekend–October. Whether on a shuttle or on your cycle, when you head north on this road you'll pass the Zion Lodge. Keep going and eventually you'll reach beautiful sites like Angels Landing, Weeping Rock, and the Temple of Sinawava.

Plan to pull over frequently—around each bend, another perfect photo beckons. To really give you a sense of the park, rangers offer programs and lead guided hikes from May through September, which will get you beyond the implied barriers and into places like The Narrows, rock passages that are 60–100 million years old and tower 1,500 feet overhead. You've come this far. Don't blow it.

PULL IT OVER: ZION HIGHLIGHTS
Attractions and Adventures
For a basic understanding of what you'll see, there's a free orientation film shown in the park's **Zion Human History Museum** auditorium on the hour and half hour throughout the day. It's located a half-mile north of the park's south entrance on the main park road. Another option is watching the film *Zion Canyon: Treasure of the Gods,* an impressive—although often fictionalized—introduction to the park. The 40-minute shows are daily on the hour between 11 A.M.–7 P.M. at the **Zion Canyon Theatre** (145 Zion Park Blvd., 435/772-2400, www.zioncanyontheatre.com, $10). Few things can do justice to the beauty of this park, but this large-format film comes close. You'll travel back to meet the Ancestral Puebloans (or ancient Anasazi) and in some stunning footage experience what it's like to be a high altitude rock climber.

I learned a good lesson here from a local: The average tourist heads down the scenic drive, walks down a sidewalk, sees some steps, and turns around. Zion boasts the best canyons in the world, most of which are hidden behind the hills. If you get off your bike, carve out some time to see what everyone else is missing.

The first stop you should consider making before wandering into the wilderness on your own is the **Zion Adventure Company** (36 Lion Blvd., Springdale, 435/772-1001, www.zionadventures. com), which (for $19) provides the maps and gear you'll need to hike through the Narrows. Donning a drysuit and carrying provisions and a walking stick, you'll trudge through thigh- to waist-deep water and enter silent, sublime passages. This is the signature Zion experience; it may whet your appetite for its Jeep tours and rock climbing classes. Guided Narrows tours are also available, although the price leaps. If you'd rather let a horse do the walking, **Canyon Trail Rides** (Zion Lodge, 435/679-8665, www.canyonrides.com) offers one-hour ($40) and half-day ($75) tours through the park.

Shopping
Since it's nearly impossible to capture nature's intricate beauty with a disposable camera, Michael Fatali has done the work for you. Lugging his camera to canyons and mountains you don't even know exist, he has spent years looking for the perfect shot. His efforts show in the colorful, passionate photographs on display at **Fatali Gallery** (145 S. Zion Park Blvd., 435/772-2422, www.fatali.com). Using just the right light (no filters or digital enhancement) he captures exquisite shadows and surreal natural colors to give ordinary objects a different and far more interesting visage.

Blue-Plate Specials
The **Bit and Spur Restaurant and Saloon** (1212 Zion Park Blvd., 435/772-3498, www.bitandspur.com) claims to be one of the best Mexican restaurants in Utah, but it's hard to judge since it's so packed it's hard to get inside to eat the food. Serving

dinner daily and breakfasts on weekends, the eatery uses locally grown produce in traditional Mexican favorites, and it pours a great selection of Utah microbrews like Provo Girl Pilsner, Squatters Hefeweizen, and the Mormon favorite, Polygamy Porter—why have just one? To top it off, the restaurant features a garden patio, billiards, and sports TV.

Zion Pizza and Noodle Company (868 Zion Park Blvd., 435/772-3815, www.zionpizzanoodle.com), in an old church, serves lunch and dinner. Along with creative pasta dishes, salads, and Utah microbrews (Wasatch and Squatters), the menu features specialties like Thai chicken pizza and hot and spicy Southwestern burrito pizza. A back porch patio and front porch deck are perfect when the weather is right, and it usually is.

Shut-Eye

The only place to stay inside the park, **Zion Lodge** (435/772-3213 for same-day booking, 303/297-2757 or 888/297-2757 for advance booking, www.zionlodge.com, $159 and up) was designed in the 1920s, destroyed in 1966 by a fire, and rebuilt without the classic rustic design and historic appearance. The oversight was corrected in 1990, and now it looks as it should—an outdoors lodge in the heart of beautiful country. With only 120 rooms and a restaurant, the lodge often fills up, so don't be disappointed if you can't get in.

In the town of Springdale, your choices of lodging are surprisingly diverse. The **Zion Park Inn** (1215 Zion Park Blvd., 435/772-3200, www.zionparkinn.com, $110 and up) is a link in the Best Western chain, but in a small town where conveniences are hard to come by, it's a nice option. The inn features a pool, hot tub, gift shop, guest laundry, state liquor store, large and comfortable rooms, and a terrific restaurant—the Switchback Grille. Slightly more upscale, yet surprisingly reasonable, is the **Desert Pearl Inn** (707 Zion Park Blvd., 435/772-8888 or 888/828-0898, $148 and up). Swank, cathedral-ceiling rooms come with a TV, fridge, and microwave; outside are a waterfall and sparkling blue pool. The rooms are not quite suites, but with growth hormones, they would be. Old-fashioned describes the **Pioneer Lodge** (838 Zion Park Blvd., 435/772-3233 or 888/772-3233, www.pioneerlodge.com, $129 and up high season, $69 and up off-season). It gives you what you want, if you just want a bed, a pool, and a neat old motel diner that claims to be the "home of home-cooked cooking."

Resources for Riders

Red Rocks Run

Arizona Travel Information
Arizona Association of Bed & Breakfast Inns—www.arizona-bed-breakfast.com
Arizona Road Conditions—888/411-7623, www.az511.com
Arizona State Parks—602/542-4174, www.pr.state.az.us
Arizona Travel Center—866/275-5816, www.arizonaguide.com

Utah Travel Information
Bed & Breakfast Inns of Utah—www.bbiu.org
Utah Road Conditions—800/492-2400
Utah State Parks—801/538-7220 or 877/887-2757, www.stateparks.utah.gov
Utah Travel Council—801/538-1030 or 800/200-1160, www.utah.com

Local and Regional Information
Grand Canyon Chamber of Commerce—928/638-2901 or 888/472-2696,
    www.grandcanyonchamber.com
Grand Canyon Road and Weather Conditions—888/411-7623
Grand Canyon Switchboard—928/638-7888, www.nps.gov/grca
Grand Canyon Visitors Center—928/638-7644
Page/Lake Powell Chamber of Commerce—928/645-2741 or 888/261-7243,
    www.pagelakepowelltourism.org
Sedona–Oak Creek Canyon Chamber of Commerce—928/282-7722 or
    800/288-7336, www.sedonachamber.com
Zion Canyon Information—435/772-3256, www.nps.gov/zion
Zion Canyon Visitors Bureau—888/518-7070, www.zionpark.com

Arizona Motorcycle Shops
Grand Canyon Harley-Davidson—I-40 at Exit 185, Bellemont, 928/774-3896,
    www.grandcanyonhd.com
Northland Motorsports—4308 E. Rte. 66, Flagstaff, 928/526-7959,
    www.northlandmotorsports.com
Outdoor Sports Lake Powell—910-B Coppermine Rd. Vista Ave., Page,
    928/645-8141, www.outdoorsportsaz.com
Sedona Motorcycles—6560 SR 17, Sedona, 928/284-3983

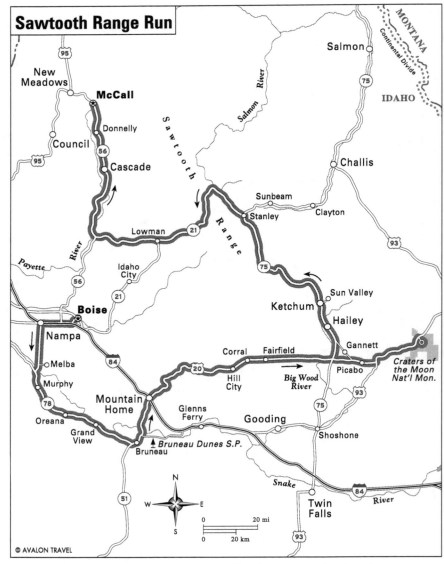

Sawtooth Range Run

Route: Boise to McCall via Nampa, Bruneau, Mountain Home, Ketchum, Sun Valley, Stanley, Banks, Cascade

Distance: Approximately 450 miles

First Leg: Boise to Ketchum (235 miles)

Second Leg: Ketchum to McCall (215 miles)

Helmet Laws: In Idaho, helmets are optional if over 18.

Sawtooth Range Run
Boise, Idaho to McCall, Idaho

Remote and expansive plains usher you into sometimes intricate yet always scenic low-mountain riding. Start with a wide-open ride custom-designed to relieve stress and cleanse your mind, and then cruise across the charcoal-black cinders of an ancient lava bed. After rolling into a valley retreat favored by cowboys, skiers, and America's most powerful people, ride out on a final run combining the majesty of wild rivers and scenic byways.

ON THE ROAD: BOISE TO KETCHUM/SUN VALLEY

If you're heading to Idaho specifically for this ride, odds are a major road will lead you toward Boise. It's a nice city, but doubtful one that you'd explore on a motorcycle, so look at your map and consider following a roundabout counterclockwise route from here and then into the heart of Idaho.

There's not a scenic way to exit Boise, but in a state of only 1.4 million residents, even the interstates are relatively empty. It's much faster to reach the junction of U.S. 20 at Mountain Home by taking I-84 East, but a better alternative is enduring a little bit of congestion to reach some more good stuff on the horizon.

Set your coordinates and depart Boise via I-84 West, riding toward the suburb of Nampa, where Route 45 drops due south. After about 30 minutes into the ride the last residue of urban traffic dissolves and you are in farm country, where the hills and valleys are the Gem State's finest welcoming committee.

If you were watching television on September 8, 1974, the sight of Snake River should ring some bells. This is the river Evel Kneivel planned to clear aboard a rocket-powered motorcycle called the X-2 Skycycle. Although Evel had trouble crossing the river from his launch pad near Twin Falls, thanks to a well-placed bridge, you'll have no difficulty whatsoever.

More impressive than memories of Kneivel's jump is the terrain Snake River helped create. Where Route 45 joins Route 78, the landscape is slowly washed clear of everything, including the constricting sights of strip malls, stores, and city traffic. Free of all this, you can gun it and pour yourself into the wind, taking advantage of the highway where speed limit signs should include the promise of "100 percent satisfaction guaranteed."

The town of Murphy is here…and gone, memorable if only for a nice dip that hugs both the summit and plummet of a hill. By the time I reached Oreana, the land had worked its magic on me. I looked at the road leading to the horizon and, for the first time in my life, I had a new appreciation for an old song. As I watched the world through the windscreen, Woody Guthrie's endless skyway and ribbon of highway were no longer just lines from "This Land Is Your Land"—they were a very real part of this ride.

Ahead there was a sparse desert region that led me into one of my favorite environments. As a solo rider, I find that deserts invariably match my mood and desire for privacy. While this stretch gave me enough curves to keep me alert, at times I rode upon straights that pierced the land for as much as six arrow-true miles. And when the road turned and decided to sneak up on Snake River, it revealed the nice high walls of the canyon. Between Grand View and Bruneau, the 20 or so miles that divide the towns give you a perfect mixture of riding as you reach a weird confluence of mountains and desert and fertile farmlands irrigated by 300-yard long sprinklers poised above the fields.

In addition to the scenery (or lack of it), what also impressed me about Route 78 was its speed. There were few towns and no switchbacks, and since I couldn't recall passing any troopers, Route 78 became a very fast road. If you've ever thought about setting a land speed record, forget the Salt Flats and consider Idaho.

Near Bruneau, Route 78 swings to the north, where it wants you to cross Snake River and roll onto Highway 51. Don't go yet. Stay on Route 78 for two more miles for a stop at **Bruneau Dunes State Park** (27608 Sand Dunes Rd., 208/366-7919). When you enter the park, a winding road leads to the park office, which has information on what's ahead. Until you get there, here's the skinny: It's a five-mile run to the end of the trail, and along the way are 12,000-year-old soot-colored dunes, one of which—at 470 feet—is the largest single-structured sand dune in North America. Unlike the dunes of Florence, Oregon, though, there are no dune buggies here—but there are lake, marsh, desert, prairie, and dune habitats to explore. If you decide to bunk down at the campground or cabins here and stay the night, the popular Bruneau Dunes Observatory has a collection of telescopes that'll help you see into the clear country skies.

Returning to Highway 51, the road spans Snake River (take that, Evel) and points you north toward Mountain Home. Here the highway is marked with periodic "open range" signs that I'm sure refer to livestock, but you'll get the sense that it also means free-range motorcycling.

On this open road, the lure of the landscape will find you twisting the throttle to rocket down the road. The intensity of the ride may be tempered if you're lapped by one of the jets screaming back to the neighboring Mountain Home Air Force Base. Aside from the random jet, there is nothing—nothing—here except the flat, endless prairie and the strip of asphalt that divides it. The emptiness continues until you hit a touch of density in and around Mountain Home, after which you squeeze under I-84 and work your way toward U.S. 20 East, at which point you're bound for glory. For an alternative route, swing southeast on I-84 toward Twin Falls, near the center of the Great Rift. This 635-square mile geological phenomenon spreads across the Snake River Plain to create one of the earth's most impressive plumbing systems; it's a series of fissures, spatter cones, and lava tubes from 60 lava flows and 25 volcanic events.

When you're back on U.S. 20 once again, the road ahead is clean and spare. You may spy a home every 10 miles or so, and when a curve does appear, its arc is so long and slow that you may think you're still on a straight. Rolling on toward an area called Tollgate, you can look around and realize this desert was once the floor of an ancient ocean, as shifting sands and the trails of long-evaporated streams lead off to the horizon. You can you see all of this as the road slowly elevates you above the landscape and presents wonderful aerial views of the ride ahead.

There's not much shaking in Hill City or Corral or Fairfield, save for the random gypsy wagon parked in the middle of a field. The hills are snug, low, and packed tightly together to create repetitive, easy corners. Creeks and ravines intersect the land, and wonderful scenes that were new to me appeared, like the random woodchucks that crept toward the road before dashing away from the growl of my bike.

U.S. 20 becomes increasingly more alluring, no thanks to any magnificent formations but really to the lack of them. This lasts for about 20 miles until you reach the junction of Highway 75 and well beyond it. Trust me—after the months you've spent planning and then waiting for the office clock to tick down to the zero hour, wonderful emptiness like this is what you need.

Depending on your schedule, you may want to invest time to ride over to yet another unusual parcel of real estate. To see it, pass the junction of Highway 75 for now and stick with U.S. 20 toward Picabo. Along the way, there is almost omnipresent desolation. To your right, the southern horizon is flat and endless. From horizon to horizon, you will not see a living soul; and clouds probably 50 miles away look quite strange and surreal, since there is nothing at all to break the view. Gradually, scrub brush and desert sand are replaced by black lava rock, and off in the distance at about 2 o'clock, there's an ancient volcano that looks as if it coughed up this very ground.

The artificially-made views here are limited to a few service stations, homes, and ranching supply stores. But nature delivers towering formations lacerated by rocks piercing through the grass, and more beds of crisp black lava tell you you've reached the entrance of the mysterious **Craters of the Moon National Monument** (U.S. 20/26/93, 208/527-1300, www.nps.gov/crmo, $4). Before heading down the loop road, stop at the visitor center where you can get a basic education on what happened here. In short: Several times during the past several thousand years, a parallel line of fissures in the area erupted through volcanic buttes and cones to spread a flow of lava that cooled into either pahoehoe (pa-HOY-hoy), a ropelike lava, or Aa (AH-ah), a rough, jagged rock. No one was here to see the last eruption 2,000 years ago, but you can check out old volcanoes and see where lava beds created caves that you can explore.

So unusual is this area that Apollo XIV astronauts came here to study geology when training for their moon mission, to get a sense of what the moon's surface would look like. So, in a sense, for the next few hours, your bike will become a lunar rover.

There are several stops on the seven-mile loop, such as Big Craters, Devils Orchard, and an extinct 6,181-foot tall volcano called Inferno Cone. Since you're already just a few hundred feet from the summit, you can hike to the top of the cone fairly quickly and easily, although the pebblelike consistency of the black gravel contrasts with the steep 14-degree grade of the hill. And when you reach what you thought was the summit, you'll see another plateau ahead. To a chorus of crunching rocks, swift winds, and your own chuffing breath, you pass several peaks before reaching the final one to find that the reward is a view well worth the effort. There is no crater left here, just a few flat boulders and a lone tree that draws your eyes to the east, where another extinct volcano rests far, far, far away. On a quiet day, you may be the only fool on the hill. Alone in private, you can scan the entire world. If you've ever considered meditation, there's no better place where you can reflect on your ride and your life.

Back down the hill, the loop road leads to other overlooks and then to the enticing "lava tubes"—caves hidden beneath a crust of lava. It may be tempting, but if you're alone or lack the right gear, such as a hardhat and lantern, heed the warning signs that remind you help may be a long time coming. And if you're wondering if you'll be able to leave the park with a few lumps of lava—the answer is no. Every year a few truckloads of rock are collectively pilfered from the park, and some even chip souvenir chunks off delicate formations. Keep in mind that what erupts in Idaho should stay in Idaho. So take pictures, and file away mental images, but leave the lava alone if you want to avoid a $250 fine.

Now you have the pleasure of backtracking to Highway 75, one of the nicest roads in Idaho, which takes you to Ketchum and beyond. Rather than riding U.S. 20 all the way, watch for a spur road to the right just past Picabo that'll take you northwest on Gannett Road (Route 23) toward Bellevue and Hailey. At Highway 75, head north toward Hailey, where today's downtown bears little resemblance to the Hailey of yesteryear. What changed? Bruce Willis. He and Demi Moore moved here to raise their kids, and even though they split, their presence helped put a little Hollywood hep into the Wild West.

From here, it's just another 10 prairie-rich miles to Ketchum and Sun Valley, one of the leading "lucky break" stories of the 20th century.

KETCHUM/ SUN VALLEY PRIMER

Ketchum has always had a penchant for wealth. Originally known as Leadville, back in 1879 prospectors came here to rip gold, silver, and lead ore out of the mines—but only after they had ripped the Tukudeka Indians from the land. After the tribes were gone and the mines were spent, Basque sheepherders from Spain showed up and began guiding their flocks through the crossroads of Wood Valley.

Aside from silver and sheep and a stab at creating a spa from local hot springs, Ketchum didn't really catch on until 1936. That's when Averell Harriman, the chairman of the Union Pacific Railroad (and later Secretary of Commerce under Harry Truman), sent Austrian Count Felix Schaffgotsch on a mission to find one place in America that could rival European ski resorts such as St. Moritz. After several months of scouting, the Count was getting ready to wire Harriman that he had failed when an Idaho rep of the railroad directed him to the old mining town. Fewer than 100 people lived in Ketchum then, but the site was perfect.

Backed by his fortune and connections,

The Dawn of Sun Valley

So what's the appeal of Sun Valley, the place that's accepted as "America's First Destination Resort?" You can find out for yourself by taking a short walk east of downtown Ketchum.

Sun Valley (208/622-2001 or 800/786-8259, www.sunvalley.com) is centered around the main hotel that was built in 1936, and at the lodge are a few restaurants, a sports lounge, and a circular heated pool that looks hedonistic when it's steaming up in the cool months. There's a vintage six-lane bowling alley in the basement, and behind the lodge is an ice-skating rink where Olympic skaters practice during the day and appear in a popular, free ice show each Saturday in the summer. On the second floor, Room 206 was Ernest Hemingway's favorite and where he wrote *For Whom The Bell Tolls.*

Down a winding sidewalk, a mock Alpine village features more of the resort's dozen stores, 13 restaurants, and five bars, as well as a theater where, each afternoon at 5 P.M., you can watch *Sun Valley Serenade,* filmed here in 1941. Elsewhere, you'll find a shooting club, trail rides, ski lifts, and golf.

It's a neat little operation, and the best part of it all is that it's not always so expensive. Travel between seasons and you can get one of its 500 rooms for less than a hundred bucks.

Harriman bought the 4,300-acre Brass Ranch and, just 11 months and five days after the count hit town, millionaire socialites from the east and stars from Hollywood hit Sun Valley. The blend of money and celebrity worked and today's Ketchum was born. Called the "American Shangri-La," in 1941 Glenn Miller came here to film *Sun Valley Serenade* with Sonja Henie. Clark Gable, Robert Kennedy, Ginger Rogers, and Lucille Ball were frequent guests and even he-man Gary Cooper came by to go duck hunting with pal Ernest Hemingway who liked shooting ducks and, apparently, himself. After his 1961 suicide he was buried in the last row of the Ketchum Cemetery on Highway 75.

The popularity of this hole-in-the-wall resort has seldom abated. Power players from Washington and Hollywood have made this a favored retreat, and the power surges each summer when CEOs and CFOs from leading entertainment, technology, communications, and computing companies arrive for a summit at a Sun Valley retreat.

After the business leaders jet out, long-term residents and annual visitors stick around so there's always a chance you may run across a generous share of celebrities that call this home. Despite the panache of the town, prices on basic goods and lodging are still reasonable—just don't plan on buying a home and settling down. Why not? Here in Ketchum, revealed a local, "The billionaires are pushing out the millionaires."

ON THE ROAD: KETCHUM/SUN VALLEY

The surrounding area has more than enough to keep you occupied for a day—perhaps even a few years if you happen to bump into Oprah and she wants to marry and support you. If you're here for one day, though, half the day will keep you grounded, and the other half should have you heading for the hills.

If I were in your boots, I'd start at the **Visitors Center** (491 Sun Valley Rd., 800/634-3347, www.visitsunvalley.com), which has a library's worth of brochures and information on the local area, as well as maps and guides for sites on the outskirts of town and across Idaho. Then take your pick. There are mountains all around you and even in the summertime the ski lift still clips along to the top of Bald Mountain. What does that mean to you? While you can't get your bike to the top of the peak, you can get a *bicycle* there.

There are several rental shops in Ketchum, and one of the largest and oldest (since 1948) is **Sturtevants** (340 N. Main St., 208/726-4501 or 800/252-9534, www.sturtos.com). Provided you're not the size of Billy or Benny McCrary (the world's fattest twins), for about $35 a day you can rent a sturdy cross-country mountain bike and ride the high-speed quad lift to the top of Bald Mountain. During the summer, the lift station at River Run lets you slap your bicycle on a rack, take a 10-minute ride to the peak, and then hop off at Lookout Lodge where you can grab a light lunch at the grill and settle back with some outstanding views of the surrounding Pioneer and Sawtooth ranges. After living in the moment for a moment, spend the next hour riding down from 9,000 feet, burning off lunch as you navigate foot-wide trails carved out by animals and motocross riders.

If the idea of riding a bicycle down a steep hill strikes fear into your heart, here's an alternative: Jump off the mountain. *Oui, monsieur, c'est ci bon.* Sure, it's expensive (about 200 bucks) but you'll never forget it. When the weather's right, you can sign up for a tandem paragliding leap with **Fly Sun Valley** (160 W. 4th St., 208/726-3332, www.flysunvalley.com). Strapped to your guide, you literally step straight ahead as the winds lift you off the side of Bald Mountain. You'll swirl through the air for up to an hour before swooping in for an approach at a nearby parking lot or soccer field. What about your friends on the bicycles? Those poor bastards are still pedaling.

PULL IT OVER: KETCHUM/SUN VALLEY HIGHLIGHTS
Attractions and Adventures

If you're active, there are enough outdoor adventures to keep you occupied for well over a week. Within a five-mile radius of Ketchum there are more than 100 miles of hiking trails: Fox Creek, Adams Gulch, Trail Creek, and others at Sun Valley. They're all free and maps are available at the **Ketchum Ranger Station** (206 Sun Valley Rd., 208/622-5371).

There are a host of organized options available at **Sun Valley** (www.sunvalley.com). A few that may do it for you are **guided trail rides** (208/622-2387) on horseback up to Dollar Mountain and skeet shooting at its **Gun Club** (1.5 miles east of Sun Valley Lodge, 208/622-2111). Rent one of the Beretta shotguns and try trap, double trap, wobbletrap, and duck tower shooting. Smack a few clay pigeons, and you've got yourself a dinner. Good eatin'.

Shopping

With about 20 square blocks of stores, galleries, thrift stores, and restaurants to see, shopping is a significant part of life in Ketchum. I didn't hit all of them, but the few that I did visit seemed pretty all right.

For a comprehensive listing of galleries in town, pick up a *Sun Valley Gallery Association* guide (208/726-5512, www.svgalleries.org) at any of the galleries the chamber of commerce, or a grocery store.

At heart, this is a tourist destination which means that someone *has* to sell T-shirts. Here, the store is **T's & Temptations** (Giacobbi Square, 4th and Leadville Sts., 208/726-9543). Along with T-shirts and sweats, it also sells baseball caps, stickers, and other Ketchum and Sun Valley souvenirs.

A jim-dandy bookstore (and a bookstore *can* be jim-dandy, dammit) is **Iconoclast Books** (671 Sun Valley Rd., 208/726-1654, www.iconoclastbooks.com). If you fall ass-over-teakettle for Idaho, odds are you'll want to peruse the new and used volumes here. They provide great historical and photographic references of the state and, most important, the areas you'll explore. It's not just regional guides, either—there are volumes on philosophy, art, history, and literature, as well as collectible first editions.

If you're staying in a cabin or efficiency or plan a picnic out in the wilderness, **Atkinson's Market** (4th and Leadville Sts., 208/726-5668), is a large market that has aisles of groceries, coolers of beer, a full-service deli, and drugstore.

Blue-Plate Specials

Ketchum is an important part of a well-balanced diet. There are some great restaurants here, and despite the deep pockets of many locals, prices at most places felt pretty fair to me.

Looking upscale is the affordable **Sawtooth Club** (231 N. Main St., 208/726-5233, www.thesawtoothclub.com), which opens into a cool bar, with the dining area on the second floor. It puts a creative spin on basic dishes to create super good chicken Senegalese, mesquite-grilled steaks, chops, ribs, and wood-grilled duck and lamb. Often voted the Valley's best overall restaurant, the food's so nice I ate here twice.

Completely starving, I dined at **The Kneadery** (260 Leadville Ave., 208/726-9462) and fully expected to finish just a single sandwich. I couldn't. It was way big, as were the massive home-style breakfasts that were defeating other diners. The portions are large and the prices medium, and the Rocky Mountain lodge look went a long way to please this rider.

For a fresh and inexpensive Mexican meal, try **Desperado's** (211 4th St., 208/726-3068, www.despossv.com). Founder and owner Jim Funk believes in fresh ingredients and fresh salsas, a recipe that's worked for him—and has pleased a fan base of locals and visitors—since the mid-1980s. There are plenty of beers on tap (including Tecate and Dos Equis) and a patio for dining out when the weather's right.

Watering Holes

You've probably realized that Ketchum has just about everything you need. At night, it has even more. Every bar and saloon in sight is built for locals, and they all have at least two things in common: a real good vibe and a moose head on the wall. Even if you don't imbibe, these are some good places to hang out with locals—and each saloon complements its drinks with an impressive menu.

As mentioned, the **Sawtooth Club** (231 N. Main St., 208/726-5233) is a wonderful restaurant, but there's an even better bar and lounge downstairs. Fat, padded armchairs and couches around a fireplace make it seem like a combination dorm room/gentlemen's club.

Stumble across the street to **The Roosevelt Grille** (280 N. Main St., 208/726-0051, www.therooseveltgrille.

com), another restaurant whose twin is a lounge (Roosevelt Tavern). A Western theme is the obvious choice, accented by a sign asking what is now so very clear: "24 hours in a day, 24 beers in a case. Coincidence? I think not." Count on at least 10 beers on tap, 15 brands in bottles, and specialty martinis. In good weather, head on upstairs—way up—to the roof to drink a brew under clear Ketchum skies.

The Casino (351 Main St., 208/726-3200) isn't a place where you'd really gamble, but you can bet on it. Here since 1936, it's had decades to become what it is: a place with three pool tables, a long, long bar, $2 Pabst on tap, and some micros. Down the street you'll discover that The Pioneer Saloon (308 N. Main St., 208/726-3139) is just that. Once a place where mountain folks and people of the frontier hung out and conducted business over a drink and a handshake, it still has an authentic saloon-style atmosphere. The restaurant's fancy, although the lounge and bar are where you'd want to relax at the end of the day.

Shut-Eye

You shouldn't have any trouble finding a place to bunk down. Even if everything's full in Ketchum, you have two options: Lodging's available and less expensive 10 miles south in Hailey and 15 miles south in Bellevue. In addition to motels, in Ketchum you're surrounded by the Sawtooth National Recreational Area—which is government-owned land, so camping's free in the wilderness (although there's a charge at serviced campsites).

Here and throughout Idaho, a *free* service that'll save you the trouble of finding the right lodging is the McCall-based **www.inidaho.com.** One call or email will provide rates and references to hotels, cabins, condos, and inns, call 800/844-3246 or

check online. The service also creates packages that combine lodging with outdoor adventures such as rafting and trail rides.

Chain Drive

These chain hotels are in town, or within 10 miles of the city center: **Best Western, Clarion** For more information, including phone numbers and websites, see page 151.

ON THE ROAD: KETCHUM/ SUN VALLEY TO McCALL

Somewhat challenging and almost always picturesque, the trip north will put you in the midst of some tricky riding and the beauty of four scenic routes.

As you get started on the Sawtooth Scenic Byway (aka Highway 75), the often elaborate homes and condos of Ketchum will fill the roadside. Some are delicately and expertly constructed for CEOs and CFOs, while other older shacks look like shopclass projects after the kids got hold of a case of wood glue. The residences gradually taper off and disappear and are replaced by wooden structures known locally as spruce, aspen, fir, ponderosa, and lodgepole pine.

If you plan on camping or spending more time in the region, about eight miles north of Ketchum, just past the Big Wood River, is the headquarters of the **Sawtooth National Recreational Area** (208/727-5013 or 208/727-5000, www.fs.fed.us/r4/sawtooth), a great stop for information. There's a steady incline to the road, and while it's not a dramatic ascent, what it delivers for the next 20 miles is the money shot. As you ride, the breadth and width of land are sensational, with straights stretched taut across the plains. As this rekindles memories of the road from Boise, you'll run into steeper drives that haul you into the heart of the Sawtooth Mountains.

If viewed from space, the road ahead

would appear to be scribbling back and forth like a seismograph needle during an earthquake. Now you get to take full advantage of it. For several miles, your attention will switch from the road to the drops to the curves, and as you navigate these jigsaw ridges and twisted corners, you may be looking at high-elevation pine trees still sugar-coated with snow. Eventually, you'll reach the road to the **Galena Lodge** (Hwy. 75, 24 miles north of Ketchum, 208/726-4010, www.galenalodge.com), an old resort that's managed to survive and become a landmark destination.

Racing another five miles and several hundred feet higher into the atmosphere, you'll tackle six-degree grades to reach the 8,701-foot summit at Galena Pass. Two miles ahead, your reward is reaching one of the nation's finest overlooks. More than a mile below and shooting clear to the northern horizon is Sawtooth Valley. I'd argue that scenes like this have appeared on too many postcards, calendars, and inspirational bookmarks, but the real-life sight of this hallowed ground drives home the absolute beauty we're blessed with in America. Quite a while passed as I contemplated this vision, and even though the miniscule images I collected on camera will never do it justice, I hope they add something to my new calendar of postcard-sized inspirational bookmarks.

After meditating, you and your bike fall down the mountain, rolling swiftly around corners that lead to Smiley Creek, an out-of-place place marked by the **Smiley Creek Lodge** (16546 Hwy. 75, 208/774-3547, www.smileycreeklodge.com), a store, restaurant, and lodge that offers cabins and teepees. Now there's nothing between you and the town of Stanley. Really, *there's nothing.* Around you, it's a Cinemascope view of the world, with nothing for more than 20 miles except flat-open land

stretched across the earth, tacked down by mountains on the horizon. Just south of Stanley, though, on the laserbeam straight near mile marker 174, look for the pullout where you can park and look around. Do this and shut off the bike. With pure silence as a soundtrack, tune into the sound of the wind and birds you can hear, but which may seem lost in the emptiness. Around you is an almost complete circle of the mountains, which pulls your view from side to side to see the sharp peaks of the Sawtooth Range and then to the Salmon River that leaps into view, kept at a distance behind a crisscrossed timber fence.

Only a mile ahead at the junction of Highways 75 and 21 is the town of Stanley. Stanley gets an unusual amount of attention, roughly as much as Chicago, but when you ride in, you may wonder why. It's quite desolate and quite strange, and even though it's as small as a residential subdivision, there are tens of thousands of travelers who join Stanley's 100 residents for backcountry hiking, rock climbing, whitewater rafting, and all the things outdoor adventurers do outdoors. If this style of solitude appeals to you, the **Mountain Village Resort** (junction of Hwys. 75 and 21, 208/774-3661 or 800/843-5475, www.mountainvillage.com) anchors a combination market, service station, motel, and restaurant, all run by the same family. Make use of the gas pumps—there won't be any for quite a while.

By now you've completed the fantastic Sawtooth Scenic Byway, and the next stage takes you west on Highway 21 to put you on the Ponderosa Pine Scenic Route, the habitat of eagles, osprey, heron, elk, deer, bear, and fox. For several miles, though, scenic is just a rumor. Routine views and mile after mile of straight riding through a low-key forest sets the tone as you enter what should be grazing land but where nothing's grazing. As on the ride out of

Ketchum, though, things are happening behind the scenes. You are in the Salmon-Challis National Forest on a plateau that's slowly and surely increasing in elevation. The lack of traffic may trigger the part of your brain that says "ride faster," and if you do, you'll quicken your arrival to Banner Summit, at an elevation of 7,200 feet.

Although there are no open views from the summit, what did draw my attention were the snow drifts that, I learned, had shut the road down only a few days earlier. Keep in mind this was in late May. The weather here can get squirrelly, and had the gates been down to block my path, I'd have been forced to double back to Ketchum. To be safe, contact the **Idaho Transportation Department's Road Reports** (888/432-7623, http://511.idaho.gov) to check on road conditions and closures.

As you ride, on your left is the Sawtooth Wilderness Area and its 217,000 acres of ponderosa pine and steelhead fishing. On the right is the Challis National Forest, gateway to the 2.3-million-acre Frank Church River of No Return Wilderness Area, where there are fewer roads than anywhere else in the Lower 48. Nearly 40 miles out of Stanley, the mountains become steeper and more angular, and the South Fork of the Payette River introduces itself and decides to stay with you for the next 50 miles to Banks. It's a great riding partner, sticking with you when it narrows to a mere stream just a few feet from the road, and still hanging around when it switches to furious rapids in a chasm far below.

The cliffs and low mountains, jackstraw pines, and loneliness of the ride continue for 20 more miles to Lowman, which is a town like Stanley's a town. You've ridden 120 miles now, and although Highway 21 makes a slow curve to the south at Lowman to head back towards Boise, take a quick jog to follow a new part of the route, the Wildlife Canyon Scenic Byway. For quite a stretch, this is a paved pep pill, with 25-mph curves and fast ascents that bring to mind the Scottish Highlands as the lanes reach higher and the canyons plummet deeper. Signs warn you to watch for hikers and falling rocks, and with the pitch of the terrain, you'd expect to see falling hikers. Seriously, what you need to watch for are not huge boulders that'll knock you off of your bike, but the hundreds of small chunks of gravel that'll knock your bike off of you.

Curves start shaking fast and furious here because—as you've probably learned—the roads that always seem right are the ones that follow the free-form flow of a wild river. It's true in the Smoky Mountains, in Arizona, and right here. The Payette River leads through remote country, even more remote than what you challenged south of Stanley.

The land changes again, with green swaths created where the Payette meets another creek, and civilization comes back near Garden Valley, with its churches and sporadic log cabins. After 10 miles of this high-test scenery, the byway spits you out at Highway 55 and the town of Banks. Although you'll be heading north, just a few hundred yards south is the kind of diner that you've frequented from Acadia to San Simeon. The **Banks Country Store and Café** (208/793-2617) has been here since 1915, serving its first guests slightly more than a decade after the invention of Ford's motorcar. With nearly a century of experience, it's learned its lessons well. When you stop for lunch (no gas), you can recall the beauty of the ride so far and enjoy the freedom of feasting on a Big Bubba burger at a table by the river.

Turning true north once again, you've reached the fourth of the day's scenic runs: the Payette River National Scenic Byway. Like Cash's ring of fire, you're going down, down, down, swallowed by

© NANCY HOWELL

When there's not much to look at, you notice things like this: an old hotel with a retro sign.

the gravity of the river in the heart of a gorge. There's not much to look at, but there's so much to see, like the old swinging bridge and the pullout where you can stop and listen to the crushing sounds of the river. The pine forest layered through here creates a nice wooded ride within the Boise National Forest, and the river and a railroad track on the far bank follows you around curves and across bridges and into the backcountry.

This joy continues for miles and slowly gives way to flatlands near Smiths Ferry, where the **Cougar Mountain Lodge** (9738 Hwy. 55, 208/382-4464) is a convenient market and bar that appears out of thin air. Surrounding you is the Round Valley, an area that takes on a Swiss, rather than Scottish, visage—which is important because it gives me the rare opportunity to use the word "visage." The thin river that you recall from earlier is now the wide North Fork of the Payette, seen across the pastures far to your left. The ground is coated with sandbars, driftwood, and rocks. A waterfall appears as you close in on the start of a four-

mile stretch of S-curves and vertical mountain slopes that make you feel somewhat vulnerable until you reach a safe pocket of civilization in Cascade. I'm sure there are things here besides the retro Chief Hotel sign, but that's all I remember about it.

North of town, the swift and sharp road darts through the center of hills and beside a lake. Horses graze and trot on the plains, but they're enjoying the outdoors only half as much as you. The wide-ranging range is split by the Gold Fork River, where you'll see the entirety of Donnelly and its little red schoolhouse before graduating, 13 miles later, to the second-most popular tourist destination in Idaho.

Last call for McCall.

McCALL PRIMER
Like nearly every area in the nation, the Long Valley region of Idaho was populated by Native Americans; in this case, the Shoshone, Bannock, and Nez Perce tribes. Eventually, as Chief Joseph of the Nez Perce was pursued into submission, there was a void to fill. So, in 1891, on the shores of Payette Lake, homesteader Tom McCall arrived in the area that would become his namesake. Thanks to help from more than 30,000 Chinese workers, the Warren and Marshall Mountain Mining District fueled the area's economy, with McCall's Brown Tie and Lumber Company hiring the bulk of the town's citizens. Naturally, the twin industries sparked a loose and open society highlighted by lakeside whorehouses, dance halls, and casinos. Sadly, they are gone now, but their effects lasted for decades. Guns were finally banned from local bars only in the early 1980s.

Relatively recently the arrival of the Tamarack Resort, about 15 miles south, helped elevate McCall's profile—but the relationship wasn't reciprocal and after a rough run the resort declared bankruptcy in 2008. Regardless of Tamarack's fate, McCall remains the second-most popular resort destination in the state, which begs the question: Why is it so small? I cannot tell you.

ON THE ROAD: McCALL

As I hinted, the center of town is about the size of a walnut, and there may not be much to hold your interest—but after a great ride up here, you may be satisfied with just walking around town. Another option is cruising up the west shore of Payette Lake on Warren Wagon Road, en route for a circle tour up and around the lake. Pick up a map at the visitors center, and you'll see that, near the terminus of the loop, a scenic overlook on a peninsula is accessible via Scenic Drive.

If you do walk around town, you'll be surprised to find you can cover the whole thing on foot in a few hours, tops. In the center of town, you're at the south end of the lake. A few blocks west is the **Manchester Ice and Event Centre** (200 E. Lake St., 208/634-3570, www.manchester-icecentre. com), an impressive facility that occupies a good chunk of prime real estate and is open for ice hockey, curling, and skating.

From here on out, the day is yours.

PULL IT OVER: McCALL HIGHLIGHTS
Attractions and Adventures

McCall is within the **Payette National Forest** (208/634-0700), a massive parcel of land that contains more than 2,100 miles of trails, 2,500 miles of roads, 15,000 miles of streams and rivers, and 30 campgrounds. Within the national forest on the eastern and northern shores of the lake is the **Ponderosa State Park** (208/634-2164), the peninsula that leads to the scenic overlook.

The park is on the shores of Payette

Lake, a 5,377-acre playground that's nearly two miles wide, more than six miles long, and as much as 300 feet deep. With that in mind, you'd be missing a lot if you didn't check in with **Cheap Thrills Rentals** (303 N. 3rd/Hwy. 55, 208/634-7472 or 800/831-1025, www.cheapthrillsrentals.com) which rents boats, wave runners, and water tow-toys that'll get you cooled off while heating things up in the middle of the lake.

Shopping

With so little ground to cover, there are just a few places to hit. One, in my opinion, was a pretty cool shop called the **Granite Mountain Nature Gallery** (317 E. Lake St., 208/634-1111), in the small McCall Mall. Dennis DeLaet turned his passion for collecting one-of-a-kind fossils of starfish, trilobytes, and plants into a profession. What's so cool about all of this is the age of his inventory: between 40 million and 500 million years old. He also peddles shadowboxes of butterflies and butterfly wings (made in Mexico—illegal here), as well as displays of some of the creepiest-ass insects I've ever seen, including the cave spider, a grossly overgrown arachnid nearly 10 inches in diameter.

Aside from the standard gift shops in town, **McCall Drug** (1001 2nd St., 208/634-2433) may look suspiciously familiar if you can recall drugstores from the 1950s. This place encompasses everything, including a pharmacy, toy department, a record store, office supplies, a bookshop, a candy counter, and a soda fountain that serves huckleberry milkshakes. Dig the nostalgic Johnson's Toasted Nut display case with a rotating pan.

Blue-Plate Specials

A few miles from town on the west side of the lake is **Lardo's** (600 W. Lake St., 208/634-8191), a big, barnlike restaurant and saloon where locals hang out. The name, by the way, stems from the tale of an overturned wagon that dumped out a shipment of fat here. The entrées, though, are more appetizing, with the menu listing "old-time spaghetti" (whatever that means), as well as assorted configurations of the "famous" Lardo Burger and fries. After dinner, you may find yourself hanging out at the bar.

The Mill (326 N. 3rd St./Hwy. 55, 208/634-7683, www.themillmccallidaho. com) seems to be at the center of McCall's social circle. It's usually the first place locals recommend, although after looking at the prices on the menu, you may want to check on your credit limit. Of course, you'll get what you pay for—a quality dining experience. You enter what feels like an old mine and arrive at a circular fireplace where chairs, some made from old ski lifts, provide a comfortable place to hang out and go to work on a drink. The low-ceiling dining room's down another mine shaft, where you sit down to a big dinner of Western beef: strip steak, ribeye, tenderloin, porterhouse, and prime rib. Connected to the restaurant, **Beside the Mill** is a sports bar with seven televisions, cocktails, specialty drinks, pool, and darts.

Watering Holes

In addition to hunkering down at the warm bars of Lardo's and The Mill, the local brewpub is the self-explanatory **McCall Brewing Company** (807 N. 3rd St., 208/634-3309), where cowboys, blue collars, and mountain folks hang out and watch sports to the accompaniment of the pub's eight brewed beers. To temper the effects of the alcohol, the kitchen whips up burgers, sandwiches, prime rib, and sirloin. Dine inside or grab some basic grub on the rooftop beer garden.

Shut-Eye

As in Ketchum, when in McCall consider checking with **www.inidaho.com** (800/844-3246), which is a free service that can give you rates and references to hotels, cabins, condos, and inns here in McCall and throughout the state.

Motels and Motor Courts

One of the smartest-looking motor courts I've seen is the **Brundage Bungalows** (1005 W. Lake St., 208/634-2344 or 800/643-2009, www.brundagevacations. com, $79 and up high season). The rooms are across the street from Payette Lake and have that cool old-fashioned knotty pine or log interior. Some have fireplaces and some have a kitchen or kitchenette—but all are really cool. The same folks also rent rooms at the Brundage Inn and Brundage Motel. The larger cabins sleep as many as six.

Inn-dependence

Opened in 1904, the **Hotel McCall** (1101 N. 3rd St., 208/634-8105 or 866/800-1183, www.hotelmccall.com, $135–150) is close to an inn—it's the largest hotel in town and sits within a few feet of Payette Lake. In addition to a clean, old-fashioned feel in its 34 rooms, there's a library; lounge; and the Epicurean, the in-house restaurant that serves award-winning beef Wellington, chicken and crawfish crepes, rack of lamb, and New York strip.

Chain Drive

These chain hotels are in town, or within 10 miles of the city center:
Holiday Inn, Super 8
For more information, including phone numbers and websites, see page 151.

Resources for Riders

Sawtooth Range Run

Idaho Travel Information
Idaho Outfitters and Guides Association—208/342-1438 or 800/494-3246,
www.ioga.org
Idaho Parks and Recreation—208/334-4199 or 888/922-6743,
www.idahoparks.org
Idaho Road Conditions—888/432-7623, http://511.idaho.gov
Idaho Tourism—208/334-2470 or 800/494-3246, www.visitidaho.org
Idaho Vacation and Travel Assistance—800/844-3246, www.inidaho.com

Local and Regional Information
Boise Convention and Visitors Bureau—208/344-7777 or 800/635-5240,
www.boise.org
McCall Chamber of Commerce—208/634-7631 or 800/260-5130,
www.mccallchamber.org
Payette National Forest—208/634-0700
Sawtooth National Recreation Area—208/727-5013, www.fs.fed.us/r4/sawtooth
Stanley Ranger Station—208/774-3000
Stanley-Sawtooth Chamber of Commerce—208/774-3411 or 800/878-7950,
www.stanleycc.org
Sun Valley/Ketchum Visitors Bureau—866/305-0408, www.visitsunvalley.com

Idaho Motorcycle Shops
Adventure Motorsports—2469 Kimberly Rd., Twin Falls, 208/733-5072,
www.ams-twinfalls.com
Big Twin Cycle Center—2816 S. Orchard St., Boise, 208/336-0367,
www.bigtwincycles.com
Boise Cycle—9621 Ustick Rd., Boise, 208/375-9431, www.boisecycle.com
Carl's Cycle Sales—5550 W. State St., Boise, 208/853-5550, www.carlscycle.com
High Desert Harley-Davidson—2310 E. Cinema Dr., Meridian, 208/338-5599,
www.highdeserthd.com
Hinson Power Sports—13924 Hwy. 55, McCall, 208/634-7007,
www.hinsonpowersports.com
KTM MotoSports—6481 Overland Rd., Boise, 208/375-5660 or 800/203-2353,
www.ktm-motosports.com
Snake Harley-Davidson—2404 Addison Ave. E., Twin Falls, 208/734-8400 or
888/788-9809, www.snakehd.com
Woodside Motorsports—4040 Glenbrook Dr., Hailey. 208/788-4005,
www.woodsidemotorsports.net

Washington State Run

Seattle, Washington to Port Townsend, Washington

Washington is a big state with more than its share of natural beauty. The mountains are snowcapped even in summer, and the bays, islands, and glacier lake are more striking than any postcard you've seen.

There are a few downsides to this tour. There was no perfect starting point, although Seattle's legend is so large I started there. In the countryside, I learned that many back roads are either poorly marked, clogged with logging trucks or, off-season, blocked by snow. But trying to stick with tradition, I created this to get you to some neat towns and onto some back roads.

I gave it my best shot.

Now it's your turn.

ON THE ROAD: SEATTLE TO LA CONNER

From Seattle, you can point your bike in any direction and find great destinations: Mount Rainier, Mount St. Helens, or the Olympic National Forest. The challenge is getting there via a combination of cool roads and decent walking towns. Regardless, there are some options.

When you leave Seattle via I-90 you'll understand why this state is so popular—even the federal highway is scenic. By the time the road has extricated you from city traffic, suddenly you're riding on a wide road that flows past lakes and mountains. About 30 minutes later when you reach the turn off for Snoqualmie at Exit 25, you're entering even more desolate countryside. The country road winds around to reach the speck of a town known as Snoqualmie and its main attraction: Snoqualmie Falls. If you ever watched the cult favorite program *Twin Peaks,* you'll recognize this water feature. At 270 feet, Snoqualmie is 100 feet higher than Niagara and the spray kicks out for hundreds of yards. If you've stowed some food, settle down at a picnic table by the gazebo. If you have time and a healthy heart, hike the half-mile trail that winds down to the riverbanks. Add the fragrance and brilliance of the flowers and the sounds of

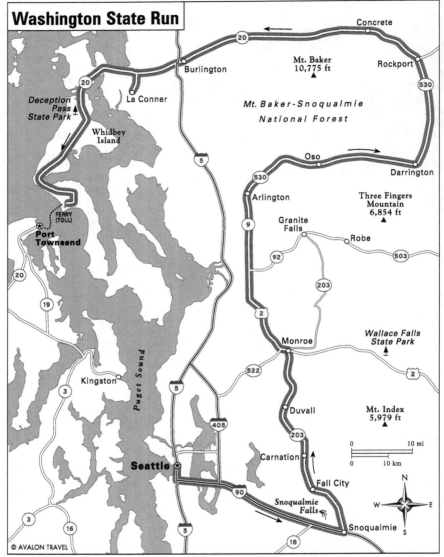

Washington State Run

Route: Seattle to Port Townsend via Snoqualmie, Fall City, Carnation, Duvall, Monroe, Arlington, Darrington, Whidbey Island

Distance: Approximately 245 miles

First Leg: Seattle to La Conner (196 miles)

Second Leg: La Conner to Port Townsend (46 miles)

Helmet Laws: Washington requires helmets.

nature and this is a must-see and a nice marker for the real start of your ride.

When you're ready to move on, the road runs briefly through a dynamite combination of woods, rivers, and hills. Canopy roads give way to country roads, and soon you reach the junction of Route 203 at Fall City. Turn right onto Route 203 and head north on the low and level two-lane road that winds ever so slightly toward the towns of Carnation and Monroe. Carnation is a nice little town, but I was more impressed by what I saw as I was riding out of town—open fields and wide valleys that reminded me of Vermont's classic Route 100.

There's not much to note between here and Duvall aside from noticing that you're actually in the country and on your motorcycle and miles away from the pressure and politics of work. So settle back and roll through Monroe which features a few restaurants and pubs and brings you to U.S. 2, where the ride northwest will have you navigating some dense growth before freeing you into mile after mile of farmland to reach Highway 9 North. This isn't a great road, but the Mountain Loop Road to Darrington usually is not an option, since long sections of gravel (or late snows) often make it impassable. Option B (Highway 9) takes you up to Arlington, where the ride gets nice in a hurry.

At Arlington look for Route 530, which will guide you straight toward Darrington, a short 25 miles away. While there had been some spells of good roads, this is more consistent and what you've been waiting for. Instantly, the road gets better and wider, and you're riding between majestic Washington mountains. The smells are hearty; the grass is plump. Tufts of clouds stuffed between the summits slowly tug at their granite moorings, break free, and drift away. Even in early summer,

slivers of snow from the peaks pierce into the woods below.

Past the town of Oso, pull off alongside the creek, and everything is perfect—with the glaring exception of clear-cut forests that have scarred the mountaintops. Why this makes any sense to anyone is beyond me.

Then comes Darrington where there's a quick jog north on Route 530 that puts you in the Sauk Valley of the Mount Baker-Snoqualmie National Forest. This is a fun road, delivering another boost of good riding as every slow corner leads into a magnificent run through a tunnel of 50-foot straight-as-nails pines. This wonderful road runs beside and over the Sauk River; it's a brilliant forest run. Regardless of the dense urban traffic surrounding nearby Seattle, here there is nothing but woods on both sides and fresh air all around you. At mile marker 60, the river, woods, and mountains converge and the twisty road drops you past meadows, moss, and an almost fluorescent green landscape.

When you reach Highway 20 at Rockport turn left. Around here, natural beauty takes a backseat to small towns like Concrete and larger ones like Sedro Woolley. So you'll enjoy only a decent, not breathtaking, ride. But once you cross beneath I-5, the mood of the road switches instantly from commercial to agricultural.

Farmland stretches from horizon to horizon and when you reach the community of Whitney, you'll see the turnoff south to La Conner. From here it's a quiet country ride down to tulip town.

LA CONNER PRIMER

It was a town built on a trading post and then evolved to focus on the shipping industry, canneries, and farms. Ultimately, La Conner became a retreat for artists and writers. It was a great place for a retreat since it occupied a point of land inaccessible by rail and folks had to make an effort to reach it.

Not much has changed since those early days. Commercial development hit Skagit County, but distance has preserved La Conner. It remains a waterfront community relatively unaffected by the explosion of technology and music a few hours south in Seattle. Victorian-era buildings are still in use more than a hundred years later; pleasure boats are moored in the Swinomish Channel; and countless acres of fields burst into a rainbow each April when the tulips are in bloom.

ON THE ROAD: LA CONNER

At first glance, it doesn't seem as if La Conner would be intriguing or popular. But it is, and there are reasons why.

In addition to presenting springtime's kaleidoscope of tulips, the town has re-invented itself as an artists' colony. There are more than 20 galleries, pubs, antique shops, and restaurants packed into one condensed area, so you can park your bike and easily explore everything on foot. Another advantage of La Conner's is its location. Equidistant from Seattle and Vancouver, nearly every Friday it's one of the most popular destinations for week-enders arriving from both cities.

This is the kind of town I prefer on a ride—not so large you think you've missed something, and not so small you go stir-crazy. La Conner can easily fill an afternoon and give you a place to relax at night. You can ride past the flower fields on the way out of town, but first just park your bike and walk down Morris and 1st Streets. Notice the street window artwork displays, most of which are based on the nature of Washington state, with wood carvings, glassware, and paintings featuring grizzly bears, eagles, wolves, or a combination of the three.

For details on walking tours, trails, and whale-watching excursions, stop by the **Visitor Information Center** (606 Morris St.). Sometimes, though, you may have other priorities. In La Conner, you can just enjoy the town at a leisurely pace, give yourself time to relax, ride across the Rainbow Bridge once or twice, and then just kick back and watch the flowers grow.

PULL IT OVER: LA CONNER HIGHLIGHTS
Shopping

There's a whole grab bag of shops and galleries around town, and you'll probably just park your bike and wander around until you find something that catches your attention. There were a few I found interesting, like the shop owned by Jon Peterson. He's got a limited market, but if you collect antique fishing tackle, pay a visit to **Plug Ugly** (313 E. Morris St., 360/466-1212). Open 11 A.M.–5 P.M. Thursday-Sunday, this place sells duck decoys and marine gear as well.

Good thing La Conner has a well-stocked grocery store like **Pioneer Market** (416 Morris St., 360/466-0188). This way, you can stock up on road food and supplies before you go. Even better, it's open 'til 10 P.M. every night.

Blue-Plate Specials

On the outskirts of town just off Highway 20, **The Farmhouse Restaurant** (13724 La Conner-Whitney Rd., 360/466-4411, www.thefarmhouserestaurant.net) serves old-fashioned big road food for breakfast, lunch, and dinner. Within this cavernous restaurant, you can get platters filled with steak, ham, chicken 'n' dumplings, grilled pork chops, hot turkey sandwiches, pies, and cakes. After dinner here, I puffed up to 438 pounds.

Not only is **La Conner Brewing**

Company (117 S. 1st St., 360/466-1415, ww.insidelaconner.com/LaBrew.html) a warm and intimate family restaurant serving wood-fired pizzas, soups, wings, quesadillas, and salads for lunch and dinner, it also has a great and active bar serving wines, ales, lagers, porters, stouts, pilsners, and dopple bocks. Can you believe it? Dopple bocks!

La Conner Seafood and Prime Rib House (614 1st St., 360/466-4014, www.laconnerseafood.com) is a traditional waterfront hangout open for lunch and dinner. Using only two base ingredients—fish and meat—this restaurant has created about 100 different dishes, including firecracker prawns, shrimp-smothered red snapper, Cajun prime rib, and more. If you have a hearty appetite, sample the buffet.

Watering Holes

If the Brewing Company's too tidy, **La Conner Pub** (702 S. 1st St., 360/466-9932) is the alternative. This blue-collar bar has two pool tables, some old folks, a few young'uns, bottled and tap beers, and a full bar open until at least 1 A.M. Try to ignore the family restaurant in the next room.

Shut-Eye

La Conner has relatively few lodging choices, with most options being inns. For a chain motel or hotel you'd need to travel more than 10 miles out of town. Contact the **La Conner Chamber of Commerce** (360/466-4778 or 888/642-9284, www.laconnerchamber.com) for assistance in finding a room.

Inn-dependence

The **Wild Iris Inn** (117–121 Maple Ave., 360/466-1400, www.wildiris.com, $109–189) has 18 large rooms—12 with hot tubs—and provides a full breakfast. More

basic, the **La Conner Country Inn** (107 S. 2nd St., 360/466-3101, www.laconner-lodging.com, $159 and up high season) provides generic, motel-like rooms (some with king beds) and then adds a continental breakfast.

ON THE ROAD: LA CONNER TO PORT TOWNSEND

When you're ready to leave La Conner behind, look for Morris Street, which bypasses Highway 20. This short detour will take you to a patch of beautiful farmland, which, in the spring, will likely provide you with a fantastic photo op of your bike poised before a spectacular field of flowers. Less than a half-mile from town, Morris Street zigzags and turns into Chilberg Road; once you've ridden past Best Road, start looking for Beaver Marsh Road. I suggest this little detour because when you turn left here, you'll be able to see why La Conner's earned the reputation for its proliferation of tulips.

It's a few miles to reach **Roozengaarde** (15867 Beaver Marsh Rd., 360/424-8531), where even in the off-season a small garden of multicolored tulips will give you an idea of what the fields look like when they're in full bloom. It's open 9 A.M.–5 P.M. Monday–Saturday. Admission is free.

When you leave, follow Beaver Marsh Road north and watch for McLean Road and make a right onto it. If you need some last-minute supplies, you can stop in at the old-fashioned **Evergreen Grocery Store** (16016 McLean Rd., 360/424-4377). After stocking up, head out a few blocks more to Avon-Allen Road where you hang a left to wind up on CR 536 en route to Highway 20—which is the last number you'll have to think about for the next several days.

With the Washington breeze in your face, you'll pass sporadic mountains and a few commercial enterprises before turning left to follow Highway 20 west toward Whidbey Island. The island's just about a dozen miles away and marks the entrance to the Olympic Peninsula. Near Sharpes Corner there'll be a sharp corner as Highway 20 drops south where, almost immediately, images from rides of motorcycling past will flash into mind since this stretch looks comparable to the Berkshires, Yosemite, and the Blue Ridge Parkway.

On your right, you'll see a glacier lake that looks frigid even at the height of summer. Several miles ahead near mile marker 43, watch for Pass Lake and a pullout where, if you're riding in a group, you can grab a wonderful shot that uses the lake and mountain as a backdrop.

This level of scenery continues for several miles and it all brings to mind the look of a 1940s *Field and Stream* magazine. Ahead, the Straits of Juan De Fuca can be seen to the right, but one of the most impressive sights of the trip arrives as you round the corner and approach Deception Pass. At the spot where the Canoe Pass and Deception Pass bridges span a huge gorge, the vista is breathtaking. At the bottom, blue-green water floods back to the sea and the shores are packed with massive trees washed ashore like twigs. It's all a larger-than-life scene and there's another convenient pullout if you want to park your bike and grab a shot with the bridge in the background.

When you ride across the span it seems more thrilling than running the Golden Gate. At the opposite side of the 976-foot bridge are restrooms, a parking area, and a trail that you should walk down even if you have a heart condition, gout, and a wooden leg. The views around each bend in the trail are fantastic, and the pine forest scents are reminiscent of a Christmas tree farm.

Less than a mile later, consider pulling into the 4,128-acre **Deception Pass State Park** (360/675-2417 or 360/675-7277, www.parks.wa.gov, free). Built primarily by the Civilian Conservation Corps in the 1930s, this marine and camping park boasts 30 miles of hiking trails, 19 miles of saltwater shoreline, three freshwater lakes, 246 campsites, freshwater swimming, fishing, and canoeing. The old-growth forest is sprinkled with cedar, spruce, yew, apple, and cherry trees, as well as fields of foxglove, lupines, rhododendron, and roses. Due to the temperate climate here, wildlife thrives and there's a strong chance you'll spy bald eagles in flight.

Now I hate to have to break this to you, but following this spectacular introduction to Whidbey Island, the scenery fizzles. From here to Port Townsend, the landscape is pockmarked by random development, so even after you get your mojo going on a good run, it withers out when you encounter trailer parks and hideous commercial sprawl.

From south of Coupeville, all you need to do is watch for the turnoff to the **Port Townsend Ferry** (206/464-6400). For about $5, you and your machine can take a 30-minute sea cruise to one of the nicest towns on the peninsula.

PORT TOWNSEND PRIMER

Before Port Townsend was infected with quaintness, it was a real town—a real get-drunk-in-the-bar-get-laid-upstairs kind of town. A century ago, Port Townsend was home to 40 saloons and 17 brothels (the most prosperous of which was adjacent to City Hall). A writer visiting town remarked that the "stench of whiskey permeates Port Townsend to a depth of nine feet"—although no one knows how he measured it. I lost the scent at four feet.

It was an affluent town that accommodated a thriving maritime port and the consulates of 17 countries. As in other resurrected cities, a period of decline was eased by the arrival of hippies in the 1970s. From the luxury of their smoke-filled VW buses, artists and writers emerged and fueled a creative spark that sustains itself today. The hippies grew up and learned the rules of business and restored old homes and then rich Californians came in and bought the homes and turned them into inns. And the town was turned around.

One unusual quirk you may notice is that citizens seem to take obsessive pride in the movie *An Officer and a Gentleman,* which was filmed around here in the early 1980s. If a cardinal from Port Townsend were ever elected pope, you can bet the new pontiff would recall Richard Gere's character and adopt the name Pope Zack Mayo.

Aside from that devotion to a long-ago film, what you'll see today is a tight-knit community that combines new money, young hippies, established businesses, and trendy shops in Woodstock-era ambience. Far out.

ON THE ROAD: PORT TOWNSEND

Like much of Washington, riding in the vicinity of Port Townsend poses a dilemma. If you check the map, **Olympic National Park** (360/565-3130, www.nps.gov/olym) seems so close, and a ferry trip to Victoria, British Columbia, looks so tempting. In the end, I chose to hang out in town for several reasons. A trip to Victoria makes for a very long day—the ferry trip lasts several hours, and reaching the boat takes about as long. Olympic National Park didn't pan out either. After riding halfway there via Highway 20 and U.S. 101, I realized that the road was beating me into submission with its slow-moving traffic and a disturbing lack of scenery. Port Townsend calmed me down and kept me entertained. I was

content. But if your schedule affords you more time, give them both a try.

Port Townsend is a great walking town, and the people are friendly. If you hang around town, definitely stop at **Bergstrom's Antique and Classic Autos** (809 Washington St., 360/385-5061). Based on the building's exterior, you wouldn't expect to find much, but inside you'll usually find a collection of old motorcycles, scooters, and classic cars as well as garage memorabilia, hubcaps, lighters, and technical manuals representing a fleet of antique vehicles.

A short ride away lies **Fort Worden State Park** (360/344-4431 or 360/344-4400, www.parks.wa.gov/fortworden), which is where they filmed...*An Officer and a Gentleman!* The 19th century base is closed now, which makes it look like Fort Knox after Goldfinger's ladies sprayed the soldiers with knockout gas. There are still parade grounds, officers' quarters, gun batteries, an artillery museum, a natural history museum, a theater, and a performing arts center, as well as nice shoreline beside the frigid waters of the straits. If you're traveling with a large group, you can reserve lodging space in some of the seriously cool renovated barracks and officers' quarters.

With a decent map, you'll likely find some nearby back roads to satisfy your desire to explore, and you shouldn't miss the stretch of restaurants and stores in the section of town known as uptown Port Townsend, which is higher up the bluff. Aside from that, just appreciate the broad waters of the Straits of Juan De Fuca and the magnificence of Port Townsend Bay.

PULL IT OVER: PORT TOWNSEND HIGHLIGHTS
Attractions and Adventures
If you don't mind devoting some touring

time to a movie, you may as well do it at the restored **Rose Theatre** (235 Taylor St., 360/385-1089, www.rosetheatre.com). Buy some licorice and Necco wafers at the counter, and then sit back in the classic theatre for the moving picture show.

A center for maritime education, the **Wooden Boat Foundation** (Cupola House, Port Hudson, 360/385-3628, www.woodenboat.org) offers several courses—each of which will get you on the water. You can learn to sail a large wooden ship, sail a small wooden boat, or rent a rowboat and explore on your own. If you appreciate fine craftsmanship and tales of the sea, hang out at the chandlery and talk boats.

You cannot avoid fly-fishing in the Northwest. Do not even try. The folks at **Port Townsend Angler** (940 Water St., 360/379-3763, www.ptangler.com) have all the gear and arrange guides for fishing in streams and on the Sound. They claim this as the best spot for wild steelhead fishing in the Lower 48. But it's an expensive hobby: A full day of fly-fishing for two will cost around $250 and up, and then you have to add the gear. If you can swing it, it'll be a memorable wilderness experience. Too much? A McFish sandwich costs two bucks.

Shopping

Joe Euro runs **Wine Seller** (940 Water St., 360/385-7673 or 888/629-9463, www.ptwineseller.com), the oldest wine shop on the peninsula. Open around 10:30 A.M.–6 P.M. daily, the small shop features an array of wines (including generic "cheap white" and "cheap red" wines), plus cigars, gourmet cheese, smoked salmon, and free back issues of *Wine Spectator*.

Blue-Plate Specials

Silverwater Cafe (237 Taylor St., 360/385-6448, www.silverwatercafe.com),

serving lunch and dinner, features creative spins on fresh seafood, meat, and vegetarian entrées that are often prepared with ingredients purchased from local farms and anglers. The meals are upscale, but the clientele casual—an unusual mix, but it works here. In its quiet corner location, you can dine in peace.

Also open for lunch and dinner, **Waterfront Pizza** (951 Water St., 360/385-6629) sells takeout by the slice downstairs, and the upstairs dining room serves pizza that keeps the locals coming back.

Watering Holes

Waterstreet Brewing and Ale House (639 Water St., 360/379-6438, www.waterstreetbrewing.com) sits on the site of the old Town Tavern and features an 1800s bar, three pool tables, two fireplaces, and a dozen beers on tap (six of them brewed right here).

With a broad deck that overlooks Puget Sound, **Sirens** (823 Water St., 360/379-1100, www.sirensbar.com) is a real great spot to work on a pitcher of beer. There are 11 micros, hot pizza, live music, and a Wednesday open mic night that turns this into a hipster's hootenanny with local musicians playing jazz, blues, or rock to a packed bar full of locals.

More coffeehouse than bar, **Upstage** (923 Washington St., 360/385-2216, www.upstagerestaurant.com) pours wine and draft microbrews. An eclectic entertainment calendar changes nightly, featuring everything from open mic to blues to swing.

Shut-Eye

Surprisingly remote, Port Townsend does not have any chain hotels. It does, however, have plenty of inns. Check with the **Port Townsend Visitors Center** (360/385-2722 or 888/365-6978, www.

ptguide.com) for the full slate, and consider this list just the tip of the iceberg.

Inn-dependence

The **Quimper Inn** (1306 Franklin St., 360/385-1060 or 800/557-1060, www. quimperinn.com, $98–165 year-round), a large 1888 home, rests on a hill overlooking Port Townsend. It's elegant without the clutter. Kick back on the second-story terrace or relax in the living room and talk to innkeeper Ron Ramage about his Porsche collection and rebuilt Triumphs.

The **Palace Hotel** (1004 Water St., 360/385-0773 or 800/962-0741, www. palacehotelpt.com, $59–109) is a nicely restored 1889 hotel on the town's main drag. Large rooms and suites (ask for a private bath) sport an Old West look.

Resources for Riders

Washington State Run

Washington Travel Information
Washington State Ferries—206/464-6400, www.wsdot.wa.gov/ferries
Washington State Parks—360/902-8844 or 888/226-7688, www.parks.wa.gov
Washington State Road Conditions—800/695-7623, www.wsdot.wa.gov/traffic
Washington State Tourism—800/544-1800, www.experiencewa.com

Local and Regional Information
La Conner Chamber of Commerce—360/466-4778 or 888/642-9284,
    www.laconnerchamber.com
Mt. Baker-Snoqualmie National Forest—425/783-6000 or 800/627-0062,
    www.fs.fed.us/r6/mbs
Olympic Peninsula—360/437-0120, www.olympicpeninsula.org
Port Townsend Visitors Center—360/385-2722 or 888/365-6978,
    www.ptguide.com
Whidbey Island Information—www.visitwhidbey.com

Washington Motorcycle Shops
Bellevue Kawasaki—14004 N.E. 20th St., Bellevue, 425/641-5040,
    www.bellevuekawasakiwa.com
Downtown Harley-Davidson—3715 E. Valley Rd., 425/988-2100 or
    800/474-4647, www.dowtownhd.com
Eastside Harley Davidson—14408 NE 20th St., Bellevue, 425/747-0322,
    www.eastsideharley.com
Eastside Motorsports—13029 NE 20th St., Bellevue, 425/882-4300,
    www.eastsidemotosports.com
Everett Powersports—215 SW Everett Mall Way, Everett, 423/437-4545,
    www.everettpowersports.com
I-90 Motorsports—200 NE Gilman Blvd., Issaquah, 425/391-4490,
    www.I-90motorsports.com
Lake City Powersports—12048 Lake City Way NE, Seattle, 206/364-1372,
    www.lakecitypowersports.com
Port Townsend Honda—3059 Sims Way W., Port Townsend, 360/385-4559
Renton Motorcycle Co.—3701 E. Valley Rd., Renton, 425/226-4320 or
    800/460-6451, www.rmcmotorsports.com
Seattle Cycle Center—10201 Aurora Ave. N., Seattle, 206/524-0044,
    www.seattlecycle.com
Skagit Harley-Davidson—1337 Goldenrod Rd., Burlington, 360/757-1515,
    www.skagitharley.com
South Sound BMW—3605 20th St. E., Fife, 253/922-2004,
    www.southsoundbmw.com

Oregon's Best Run

Cannon Beach, Oregon to Sisters, Oregon

Incredible coastal scenery preserved a century ago by a visionary governor creates a ceaselessly awe-inspiring tour. Begin in a beachside community that could serve as the model for future coastal towns, and then enjoy the finest 160-mile stretch of two-lane you may ever ride. Stop in a character-filled old town enveloped within a larger town lacking the same; hang around for an adrenaline-pumping, mind-blowing dune buggy attack on the sand; then head east where the forests, falls, and mountains herald your arrival in a new Old West village.

CANNON BEACH PRIMER

There are several dozen communities along Oregon's coast, and whether it was a river, a ravine, or a forest, each needed something to root the town as it grew. In Cannon Beach, it was a rock. Granted, it is not your ordinary rock. First of all, Haystack Rock really looks like a stack of hay. Second, it happens to be 235 feet tall, which makes it the third-largest coastal monolith in the world.

In addition to this icon, which you may have already seen on countless postcards and calendars, consider the origin of the town's name. In 1846, the U.S. Navy schooner *Shark* was pulling out of the Columbia River into the Pacific Ocean. After waves tore the ship to shreds, a section of the deck with a cannon and capstan on it floated down the coast and came to rest on a stretch of shore that would become known as Cannon Beach. Thank god it wasn't the poop deck.

Also ranking high in the town's history is the Lewis and Clark Expedition. Cannon Beach was the farthest south the explorers traveled, venturing here for an overnight in 1806 when they heard they could carve some blubber off a dead whale. And that's it. A shipwreck, a rock, and a rotting whale anchored the town long enough for it to evolve into a natural preserve that some folks consider a mini-Carmel. It has art galleries, bistros, bookstores, kites, sandcastle contests, tide pools, hiking trails, natural sanctuaries,

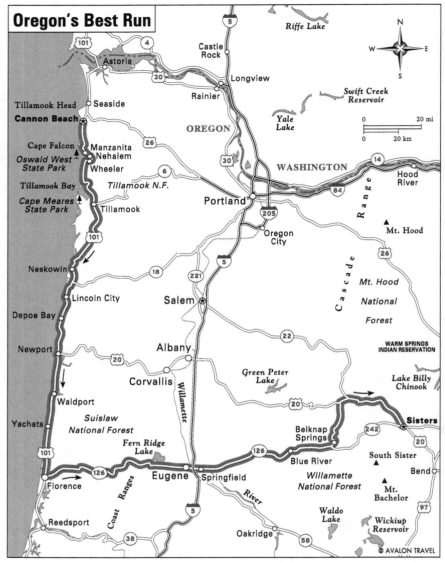

Oregon's Best Run

Route: Cannon Beach to Sisters via Manzanita, Tillamook, Lincoln City, Newport, Florence, Eugene, Vida, Santiam Pass

Distance: Approximately 325 miles

First Leg: Cannon Beach to Florence (160 miles)

Second Leg: Florence to Sisters (165 miles)

Helmet Laws: Oregon requires helmets.

Oregon's coastline is visually dynamic; and nowhere more than at Cannon Beach. At 235 feet tall, Haystack Rock is the third largest coastal monolith in the world.

and a migration of tufted puffins that flock to Haystack Rock each year to lay their eggs.

That's been enough to see Cannon Beach through its sesquicentennial—and it should keep you satisfied for a few days.

ON THE ROAD: CANNON BEACH

Cannon Beach is a place where you go to avoid having to go to your room. Each minute you're here, outdoors is where you want to be. To get outdoors, Hemlock is the street you'll need to know, since it's the main coastal route that leads to and through the center of town. With it, you can ride north to Ecola State Park or south to the beach, or stop in the middle and see the town. And it's worth seeing. After I get done cleaning out my gutters, I'm going to get started on building a beachside community of 1,600 people, and I'll use Cannon Beach as a blueprint. It's not so large as to be impersonal, or too small to be dull.

Another bonus is that no building here is more than three stories tall, a far different architectural principle than you'll find on coastlines in Florida and California. In Oregon, the ocean is for everyone.

That said, the best way to see the best of Cannon Beach is to check out the attractions and adventures that follow.

PULL IT OVER: CANNON BEACH HIGHLIGHTS
Attractions and Adventures

When I asked at the visitors center how someone would spend a perfect couple of days in Cannon Beach, I was sure they were wrong telling me to just head to **Ecola State Park** (503/436-2844 or 800/551-6949) and see the tide pools at Haystack Rock. Then I went.

From the center of town, the road north connects with a fork that leads right onto Ecola Park Road and into the woods. Accustomed to Florida scrub pines, I had never seen anything like what was ahead:

an old-growth rainforest where the trees were a near-luminescent green, which, when mixed with the fog and mist and the moisture, seemed strangely prehistoric. Riding this land of the lost in the midst of a stalled storm when the midday sun was hidden by rolling clouds was an exciting and, to be honest, eerie experience. The warped road passes massive trees and a forest bed of ferns before it reaches the ranger station, where you'll pay $3 for the day. What you'll see in a few minutes is worth that and far more.

From the parking area, a walkway leads to a lookout point, where you'll savor a vision that will last a lifetime, especially if you've never had the privilege of seeing the Pacific Ocean. The ocean is massive and awe-inspiring, with views seeming to last for billions of miles. To the south, several miles of arched shoreline are swept by an infinite series of waves. To the west, a column of curving rocks slips into the ocean like a dragon's tail. To the north, an inlet

What's so special about riding in Oregon? Take a look at this road and you'll know.

© NANCY HOWELL

dips into shore and springs out again, directing your view to the Tillamook Rock Lighthouse, perched on a rock 12 miles offshore. Construction of the lighthouse began in 1879 and took two years and the lives of a few workers before it went into service. Decommissioned in 1957, in 1980 it became—can you believe this—*a columbarium.* Twice a year, cremated ashes are flown out and deposited for an eternity at sea.

Sublime and weird things like this aren't all Ecola gives you. From the parking area, the Tillamook Head trail is an eight-mile walk to Seaside, while the Clatsop Loop Trail is a short, two-mile hiking path that connects Ecola Point to Indian Beach, following a path blazed by members of the Lewis and Clark Expedition. Elk graze in the meadows, eagles and falcons catch the currents, and in winter and summer, more than 20,000 gray whales pass by in the midst of a 12,000-mile migration. The spiritual effect of it all is ceaseless, magical, and a miracle. You'll be pleased to hear that you can look forward to 160 miles more of this on your journey south.

Descending from the hill, ride south again to the second stop: **Haystack Rock.** There are parking areas along Hemlock Street, although if you're staying at a beachside lodge, you'll just walk along the shore to reach it. What will you see when you're there? Tufted puffins, possibly. The chunky, pelagic seabird lives on land only when it's time to nest, hanging out here from the end of April to late July. Bring binoculars to spot the squat black body, white face, bright orange bill, and tufts of feathers above the eyes of the bird sailors call the "sea parrot." Sharing a piece of the rock with the puffins are pigeons, guillemots, cormorants, and seagulls, whose leisure time is occasionally interrupted by eagles that swoop to the ground, isolate a gull—like fighter pilots peel off bombers—and take it down.

It's unusual to admit there's pleasure in looking at a rock, but there is, although you may need the assistance of a ranger to understand what you're looking at. During the summer, volunteers are on the beach to host **Haystack Rock Awareness Programs** (503/436-1581) and explain the intricate ecosystem that supports dozens of creatures living in tide pools left by the receding ocean. Look closely, and in the shallows you'll see limpets, barnacles, starfish, hermit crabs, sea sculpins, and anemones. Be careful where you walk, and leave the creatures where they are.

If you have a hard time leaving the beach, plan to come back later. The oldest business in town is **Sea Ranch Resort** (415 Fir St., 503/436-2815, www.searanchrv.com). Here since 1927, it rents horses for daytime group rides between mid-May and Labor Day that follow the Ecola Creek to Chapman Point and south to Haystack Rock. When there's a low tide, moonlight rides are offered.

Shopping

Remember this while you visit Oregon: There's no sales tax. Keep this in mind when you buy food or souvenirs or a new bike. While you're in Cannon Beach, your best investment is walking around Hemlock Street. Granted, this delivers all the things a tourist town should (taffy kitchens, T-shirt shops), but there are also places like **Mariner Market** (139 N. Hemlock, 503/436-2442). Sidewalk benches are reserved for Democrats or Republicans, and aisles are inventoried with beer, deli meals, tide charts, videos, groceries, ready-made and ready-to-be-prepared foods, and everything you'd need for a beachside cookout.

As you'll discover, the history and images of Oregon's coast, roads, and lighthouses are fascinating, and you can find good regional research materials at the library or at the **Cannon Beach Book Company** (130 N. Hemlock St., 503/436-1301, www.cannonbeachbooks.com).

Cannon Beach has earned a reputation as an artists' colony and, judging by many of the galleries here, I'd tend to agree. Not knowing your taste in art, I'd suggest you pay a pre-ride virtual visit to see some of the extraordinary paintings, ceramics, oils, acrylics, and woodcarvings online via the **Cannon Beach Gallery Group** (www.cb-gallerygroup.com).

When it's bleak and drizzly and Oregon gray, I doubt that anyone's shouting "Surf's up!" But think how cool it'd be to tell your friends that you did…Whether you're a Gidget or a Grommet, you can shred a tube on a tri-skeg stick rented from **Cannon Beach Surf** (1088 S. Hemlock St., 503/436-0475, www.cannonbeachsurf.com). It offers lessons and rents wetsuits, skim boards, and boogie boards.

Blue-Plate Specials

Even though Cannon Beach features several great restaurants, think about dining at an open-air café: the beach. Bonfires are allowed, and at the **Mariner Market** (139 N. Hemlock, 503/436-2442) you can stock up on hot dogs, marshmallows, corn, and everything else you'd need for a cookout. So live it up at your personal makeshift oceanside restaurant. You don't even need a permit—all you need are matches. Just keep your fire at least 25 feet from wooden seawalls, beach grass, or driftwood, and don't wait for the tide to extinguish the flames when you're done. Do it yourself.

If the weather craps out and you're locked in your room, **Fultano's Pizza**

(220 N. Hemlock, 503/436-9717, www. cbfultanos.com) delivers traditional and gourmet pizza hot—steam lines drawn on the boxes attest to this. Its dining room, too, is an option.

The Lumberyard (264 3rd St., 503/436-0285, www.thelumberyardgrill. com) is a big Pacific Northwest–style restaurant where locals gather around the bar to draw on about a few dozen beers (some brewed here) served in bottles or on tap in pint glasses. Diners settle into natural wood booths and dine on rotisserie-grilled chicken, pork loin, pot pies, turkey meat loaf, barbecue pork, oven-roasted pizzas, and plank salmon made in the open kitchen. It's also a great place to drop in for a nightcap. The Lumberyard is big and clean and neat.

Fuel up for the day at the **Pig 'N Pancake** (223 S. Hemlock St., 503/436-2851, www.pignpancake.com). There are 35 varieties of breakfast here, which is something Einstein hypothesized in 1905. The kind of diner you look for when touring,

it also offers homemade soups, chowders, and desserts, including some made from family recipes.

Watering Holes

For a small town, Cannon Beach has more than enough places to relax and map out future rides or take a break at the end of the day. Again, you'll find homemade micros at **The Lumberyard** (264 3rd St., 503/436-0285, www.thelumberyardgrill. com) or two other local hangouts that have a good vibe. The grandpappy of them all is **Bill's Tavern and Brewhouse** (188 Hemlock St., 503/436-2202), which opened as a café in 1923. The local gathering spot is in the heart of town, where you and your buddies can grab a booth and feast on hamburgers, fried oyster burgers, albacore, cod, and seafood stew. Along with beers made right here, there are about a dozen beers on tap in the warm, inviting bar.

The **Warren House** (3301 S. Hemlock St., 503/436-1130) is a smokehouse that serves burgers and steaks, which you can

Crossing through—not over—one of the magnificent mountains of Oregon.

wash down with beers brewed here. The beer garden has an ocean view.

Shut-Eye

Although there are no chain hotels in Cannon Beach, there's something better: old-fashioned motor courts.

Motels and Motor Courts

Like most things, Cannon Beach does lodging well as well—although rates can double from winter to summer, so get ready to dig deep. There are condos, inns, and places like the triplex of **The Waves, Argonauta Inn,** and **White Heron Lodge** (503/436-2205 or 800/822-2468, www.thewavesmotel.com, $119 and up high season). Under one owner, they occupy several sites and present a combination of choices that range from motel rooms to suites to home-style accommodations that have kitchens, fireplaces, and hot tubs. Rates can double for the homes and they may require a two-night minimum.

Back in the old days, folks would take motoring trips down the coast and find a place like **McBee Motel Cottages** (888 S. Hemlock St., 503/436-1392 or 800/238-4107, www.mcbeecottages.com). Even through the McBee opened in 1941, it's been gussied up a bit since which is why basic rooms that go for $65 off-season sell for as much as $140 in high season. On the plus side, they're just steps from the beach, they're cozy, some units feature fireplaces and kitchens, and all have old-fashioned touches to complete the effect.

Chain Drive

Chain hotels are eight miles north of Cannon Beach in Seaside:

Best Western, Comfort Inn, Holiday Inn

For more information, including phone numbers and websites, see page 151.

ON THE ROAD: CANNON BEACH TO FLORENCE

...And we have a winner! Of all the rides I've taken since 1974, this day's tour down Oregon's coast really did it for me. With no frame of reference to go on, nearly every turn delivered more than I thought was possible. I owe this to Oswald West and U.S. 101. When planning most rides, I'd research alternate byways and look for other routes just in case the road fizzled out. This was different. The combination of Oregon's coast and U.S. 101 delivered mile after mile. In hindsight, though, I did err. I thought the first five miles were the finest "first five" I'd ever seen. It turned out that the first 20 miles (followed by the remaining 140) were truly great. Here's how your day will unfold.

Hemlock Street rolls out of Cannon

Riding in the Pacific Northwest comes with one near certainty: perpetual rains. If you can deal with that, you'll savor the times when the weather clears and you're given exquisite country riding.

Oswald West

It's a shame that politicians these days have little interest or desire in creating something for the people. For inspiration, they should ride the Oregon Coast and think of Oswald West, described by one writer as "by all odds the most brilliant governor Oregon ever had." I learned about West at the magnificent lookout point south of Cannon Beach, where a plaque offered a glimpse of his life and a reminder of what public service makes possible. He was described as a charismatic and intelligent man, with "a keen sense of humanity and an open mind." Tired of corruption in government but undaunted by a lack of funds and influential friends, he rode on horseback to campaign in small communities across the state. He ran to make a difference, and he won.

As you ride, you're experiencing one of the greatest achievements of "Governor Oz," as another plaque here attests: "If sight of sand and sky and sea has given respite from your daily cares, then pause to thank Oswald West, former governor of Oregon, 1911–1915. By his foresight, nearly 400 miles of the ocean shore were set aside for public use, from the Columbia River on the north to the California border on the south."

All hail the great and powerful Oz.

Beach and slides into U.S. 101 about three miles south of town. Immediately the friendly scent of the pines joins you on a journey that adds close-up views of ravines, rainforests, and the Pacific on a winding stretch of two-lane traffic. The road has an old-fashioned feel to it— diners and motor courts would be right at home here. Although they were absent, what did appear before me was a magnificent tunnel punched directly through the center of a mountain; the kind Wile E. Coyote would have painted on the side of a hill. It doesn't seem real, but it is, and it is overwhelming.

Even at 45 mph, you won't ever feel rushed, because here and for the rest of the ride, there are frequent pullouts giving speeding cars the option to pass you. In these initial 10 miles, you set a pattern for the entire trek: You ride beside the ocean until the road weaves to the east,

and that's when you enter the rainforests where the trees and trunks and ferns are the same iridescent green that you found at Ecola. Past Necarney Creek, you'll enter the **Oswald West State Park,** and a few miles farther south, you can roll off to a pullout to see one of America's most marvelous overlooks. I'd like to say this panorama is picture-perfect, but a thousand pictures wouldn't even begin to convey how wonderful this is.

As a flatland Floridian, I've always had a sea-level view of the sea. Now I was hundreds of feet above a shoreline that opened up majestic views of the coast to the north and south, the endless waves flying past rocks and onto the curving beach. I stayed awhile to enjoy the free show, gave a silent thank-you, and then resumed the ride south. At 1,661 feet, upcoming Neahkahnie Mountain is one of the highest points along the coast and as the road's seven-degree grade wraps around its base, the pleasure of the path increases as you ride. Things change slightly when you pass Manzanita and then enter Nehalem, where you'll wonder when things changed. Suddenly you're aware it's not the coast any more; you're in a valley surrounded by forests, rivers, and farmlands. If magically changing views like these don't do it for you, just stop your bike right now and take a bus home.

You'll cross the Nehalem River to enter Wheeler (pop. 400), where there's a visitors center and some antiques shops and not much more than that. Afterward, as you ride to and through Rockaway Beach and Farview, the scenery suffers slightly, but you stick with it because you have no choice, and your gut tells you that soon you'll clear it to the coast. Personally, I admire the tenacity of residents in these small towns who stuck with it through financial hardships and are building communities to be proud of.

One subtle yet intriguing feature that'll hold your attention is that each of these ordinary towns has a certain presence and personality. Towns like Garibaldi where, in the middle of extraordinary emptiness, is a monumental smokestack still standing long after the lumber mill it served vanished into history. The smokestack still towers over estuaries that rise and fall with the tide, so during the day you'll ride beside a sea of mud as you cruise into the town of Tillamook, the "Land of Cheese, Trees, and Ocean Breeze." Since this was yet another place I knew nothing about, my gut instinct was to race through it and stay on my self-imposed schedule. But at the town's visitors center I was instructed to go next door to **Tillamook Cheese** (4175 U.S. 101, 503/815-1300 or 800/542-7290, www.tillamookcheese.com). Even though I really didn't want to see a cheese factory, I went, and I was honestly glad I did.

Inside, a self-guided tour leads to an observation platform where you watch a platoon of Oompa-Loompa-ish cheesemakers at belts and slicers and rollers turning single 40-pound blocks of cheese into forty symmetrically sliced one-pound units. Across the hall, workers are whipping up and packaging ice cream. I watched all of this for far longer than my doctor would have advised before heading downstairs to a restaurant for a grilled cheese sandwich and double scoop of some of the freshest, most pure ice cream I've ever tasted. A weirdly intriguing stop, I look back and see this was a reminder to lose my self-inflicted schedule and allow the day to reveal itself.

From Tillamook, there are three ways to go. The first is staying on U.S. 101 and continuing the ride south. Or you can take the Three Capes Loop Road detour to the coast, which will present a bag full of scenery while adding only an additional 10 miles before reconnecting with U.S. 101 further south. The third is mixing up the two with half a loop that'll take you to the coast and the Cape Meares Lighthouse and back to Tillamook. That was my choice.

Turning right on 3rd Avenue, which is also the Netarts Highway, I rode west where, I'm reluctant to say, the aroma of cow crap was a pleasant reminder I was back in the country. Dairy country, no less—hence all the cheese. A few miles down, Bay Ocean Road shoots off a subtle fork to the right, over a river, and into a road slipped into place beside Tillamook Bay. The fact I was now riding north on my journey south was at first disconcerting and then comforting, a fresh reminder that motorcycling is designed for the journey and not the destination.

At low tide the view of moist, soot-colored mud lasted for several miles until I reached a junction at Crab Harbor, where the road led to the left and a sign warned "rough roads for the next five miles." How true. The rough gravel road on this Alpine pitch managed to rattle my shocks and shock my rattles before a short, narrow bridge opened up a view of the coast and compelled me to ride on toward the lighthouse.

The opening to **Cape Meares State Park** (503/842-3182) is on your right, and the road to the summit, with its pitch, gravel, and twists, creates a hat trick of good riding. From the parking area, it's a short walk to Oregon's shortest lighthouse. Built in 1890, the 38-foot beacon sits 232 feet above the waves. The other attraction here, the Octopus Tree, is a multi-trunked Sitka spruce that's an equal distance through the woods in the opposite direction. Better than both, I thought, were the overlooks above inlets carved into the cliffs over the course of millions of years. Waves continued to flood in with the tides and small waterfalls poured over the ledges and added to the sea.

Back on the loop toward Netarts with the Pacific Ocean still in sight, the high-pitched roads were again perfect for riding. Netarts itself offered a gas station and then it was back to the two-lane forest run that brought back memories from a few hours earlier. At a junction immediately south of town, you can turn left and follow the Netarts Highway back to Tillamook. If you take the right fork, you'll whip into Whiskey Creek Road, which zips past Cape Lookout and eventually Cape Kiwanda before merging again with U.S. 101 just past Pacific City. If I'm lucky enough to be reincarnated as myself, I'll take that route next time around.

I made the loop back to Tillamook to catch the **Tillamook Air Museum** (6030 Hangar Rd., 503/842-1130, www.tillamookair.com). Even a blind person couldn't miss this place. On the east side of U.S. 101, this is the largest clear-span wooden structure in the world: a massive hangar built in 1943 to house U.S. Navy blimps searching for Japanese submarines. Nearly 200 feet tall and 1,072 feet long, it encloses enough space for six football fields. Today, it's a museum housing more than 30 historic aircraft, including a great assortment of World War II warbirds. Nearly as large is **Munson Falls,** which you'll find about six miles south. Tucked out of sight nearly two miles off the main road, it's worth the effort to reach it. The 319-foot waterfall springs out of a mossy cliff and is the highest in the coast range. Amazingly, everything you've seen today has been within 50 miles of Cannon Beach, and there's another hundred ahead.

Even though you're on Oregon's main coastal highway, there is little clutter to distract you from enjoying the tour, only mountains and pines spiked on the hills and rhododendrons that may be in bloom. You'll pass homes of people you'll never meet on a road you'll never forget, and you'll witness scenes that are new to you but destined to become part of this memorable experience. You'll go deep in the woods now, then south of Neskowin, where the ocean appears again, completely undisturbed—it's perhaps the longest stretch of coastline I've seen that hadn't been destroyed by development. When you enter Siuslaw National Forest, the scenery isn't thrown at you. Instead, the well-placed pullouts, small towns, farms, valleys, hills, beaches, and bays appear for you at perfectly timed intervals.

Civilization returns in Lincoln City, where you cross the 45th parallel. Back at home, tell your friends you rode across the midway point between the equator and the North Pole, and they should be impressed. Past the city, there's not much privacy until Depoe Bay, after which you'll be dipping into the woods and the water.

Pullouts sewn onto the shores of the ocean allow you to park your bike and spy lighthouses, such as Oregon's tallest, a 93-foot-tall model flashing out at Yaquina Head, followed four miles south by the Yaquina Bay lighthouse by the bridge. As you ride through Alsea and Waldport and contemplate the end of the line in Florence, you'll reflect on the ride and may agree that it's been most excellent. For a grand finale, it's about to get even better.

After Yachats (ya-HOTS) comes one of the coolest views I've ever seen: the road spinning around a curve, shooting up an incline, and hugging the side of a cliff into extreme elevations. It spun and snapped and popped across the land, and that good riding lasted for a dozen miles and beyond, all the way past the **Heceta Head Lighthouse** (541/997-3851 or 866/547-3696, www.hecetalighthouse.com), the most photographed on the Pacific Coast. Built in 1894, this light sends out a glow that can be seen 20 miles away. If you can swing it, a bed-and-breakfast is in the old lighthouse keeper's cottage.

I couldn't swing it, so I pressed on another mile to **Sea Lion Caves** (U.S. 101, 541/547-3111, www.sealioncaves.com, $11). This is the way old tourist attractions were created: Someone would find a natural phenomenon, buy the land, and sell tickets. That's what happened in 1932, 40 years after William Cox discovered sea lions in the world's largest sea cave. From the gift shop, walk down to an overlook, where, a hundred yards below, approximately a hundred Steller sea lions are sunbathing on a flat rock, their chorus of yawps and aarps sounding like a frat house after a kegger. From here, an elevator within the mountain lowers you 180 feet into a massive hollow where sea lions

The satisfaction of completing my favorite one-day ride ever—from Cannon Beach to Florence—is seen in my expression at Heceta Head.

The Siuslaw Bridge as seen from the Old Town district of Florence.

surge in with the sea and doze atop the basalt rock formations. The sound of the water adds to the impressive sight of the two-acre, 125-foot-tall domed cavern.

After passing the seals, the road swoops down from the cliffs to the dunes for the final 10 miles into Florence. A most memorable ride has come to a close.

FLORENCE PRIMER

Several hundred years before I got the idea to explore Oregon's coastline, the Spanish were doing it from the sea, creating maps as they cruised along the coast. English explorer Captain James Cook, who was used to driving on the left side of the road, headed over in 1778 to make some maps that he could read. Watching this from shore were the Siuslaws who, like nearly every tribe in America, were destined to be displaced when white settlers showed up.

By 1900, 300 residents were making a living in this remote community either by logging, fishing, or working in a sawmill, saloon, newspaper, cannery, or general store. One enterprising resident who was making a killing by opening a ferry service across the Siuslaw River was likely quite furious when the picturesque Siuslaw River Bridge opened in 1936.

By accident or design, the original village—today called Old Town—was preserved on a bend in the river and has been revitalized with shops, restaurants, galleries, and gift shops. Without this important asset, odds are you'd see Florence as just another generic village. But it's here, as is another vital attraction, the **Oregon Dunes National Recreation Area.** There are 38,000 acres of sand mountains here, and if that doesn't sound like much...then just you wait.

ON THE ROAD: FLORENCE

The previous day's ride may still have you buzzing, and it's tempting to consider zipping 11 miles north back up the coast around Heceta Head or, perhaps riding south along the Pacific for an enjoyable thousand-mile run down to San Diego.

If you just want to experience Florence, though, you can fill up the better part of the day with just two activities: shopping and sand dunes. The former is pedestrian but satisfying, a low-key, laid-back approach that won't take much out of you. The latter is one of the most outlandish adventures you'll ever experience, kind of like plunging a syringe of adrenaline into the middle of your heart.

Have a nice day.

PULL IT OVER: FLORENCE HIGHLIGHTS
Attractions and Adventures

I've had the good fortune to do a lot of cool stuff (motorcycling across America included), but rarely, if ever, have I done anything quite as cool as heading to the Oregon Dunes National Recreational Area and hitting the sands with Darin of **Sand Dunes Frontier** (83690 U.S. 101, 541/997-3544, www.sanddunesfrontier. com). I thought a dune buggy ride would include going to a clambake with Frankie and Annette, and I also thought I'd drive the dune buggy myself. Thankfully, I've never been so wrong.

Arriving early (and off-season), I was the only passenger and I was quickly in the passenger seat and neatly trussed up in a net of harnesses. Darin rode slowly through the woods, and since I thought *that* was the ride, I was creating excuses to bail. But when we reached the edge of the forest, I saw Oregon's most unusual landscape. It wasn't simply a patch of shoreline between us and the ocean, it was immense towers of sand as high as 300 feet that stretched about 40 miles north and south. He gunned the engine and the huge tires bit into the sand and sent us on a 50-degree

ascent to the peak of a dune that I knew would propel us into the unknown or on a collision course with another driver racing up the opposite side. My death grip threatened to crush the metal cage around me, but at the peak, in a split second he triggered a small handbrake that slapped the tail parallel with the seam at the top of the dune. We raced on, the dune buggy slipping over the side but clinging like a knife in the sand. For the next 30 minutes, I was driven like a maniac to peaks and then down dangerous hills and, at one monumental moment, around the 60-degree basin of a Daytona 500-style bowl called the NASCAR berm. This is where I am certain I achieved a higher level of consciousness.

Perhaps a large part of my fascination was being here when no one else was on the dunes, which made the experience seem like we were driving on the moon. In peak season, as many as 3,000 dune buggies and ATVs clog the sands each weekend, so try to get there early, invest $22, tie yourself down, and experience the motorized equivalent of a heart paddle.

A sedative about three miles south of the bridge is **Jessie M. Honeyman Memorial State Park** (800/452-5687). Created by the CCC in the 1930s, this 500-acre park has three freshwater lakes, with swimming and canoeing on 85-acre Lake Woahink. There are picnic pavilions, guided kayak tours, and a campground with 191 tent sites available for around $25 a night.

Shopping

As you ride into town, a buffer zone of new development surrounds the real and unique shopping village of Old Town which is tucked beneath the bridge on the banks of the Siuslaw River; after you park your bike you can see several blocks of stores, gadget and gift shops, and restaurants. Part of the town's appeal is its layout, with numerous old buildings recycled for today. The drawback is that after a national magazine ranked Florence as one of the best places to retire, too many merchants hoping to capitalize on the momentum rushed in and ended up selling an identical inventory of... *junque.*

One exception is the **Sticks & Stone Gallery** (1368 Bay St., 541/997-3196, www.sticksandstonesgallery.com). If you've avoided wildlife art galleries because you've seen too many paintings of mustangs galloping across the plain, this place offers a cure. There are twigs made into lamps, metallic trout leaping in a metal stream, schools of wooden salmon, driftwood eagles, and tigers painted on bird's-eye maple, as well as fish, frogs, and pheasants etched, carved, and painted in a variety of mediums.

Blue-Plate Specials

Oregon often amazed me, and it did it yet again with the **Waterfront Depot** (1252 Bay St., 541/902-9100). Roughly the size of a small home, the old train depot is now the setting for an Irish bar (which explains the Peter O'Toole/Richard Burton poster), as well as a fantastic restaurant based on an international tapas menu. For less than 10 bucks, you can mix and match entrées like crab-encrusted halibut, jambalaya pasta, and wild coho salmon. For a great experience, wait for a window seat overlooking the river.

Basic but popular meals are served at **Mo's** (1436 Bay St., 541/997-2185). Right on the river, the interior has the look and feel of a Howard Johnson's, circa 1950. That's a compliment, too, since it's packed with regular folks ordering seafood basics like clam strips, popcorn scallops, albacore tuna melts, and chowders. In addition to adding beer to the batter, Mo's also pours it into frosted mugs.

If you're craving home-away-from-home cooking, ride about two miles south of the bridge to **Morgan's Country Kitchen** (85020 U.S. 101, 541/997-6991, www.morganscountrykitchen.com). Serving down-home cooking since the 1950s, Morgan's is still at it with breakfast and lunch dishes like biscuits and sausage gravy, pecan waffles, roast beef, and chicken-fried steak.

In the heart of Old Town is the popular **Firehouse Restaurant** (1263 Bay St., 541/997-2800). Ribs, steaks, sirloin, "Code 3" burgers, salmon, halibut, sandwiches, and pasta cover most of the bases—and sidewalk dining and a lounge will take you the rest of the way home.

Watering Holes

The local favorite, **Beachcomber Tavern** (1355 Bay St., 541/997-6357) seriously exemplifies its name. A tavern since 1936, this really looks and feels like one of those places where people who like to drink, drink. It helps the cause by opening at 9 A.M., serving pub food and dishes like deep-fried prawns and Cajun-grilled oysters, and running a full bar.

Shut-Eye

Motels and Motor Courts

There's abundant quality lodging in Florence, and three great old-fashioned choices—two of which are within easy walking distance of Old Town. The **River House Motel** (1202 Bay St., 541/997-3933 or 888/824-2454, www.riverhouseflorence.com, $99 and up off-river, $125 on-river) is the best-placed place of all—less than a hundred yards from Old Town. Rooms have two queens or a king, and some have terraces to watch the drawbridge and fishing boats.

South of the Siuslaw is the **Ocean Breeze Motel** (85165 U.S. 101, 541/997-2642 or 888/226-9611, www.oceanbreeze-motel.com, $80 and up high season). Although its appearance harkens back several decades, it seems quite modern, thanks to its meticulously clean rooms, each with a queen or two.

A block from the river and a short walk to Old Town, the **Lighthouse Inn** (155 U.S. 101, 541/997-3221, www.lighthouseinn-florence.com, $84 and up) has that cool old knotty pine look working for it. Queen and king beds are offered, some rooms include sleeper sofas to add another couple to the mix, and family suites sleep five.

The **Old Town Inn** (170 U.S. 101, 541/997-7131 or 800/570-8738, www.old-town-inn.com, $79–99) is a large complex a few blocks north of Old Town. Rooms are clean and basic, and include free Wi-Fi, microwave, fridge, coffee, cable, and local calls.

Chain Drive

These chain hotels are in town, or within 10 miles of the city center:

Best Western, Comfort Inn

For more information, including phone numbers and websites, see page 151.

ON THE ROAD: FLORENCE TO SISTERS

It's hard to leave Florence behind, because this also means saying so long to the Pacific Ocean and U.S. 101. On the north end of town, Highway 126 shoots straight toward the heart of Oregon, and as the waves wave goodbye, you ride into an area of river and grass. A railroad trestle spans the river and heads into the woods for God knows where, and when that passes you look around and see a living life-insurance calendar of rivers, hills, forests, and wide-open landscape.

Within 15 miles, you'll pass the Siuslaw River and reach the low hills and a canopy road that could pass for the Berkshires of Massachusetts. Ahead there's nothing but green and the road and a tunnel to draw you farther into the ride. There's something cool about tunnels like this, and it's not just the temperature—it's the echo that makes your bike sound 10 times more powerful and muscular. Two lanes lead into more hills, and when you reach Mapleton, the road splits off to the right for a stretch of dips and nice riding. After the Siuslaw National Forest eases up, there are 40 miles of wide country riding ahead. Wide lanes and slow traffic announce the metropolis of Eugene and, as you can guess, the town doesn't offer a speck of the enjoyment you've received from the casual cruise. It's sluggish riding from about 10 miles before Eugene to about six miles past it. So now's a good time to enjoy intermission....

And we're back. I hope you enjoyed your visit to Eugene, and after you pass Springfield and enter the McKenzie State River Recreation Area, you can start to look forward to 100 miles of overwhelming Oregon riding. With the return of two-lane roads and the absence of city traffic, you'll notice a distinct change in mood that improves when you enter pristine country accented by Christmas tree farms and groves of hazelnut trees (locals call them "filberts"). There are also abundant signs of rural living, namely comparably small homes that occupy comparably vast acres of land.

The McKenzie Valley is really great and the road, of course, is just as nice. Meandering and lazy, it's bordered with ivy and wildflowers as it follows the course of the McKenzie River all the way to a neat dam that powers the town of Leaburg. Just past the town, an old wooden bridge named after racing legend Barney Oldfield crosses the Leaburg canal, but I don't know why. Vignettes like this—finding a nice little river and a walking path on its banks—are still nice discoveries.

A short distance east, the same flowing creek leads to one of the nicest covered bridges I've seen. Lane County's **Goodpasture Bridge** was built in 1938 and is one of the most photographed covered bridges in Oregon. It seems to convey the spiritual vibe of this ride with its Gothic-style louvered windows and master carpentry. From here, you may notice an unusual sensation as you ride and I think it must be that the road mimics the river, curving sharply where there are rapids and smoothing out when the river rolls out of view. All you have to do to enjoy it is hold the throttle and drift into a glide track. It's effortless riding mile after mile.

You ride past Nimrod, Finn Rock, and Blue River, and the road never fails. Before Belknap Springs, watch for **Harbick's Country Store** (541/822-3575), a well-stocked service station, restaurant, and motel that's worth a stop since there's precious little ahead in terms of conveniences. A few miles east, if weather permits, follow Highway 242—the McKenzie Pass Scenic Byway—for the final 38 miles to Sisters. Aside from summer months, though, the road is usually impassable due to heavy snows that clog the Cascades. If you can take it here, you'll be able to cross the McKenzie Pass that runs through one of the state's most recent lava flows. How recent? About 3,000 years ago. At the top of the 5,325-foot pass, the Dee Wright Memorial is a CCC-built lava rock observatory with trails to follow, and Proxy Falls is an ethereal wonder; a pair of horsetail falls just a short walk from the road.

What's more likely, however, is that between November and June you'll be sticking with the road ahead which is not a bad consolation prize. Not at all. It's a scenic arc north through the Willamette National Forest and guiding the way are enormous Douglas firs that stand like an honor guard as you roll down the blacktop. It's a magnificent experience to be heralded into the woods this way. About a dozen miles up the road is the entrance for Koosah Falls, and a half-mile later is the entrance and parking area for Sahalie Falls. Park at Sahalie and get ready for a magnificent spectacle. Just down a short wooded path you'll hear thundering waters that draw your eyes ahead to the Sahalie (Chinook for "heaven"), and when you reach the falls, you'll marvel at a torrent of water rocketing over a short cliff. It all seems more incredible and more gorgeous when combined with the mossy green rocks and trees surrounding you in the canyon. Take the time to walk the loop trail beside the frothing, tumbling whitewater cascades and you'll discover Koosah ("sky") Falls about a 15-minute nature walk away. There are few things you'll see in your life that rival finding a nice waterfall while on a forest run like this.

Back on the road, you may want to make another stop a mile or so on at Clear Lake, the headwaters of the McKenzie River. The "lake born of fire" got its start 3,000 years ago when lava from Sand Mountain reached the river and backed up water to form the lake. The water's cold as hell, and you can't swim in it, but canoeing, fishing and boating are available, and the absence of motorized boats helps keep things clear. How clear? Look into the water, and about 100 feet below the surface you'll see the remainder of tall trees submerged when the lake was formed.

Three miles north, Highway 126 laces itself up with U.S. 20 before the tandem road hooks to the right and then starts falling southeast. Highway 126 attacks the Cascades, taking you up and over Santiam Pass at 4,817 feet. The higher elevations inject clean air into your lungs and carburetors and deliver soothing views of firs and mountain hemlock, lodgepole and ponderosa pines as you ride into the high desert. It's soothing because, unlike on most mountain roads, nothing is dangerous or drastic. In fact, it's quite quiet and peaceful and calming as you snatch glimpses of the horizon across the Mount Washington Wilderness, with snowcapped mountains and miles of forests.

Take it easy, and when the road falls away to the south, you can look forward to spending the night with Sisters.

SISTERS PRIMER

I wouldn't call Sisters's theme Wild West. Maybe more like Mild West. I'll explain why in a minute. First, though, I can tell you its history includes visits by Indians and fur traders and soldiers who established soon-to-be-abandoned Camp Polk in the 1860s. In the 1880s, Sisters became a supply center for sheep shipments passing through, and after that, lumber took the lead until the 1960s, when the last mill closed.

That's when some folks in Sisters decided to create a new look for the town. But it wasn't the city council that requested the facelift. It was the owners of the Black Butte Ranch, a new local resort. It offered merchants a generous sum if they'd slap up an Old West facade over their storefronts, and everyone looked at the languishing town and agreed to go along with the scheme. The plan was implemented and in the early 1970s, the city passed a resolution dictating that future construction would exhibit an 1880s frontier theme. And whatd'ya know...it all works. When you mosey around town, you aren't wondering

why Sisters looks the way it does because *it just does.* As to why it's named this way, look to the three mountain peaks visible from town. From north to south, the "sisters" are Faith, Hope, and Charity.

Footnote: After I came home, I recalled the energy of the town. The citizens there generated such an unusual and active vibe, I assumed there were at least 20,000 residents making it all work. On the contrary. Fewer than 2,000 people are driving Sisters's mojo. And they're doing it all for you.

You go, Sisters.

ON THE ROAD: SISTERS

Although there's an all right ride out of town that will take you north to Mount Hood, in comparison to what you've already experienced, much of it's fairly routine. If you eventually have to ride north, however, within the 145-mile ride to Mount Hood and up to the Columbia River Gorge, you'll ride through the Deschutes and Mount Hood national forests to reach the communities of Hood River and The Dalles. Of this, I'd estimate that around 65 percent of it is decent riding in hills, on promontories, in canyons, and by rivers.

Since Sisters is the end of the line for this chapter, however, I'll suggest a day wandering around downtown. It may not take a full day, but from cowboy boots to fine art, the stores here can occupy a good part of the day. If you get done early, the city of Bend is only 20 miles south.

PULL IT OVER: SISTERS HIGHLIGHTS
Attractions and Adventures

In addition to the annual **Sisters Rodeo** (541/549-0121 or 800/827-7522, www.sistersrodeo.com), held in June, there's a wad of adrenaline pumping in the great outdoors. **Destination Wilderness** (541/585-2904 or 800/423-8868, www.

wildernesstrips.com) in nearby Bend plans adventures on the McKenzie, Clackamas, Umpqua, and Salmon rivers—and all over Oregon, for that matter. The streams here are filled with rainfall and melting snow from above 10,000 feet, so the waters are crystal-clear. You'll run Class II and III rapids on trips that last from half a day ($75) to two full days ($295), and include all your gear, food, and transportation. If you'd rather fish, Destination Wilderness can gear you up for fly- and spin-casting excursions. Avoid the rapids and angle for trout with the **Flyfisher's Place** (151 W. Main Ave., 541/549-3474, www.flyfishersplace. com), who can take you out on the McKenzie and Metolius rivers. This is a hugely popular sport, but the biggest catch of the day may be the day rate: from around $330 to $440 per person. Riders love to get away and **Wanderlust Tours** (143 SW Cleveland Ave., Bend, 541/389-8359 or 800/962-2862, www.wanderlusttours.com) helps you scratch that itch with a full slate of tours that take participants off trail, away from other people, and into the heart of the Cascade Mountains and Deschutes National Forest. Choices include canoe, kayak, hiking, caving, volcano exploration, GPS eco-challenge, and starlight float trips.

Shopping

Wandering around Sisters is an all right experience since, in addition to the standard retinue of ordinary inventory, there's some pretty cool stuff as well. As always, you'll be hard-pressed to find junk small enough to put on your bike, but if there's something you really dig, consider shipping it home. Some of the big stuff's at **Sisters Log Furniture** (140 W. Cascade Ave., 541/549-8191, www.sisters-logfurniture.com), where chainsaw-carved cowboys and bears and big wooden beds are sold alongside Western-themed metal and horseshoe art, paintings, rugs, and jewelry.

McKenzie Creek Trading Company (290 W. Cascade Ave., 541/549-8424, www.mckenziecreeksisters.com) carries the kind of outdoor wear you'd expect to find in the Pacific Northwest: hiking boots, Minnetonka moccasins, cowboy hats and belts. Women riders get a kick out of **Outwest Designs** (103 B Hood St., 541/549-1140, www.outwestdesigns.com) which carries crystals, trade beads, stone, glass, eclectic beads, copper, silver, and turquoise for creating your own jewelry designs.

Compared to California, New York and Florida, Oregon is such an overlooked state that it's good to find a place like the **Oregon Store** (271 W. Cascade Ave., 541/549-6700, www.theoregonstore.com) that sell goods that have style and exude a sense of place. Across Oregon craftspeople, artists, and manufacturers are creating the merchandise you'll find here—cool stuff like knives, saddle blankets, myrtlewood bowls, Oregon jams, syrups, stoneground flour, Native American robes, and Immigrant American T-shirts.

When an artist really makes it, that's really something. One who's done very well, thank you, is Lorenzo Ghiglieri. You may not know his works, but look who has: Ronald Reagan, Pope John Paul II, Tiger Woods, Al Gore, Mikhail Gorbachev, and Queen Elizabeth; they've all received his commissioned pieces. Like Remington, he's a sketch artist, oil painter, and sculptor who has a fascination with the West, as seen in pieces that focus on buffalo, cattle, elk, horses, explorers, bears, and Indians. His impressive statue *Victorious Flight* is an eagle carrying an American flag, and it would make a great gift to me. You may run across Lorenzo working at the **Lorenzo Ghiglieri Gallery** (411 E. Cascade Ave., 541/549-8751 or 877/551-4441, www.art-lorenzo.com).

For mostly everything else, there's

Sisters Drug Co. (211 Cascade Ave., 541/549-6221). The corner drugstore carries household goods, specialty foods, wine, gifts, and T-shirts, and has a pharmacy.

Blue-Plate Specials

When in Sisters, you must order up some big food at a big restaurant. **The Gallery** (171 W. Cascade Ave., 541/549-2631), a favorite with locals and tourists, serves old-fashioned family-style food like pork chops and meat loaf and soups, soft rolls, homemade pies, and cinnamon rolls. If you're riding early, it opens at 6 A.M. It's friendly and filling. A full bar and lounge are in back.

Another place with an Old West theme is **Bronco Billy's Ranch Grill & Saloon** (190 E. Cascade Ave., 541/549-7427, www.broncobillysranchgrill.com). It specializes in ribs, but it's not a rib joint—there are burgers, sirloin, tacos, pork bowls, chicken, and more. Housed in an old hotel, former rooms upstairs can be reserved for private dining. As at The Gallery, there's a jumping bar here.

Watering Holes

As I've mentioned, you may do best by looking for nightlife at The Gallery or Bronco Billy's Saloon. They're already a hit with locals, and you're bound to fit right in at these joints where the clientele seem pretty loose and friendly. Popular with local riding clubs is **Scoot's Bar and Grill** (175 Larch St., 541/549-1588, www.scootsbarandgrill.com), which encourages their dedication by adding a motorcycle theme. In addition to several dozen varieties of brews (draft, bottled, and microbrews) and half-pound burgers, Scoot's has live entertainment, pool tables, flat-screen TVs, an open patio, and afternoon happy hour.

Shut-Eye
Motels and Motor Courts

One of the friendliest motor courts I've run across is the **Sisters Motor Lodge** (511 W. Cascade Ave., 541/549-2551, www.sistersmotorlodge.com, $89 and up for rooms, $195 for extended-stay suites). Built in 1942, it's become a national historic landmark and each room has handmade quilts, cable TV, and fully stocked kitchenettes. The in-town location is conveniently close, yet perfectly secluded.

Inn-dependence

One of the best built and well-run B&Bs I've stayed at is the **Blue Spruce Bed & Breakfast** (444 S. Spruce St., 541/549-9644 or 888/328-9644, www.bluespruce-bandb.com, $169–189). About four blocks from downtown, the house was built as an inn, so rooms are large, with fireplaces. The beds are soft, the bathrooms have hot tubs and towel warmers, the den is massive, and your breakfast is as large as a water tower.

Chain Drive

These chain hotels are in town, or within 10 miles of the city center:
Best Western
For more information, including phone numbers and websites, see page 151.

Saddle Up

If the artificial Old West theme of the town seems real to you, then you may be inclined to wander over to **Long Hollow Ranch** (71105 Holmes Rd., 541/923-1901 or 877/923-1901, www.lhranch.com). This is a real cattle ranch where you'll work with wranglers, explore the ranch on horseback, dine on home-cooked meals, fish in the reservoirs, practice roping, or hang around the yard pitching horseshoes—just as they did in the Wild West.

Resources for Riders

Oregon's Best Run

Oregon Travel Information

Central Oregon Visitors Association—800/800-8334,
    www.visitcentraloregon.com
Oregon Dunes NRA—877/444-6777, www.recreation.gov
Oregon Parks and Recreation—800/551-6949, www.oregon.gov/OPRD
Oregon Road Conditions—800/977-6368, www.tripcheck.com
Willamette Forest Headquarters—541/225-6300

Local and Regional Information

Cannon Beach Chamber of Commerce—503/436-2623, www.cannonbeach.org
Cannon Beach Weather Information—503/861-2722
Florence Chamber of Commerce—541/997-3128 or 800/524-4864,
    www.florencechamber.com or www.oldtownflorence.com
Lane County (Eugene)—541/484-5307 or 800/547-5445,
    www.travellanecounty.org
Sisters Chamber of Commerce—541/549-0251 or 866/549-0252,
    www.sisterschamber.com

Oregon Motorcycle Shops

Bandit Motorsports—195-C Cap Ct., Eugene, 541/343-7433,
    www.bandit-motorsports.com
Bend Euro Moto—1064 SE Paiute Way St., Bend, 541/617-9155,
    www.bendeuromoto.com
BMW of Western Oregon—2891 W. 11th Ave., Eugene, 541/338-0269,
    www.bmwor.com
Cascade Harley Davidson—63028 Sherman Rd., Bend, 541/330-6228,
    www.cascadeharley.com
Cascade Motorsports—20445 Cady Way, Bend, 541/389-0088,
    www.cascademotorsports.net
Cascade Motorcycle—4065 W. 11th Ave., Eugene, 541/344-5177,
    www.cascademotorcycle.tripod.com
Cycle Sports—555 River Rd., Eugene, 541/607-9000, www.cyclesports.net
Doyle's Harley-Davidson—86441 College View Rd., Eugene, 541/747-1033,
    www.doyleshd.com
Florence Yamaha—2130 Hwy. 126, Florence, 541/997-1157
Motorcycles Of Bend—63056 Lower Meadow Dr., Bend, 541/617-0444,
    www.motorcyclesofbend.com
The Moto Shop—61445 S. Hwy. 97, Bend, 541/383-0828

Las Vegas–Yosemite Run

Las Vegas, Nevada to Yosemite National Park, California

Of all the runs profiled in this book, my gut feeling is that this is the most exciting, frightening, grueling, exhilarating, fascinating, inspiring, and humbling.

From the materialistic and surreal city of Las Vegas, the mood descends to the stark landscape of Death Valley. What follows are arguably the grandest vistas in America at Yosemite and, if you desire, the clear and clean waters of Lake Tahoe. It's a ride that'll test your mettle and reward your efforts.

LAS VEGAS PRIMER

Las Vegas is a town steeped in excess. From multibillion-dollar themed hotels to less-than-discreet prostitution, Las Vegas is where the circus came to town—and never left.

A little more than half a century ago, it was a way station in the middle of nowhere—until the Mafia saw an untapped oasis of cash. You know the rest: Sammy and Frankie and Dean begat Elvis and Engelbert and Wayne. When the stakes were raised, old hotels were blown up and corporations muscled in to build casinos disguised as hotels. In the late 1990s, when the local convention bureau needed to fill more beds, it decided to position Las Vegas as a great family getaway, but no one was buying it. That's when they retooled the party line and admitted it's a place where you can do all the kinds of things that you would never dare tell your wife, husband, children, employer, co-workers, priest, minister, rabbi, carwash attendant, caddy, convenience store clerk, produce manager, or a complete stranger.

So just accept that Vegas is busy, pricy, noisy, borderline profane, and no place for kids (unless you're teaching them about escort services and loan sharking). But if you're an adult who's prepared for a juiced-up, high-tension, all-night bacchanal, however, it can be the fuel for a long and winding journey.

Just don't blow your gas money.

ON THE ROAD: LAS VEGAS

It's impossible to condense and define Las Vegas, especially for motorcycle travelers.

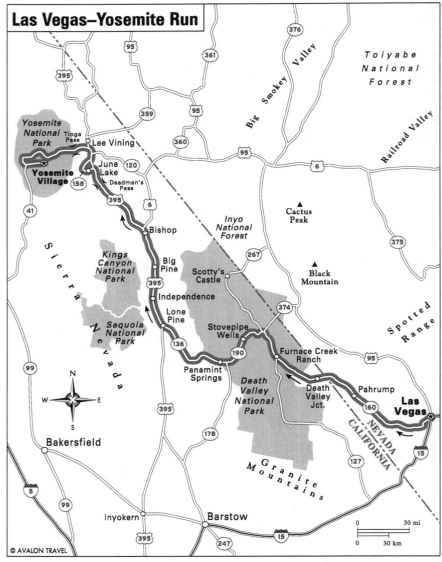

Las Vegas–Yosemite Run

Route: Las Vegas to Yosemite via Death Valley, Lone Pine, Bishop, Lee Vining

Distance: Approximately 640 miles

First Leg: Las Vegas, Nevada to Lone Pine, California (240 miles)

Second Leg: Lone Pine to Yosemite, California (200 miles)

Optional Third Leg: Yosemite to Lake Tahoe, California (200 miles)

Helmet Laws: Both Nevada and California require helmets.

© AVALON TRAVEL

Gettin' Hitched

Tying the knot in Vegas is either a romantic or pathetic blend of hormones, love, and kitsch. More than 70 wedding chapels (including ones themed for *Star Trek* and Graceland) operate in town, and if you want to get married (please, not to someone you just met through an escort service), the only requirement is a $50 license (exact change required), which you can get at the seven-day-a-week **Clark County Courthouse** (200 S. 3rd St., 702/671-0600).

You can ride your bike anywhere in the country and be content with yourself, your thoughts, and a few possessions stuffed in the saddlebags. Seconds after you ride into Vegas, you may be swept up in an orgy of greed and desire. Pray that the feeling vanishes when you leave town or you'll be the most miserable sumbitch on the road.

This concludes the warning. From here, it's a pleasant surprise to find that most employees are hospitable and the roads easy to navigate. The city is laid out roughly like a grid, with Las Vegas Boulevard as the main north–south artery. A section of this street is "The Strip," where you're most likely to spend your time and money. The magnet for tourists and conventioneers, it is where old hotels are destroyed and then rebuilt, phoenixlike, as billion-dollar resorts.

The farther north you go, the less impressed you'll be unless you're searching for vintage pre-resort Vegas. Fremont Street has been retooled as an enclosed pedestrian mall where chain-smoking seniors on gambling junkets try to score mediocre food at cheap buffets. I'm not a gambler, and it struck me that too many marathon slot-machine players press buttons in a sad choreography, looking like research monkeys awaiting the dispensation of banana-flavored pellets.

The stakes are raised as you ride south and pass the Sahara, Stratosphere, Flamingo, Aladdin, and Circus Circus casinos and when you reach the core of the Strip, you'll enter a universe of world-class hotels and high rollers. But whether you've reached Fremont Street or a deluxe resort, there seems to be a certain sameness to every venue: the ringing bells of an electronic arcade, the absence of windows and clocks, and VIP status applied based on your value as a loser.

Clearly I have mixed feelings about the town. The futile quest for quick fortune bugs me, but overall I'm impressed by the sheer magnitude of Las Vegas and its legend. Because, frankly, it's not all gambling. This is a playground for adults where you can feel the same kind of freedom you experience on your bike. Experience it for yourself.

PULL IT OVER: LAS VEGAS HIGHLIGHTS
Casinos

Larger and louder than life, the most impressive casinos are found along the Strip. Each is a community unto itself, with a distinct theme, headlining acts, guestrooms, nightclubs, restaurants, pools, and abundant services. Rates vary wildly—often daily—especially if there's a major convention in town, and suites naturally cost more. Rather than listing rates, then, I recommend you call in advance or check online for discounted prices on

© NANCY HOWELL

It takes a little while to clear Las Vegas, but along the way the congestion clears and the road travels through beautiful country... all the way to Hoover Dam.

Vegas rooms. Sunday through Thursday is a better time to look for discounts (unless a convention's in town). Even if you don't stay at a hotel, ask about the hotel's headliner—a very big draw here.

Luxor (3900 Las Vegas Blvd., 702/262-4000 or 800/288-1000 for room reservations, or 800/557-7428 for show reservations, www.luxor.com) sports an Egyptian theme and a pyramid out front. You'll see its spotlight at night.

Clean up NYC, multiply it by 10, and you have **New York New York** (3790 Las Vegas Blvd., 702/740-6969 or 800/693-6763 for room and show reservations, www.nynyhotelcasino.com).

A subtle Hollywood theme sifts through the **MGM Grand** (3799 Las Vegas Blvd., 702/891-1111 or 800/929-1111 for room and show reservations, www.mgmgrand.com), just a very large hotel with big shows and special events.

The Mirage (3400 Las Vegas Blvd., 702/791-7111 or 800/627-6667 for room reservations, or 800/963-9634 for show reservations, www.mirage.com) features the Cirque du Soleil extravaganza *LOVE*, based on the music of the Beatles. I love the Beatles, couldn't stand the show.

At **Treasure Island** (3300 Las Vegas Blvd., 702/894-7111 or 800/944-7444 for room reservations, or 800/392-1999 for show reservations, www.treasureisland.com) the big show is Cirque du Soleil's *Mystère.*

An old favorite that attracts families and fans of old Vegas, **Circus Circus** (2880 Las Vegas Blvd., 702/734-0410 or 800/634-3450 for room reservations, www.circuscircus.com) has a Big Top theme. Not real clean, not exactly dirty, it's an option.

Theoretically, there's a French Riviera theme at the **Monte Carlo** (3770 Las Vegas Blvd., 702/730-7777 or 800/311-8999 for room and show reservations, www.monte-carlo.com), which is home to popular Vegas headliner Lance Burton, Master Magician!

Caesars Palace (3570 Las Vegas Blvd., 702/731-7110 or 634-6661 for room reservations, or 800/634-6001 for show reservations, www.caesars.com) is one of the city's traditional favorites and the place where you can enjoy high-caliber performers like Elton John, Celine Dion, and Bette Midler. I'd give the waitresses here my vote for best costumes.

Excalibur (3850 Las Vegas Blvd., 702/597-7777 or 800/937-7777 for room reservations, or 800/933-1334 for show reservations, www.excaliburcasino.com) has a medieval castle theme. Why not?

A mixture of the tropical, mystical, and upscale chic, **Mandalay Bay** (3950 Las Vegas Blvd., 702/632-7777 or 877/632-7000 for room and show reservations, www.mandalaybay.com) features a House of Blues, stage shows, and off-off-off-Broadway productions.

The mighty large **Venetian** (3355 Las Vegas Blvd., 702/414-1000 or 888/283-6423, www.venetian.com) materialized where the Sands once stood. The Italian-themed resort of more than 4,000 suites gets raves on the swank-o-meter and credit for once hosting "Art of the Motorcycle."

Attractions and Adventures

If you'd like to experience skydiving and live to tell about it, **Vegas Indoor Skydiving** (200 Convention Center Dr., 702/731-4768, www.vegasindoorskydiving.com) offers a one-hour program for $75 where you don skydiving clothes and step out and float above what looks like a monstrous bathroom blow dryer. No parachute, no worries. No experience necessary.

I'm not sure if this next recommendation will fly with most riders, but you gotta give Liberace credit. In the flamboyant tradition of Gorgeous George and '70s Elvis, Liberace epitomized the vanity of Vegas and at the **Liberace Museum** (1775 E. Tropicana Ave., 702/798-5595, www.liberace.org, $15) you'll see some surprising exhibits that cannot help but impress: an Excalibur car covered with rhinestones, a customized Bradley GT, a red, white, and blue Rolls, a Rolls-Royce Phantom V Landau limousine (one of only seven, this one dons the license tag "88 Keys"), as well as a custom rhinestone-covered Stutz Bearcat with a matching rhinestone-covered toolkit. The museum is open 10 A.M.–5 P.M. Monday–Saturday, noon–4 P.M. Sunday.

The accessory branch of Las Vegas H-D/Buell, the **Harley-Davidson Shop** (4th and Fremont Sts., 702/383-1010, www.lvhd.com) carries the requisite overdone clothing, parts, and souvenirs. A bulletin board announces motorcycle-related products and services.

Blue-Plate Specials

Hundreds of restaurants line the Strip, both inside and outside the resort casinos. Surprisingly, the quality indoors is actually pretty good, and choices range from quick snacks to very elaborate meals. In fact, Vegas is gaining a reputation as a fine-dining capital, with dozens of celebrity chefs showing up to open high-end restaurants. For your purposes, however, there are lower-end choices such as the buffets offered at most major resorts. Most range between $20 and $30 and can keep you full and fueled for an entire day. Or week.

If you think that no one understands your passion for bikes, you'll find a sympathetic ear at **Harley-Davidson Cafe** (3725 Las Vegas Blvd., 702/740-4555, www.harley-davidsoncafe.com). The café boasts plenty of parking out back, while the inside looks like an assembly line. Gleaming Harleys ride up and around the room, passing before a large map of Route

66 and a giant American flag created from red, white, and blue chains. What else? Oh, yeah. Food.

Shut-Eye

In good economic times when Las Vegas turns into a convention clearinghouse, many of the 135,000 rooms are booked months in advance. That's when you should make reservations as early as you can—perhaps as part of a gambling package which will knock the rates down considerably. If not, you'll probably pay a premium to stay in a substandard hotel. Keep in mind that staying at a casino hotel can be soul-rattling after a peaceful desert ride. The local convention bureau has opened a hotel hotline and a website: 877/847-4858, www.visitlasvegas.com. Another nationwide reservation service that covers Las Vegas may help find you a room and save you some money: 800/964-6835, www.hotels.com.

Motels and Motor Courts

OK, so they're not really motels, but here are a few places I really like. For peace and quiet without a premium, **La Quinta** (3970 S. Paradise Rd., 702/796-9000, $65 and up) is a bargain and includes a continental breakfast. Just a few blocks from the action, it also has a pool. Even cheaper is the **Golden Gate Hotel and Casino** (1 Fremont St., 702/385-1906 or 800/426-1906, www.goldengatecasino.net, $39 and up). It offers cable, a free newspaper, and not much else besides a restaurant that's served 30 million giant shrimp cocktails since 1959. The **Hard Rock Hotel** (4455 Paradise Rd., 702/693-5000 or 800/473-7625, www.hardrockhotel.com, $89 and up) hits the jackpot with great accents like Flying V door handles, a Beatles display case, and an H-D Hardtail Springer owned by Motley Crüe's Nikki Sixx. It's

more inviting than the darkened casinos, but rates here leap around like Pete Townshend, so call ahead. The on-site restaurant is another reason to stay here—it displays one of Elvis's jumpsuits and Roy Orbison's Electra-Glide.

Chain Drive

These chain hotels are in town, or within 10 miles of the city center: **Best Western, Clarion, Comfort Inn, Courtyard by Marriott, Days Inn, Doubletree, Econo Lodge, Embassy Suites, Fairfield Inn, Hampton Inn, Hilton, Holiday Inn, Howard Johnson, Hyatt, La Quinta, Motel 6, Residence Inn, Rodeway, Super 8, Travelodge** For more information, including phone numbers and websites, see page 151.

ON THE ROAD: LAS VEGAS TO LONE PINE

Of all the rides in this book, this one will require the greatest degree of guts. It demands that your bike be in peak condition, that your nerves be sure, and that you are ready to face the challenge of fierce, twisting curves in the Inyo Mountains and the barren loneliness of Death Valley.

Leaving Las Vegas on Highway 159 West, it'll take a half hour to shake the Vegas glitter off your bike and reach Red Rock Canyon. This is a magnificent sight and, if you ride the scenic loop road that rolls across the conservation area, one that affords possible views of bighorn sheep, gray foxes, and wild burros. Otherwise, head south toward Blue Diamond and Highway 160, and then west towards Pahrump. Immediately, the road is a lonely stretch. There are no twists, no turns, just rolling desert. The road wakes up near Spring Mountain Ranch State Park, giving you curves to compensate.

When you reach Pahrump, it's just

a lump of a town—an embryonic L.A. that spreads across the sands. There's a well-stocked gas station at the junction of Highways 160 and 372, but mostly it seems fairly empty and akin to that classic scene in *2001: A Space Odyssey* where the caveman tosses a bone into the sky. Head a few miles north of Pahrump and watch for Bell Vista Avenue that cuts west towards Death Valley Junction. Take it.

After 4 miles of twisties and 15 miles of straightaway, the big, empty desert starts to look like the Grand Canyon (minus the canyon). It's wide, open, and empty for about 30 miles until you reach the intersection of Highways 190 and 127 where you'll find the strange and fascinating **Amargosa Opera House and Hotel** (760/852-4441, www.amargosa-opera-house.com, $60–75). Built by the Pacific Coast Borax Company in the 1920s, the combination office space and hotel had fallen into disrepair by 1967. Then New York dancer Marta Becket drove through, had a flat tire, and fell in love with its desolation. She bought the forlorn complex and now rents rooms. As if that's not enough, on Mondays and Saturdays from October to May, Marta and friend Tom Willett still perform a ballet and mime revue in the adjacent opera house. Now that's entertainment! No phones, no television, no food (a restaurant's seven miles away), but a place for some well-deserved rest before the upcoming ride.

From where you stand, you are poised for your ride across Death Valley. Now things get mighty strange here, sheriff. If you've ever judged times to reach distant points, don't expect to do it here. The land is so flat and barren, it'll take 20 minutes to ride to an object that you can see halfway to the horizon. This lasts for mile after mile after mile as you ride across the Amargosa Range and pass 20 Mule Team Canyon. If you have the time and curiosity, just before Zabriskie Point a one-way, 2.7-mile dirt loop road detours south again through the canyon until it decides to bring you back to the highway. Then in the middle of all of this nothing is really something: a four-star resort, in fact. In a desolate land where a snack machine could win an award for fine dining, **Furnace Creek Resort** (Hwy. 190, 760/786-2345, www.furnacecreekresort. com) is a mystery. You can stay the night in below-sea-level luxury, go horseback riding, or take a break on the verandah and view the upcoming 104-mile challenge. If you want to play golf on the lowest golf course in the world, the one here is 214 feet *below sea level*. Despite its existence in exile, the resort is popular and the rates prove it: from $265 at the inn and $128 at the ranch. Reserve in advance if you think you'll stay. If not, get ready for a most incredible ride.

A few miles down the road, there's a gas station that will gouge you on gas, but fill 'er up again. You're about to start a heart-stopping ride.

As you start your descent into the valley, you'll see into the future. Car headlights can be seen from 10 miles away, and when you're about 20 miles outside of Furnace Creek you'll feel the absence of life echoing around you. You may share my experience and feel a most humbling and spiritual moment here. After running a satisfying series of mountain curves, you take a wide, sweeping left and then 3, 2, 1...you've fallen hundreds of feet below sea level and are riding in the basin of Death Valley.

Picture yourself, a black speck alone in a place as flat and desolate as any on earth. Solo riders especially will feel the emotional deprivation of this silent world. If your bike is finely tuned, stop and experience the mystical solitude. It is as memorable as any experience you will have on the road.

When you turn your attention back to riding, the quiet continues until you reach **Stovepipe Wells** (Hwy. 190, 760/786-2387, www.stovepipewells.com). It has an elevation of five feet, but don't let anyone sell you lift tickets. If you're tired of riding, Stovepipe offers an Einstein-smart option. It has 83 motel rooms, an RV park, gas, a general store, swimming pool, and saloon. It's a welcome sight and rooms here go for an affordable $80–120.

Between here and the next oasis, you'll ride through the anti-valley as you face some of the most harrowing and dangerous dips and twists you'll encounter. Six-degree grades and serious shifts in terrain roll on for miles at a time. Minus any guardrails, a moment's distraction can easily turn your bike into scrap metal, but if you stay focused, this ride is rich in adventure. Accelerating drops let you click into neutral and speed through twists at 60 mph, propelling you into valleys where the emptiness is sublime in its beauty. Realize that this is the same desert you may have flown over countless times, but here and now it is a new planet that you've tamed beneath your tires.

When you reach **Panamint Springs Resort** (775/482-7680, www.deathvalley.com, rooms $79 and up, tent sites $15 and up), you have another excuse to stay the night in a 15-room motel and reminisce about the ride. You may have doubted your resolve or the belief you could find beauty in this wasteland, but by now the desert has spoken to you. Chances are you'll be keyed up for the last 48-mile leg to Lone Pine—and this will be frickin' fantastic.

From Panamint Springs, you'll ride to the backbone of a mountain range, with sheer drops on your side and no barriers to break your fall. The pavement is hyperactive as it wraps and twists around the jagged peaks like barbed wire. The road will challenge you for dozens of miles and then reward you with countless reasons to stop and shoot photos. Father Crowley Vista Point (elev. 4,000 feet) is a good bet, and when you park your bike in the middle of the road I doubt you'll be hassled by oncoming traffic largely because there is probably no traffic oncoming.

By the time you reach the intersection of Highway 136 North, take it to reach U.S. 395, and turn north for a long final leg and a well-deserved rest in the historic Hollywood cowboy town of Lone Pine.

Yippeeiyay.

LONE PINE PRIMER

Lone Pine (elev. 3,700 ft., pop. 2,060), the first town of any size west of Death Valley, flares up for a few blocks and then disappears back into the sand. Lexicographers believe the phrase "blink and you'll miss it" was coined here.

But there's more to Lone Pine than meets the eye. If you're old enough to recall matinee cowboys falling off cliffs only to return the following week, you'll have already seen Lone Pine. If you frequent antique shows, looking for a Hopalong Cassidy lunch box or Roy Rogers guitar, you'll have Lone Pine to thank.

More than 300 Westerns were filmed here, from serial episodes to full-length features. Capitalizing on this unique history, each October the Lone Pine Film Festival draws a few surviving stars of Hollywood's Old West movies.

Even if you were born too late to recall Lash LaRue and the Cisco Kid, being in Lone Pine and at the gateway to Mount Whitney is a purely American experience. After Death Valley, you deserve it.

ON THE ROAD: LONE PINE

One stoplight, three blocks, and years of history. It's enough for an interesting ride, primarily because of the Whitney Portal, a long and winding road to the majestic mountain. After defeating Death Valley, you may want to take a break from mountain roads, but if not, you can take a curvaceous 12-mile run to the base of Mount Whitney, California's highest peak (elev. 14,495). There are no mountain roads here, but a slew of hiking trails if you want to go it by foot.

Otherwise, stay a while in Lone Pine. After all, stopping in small towns offers some of the most enjoyable moments of a ride. If you're ready to rest, you can see downtown in about 25 minutes—a half hour if you take your time. One must-see is at the lone stoplight. The **Indian Trading Post** (137 S. Main St., 760/876-4726) was a favorite stop for stars such as Edward G. Robinson, Jack Palance, Errol Flynn, Chuck Connors, Maureen O'Hara, Gary Cooper, and Barbara Stanwyck, who scribbled their names on the walls and window frames while shooting in town. Today, the walls are a priceless piece of Americana.

After the mountain and the town, there's not much else to do but settle back at the diner, grab a beer at the saloon (yes!), do your laundry, and, if you share my good fortune, see a real live prospector walking down the street with his pickaxe and shovel.

PULL IT OVER: LONE PINE HIGHLIGHTS
Attractions and Adventures

You're surrounded by natural beauty, and there are two places to visit to take full advantage of this. **Mount Whitney Ranger Station** (640 S. Main St., 760/876-6200, www.fs.fed.us/r5/inyo) has maps and also issues the wilderness permits you'll need to enter the Whitney Portal area. There's no charge to enter, but if you want to camp here ($6–14), you'll need to make arrangements well in advance. A mile south of Lone Pine, at the junction of U.S. 395 and Highway 136, the **Interagency Office** (760/876-6222) stocks information about Death Valley, Mount Whitney, the Inyo National Forest, and other natural parks and sights.

Blue-Plate Specials

Besides a few pizza places and Mexican diners, eateries in Lone Pine are few, but it's easy to find some good USDA-approved road food if you know where to look. The largest joint in town is the **Mt. Whitney Restaurant** (227 S. Main St., 760/876-5751). Here since the 1930s, the family-owned diner offers—dig this—venison, buffalo, ostrich, and veggie burgers. Ask politely, and maybe they'll make you a real one with beef. Open from morning to evening, it's popular with riders thanks to the pool tables, pinball, beer and wine, and football on a 50-inch TV. Open 24 hours for breakfast, lunch, and dinner, the **High Sierra Café** (446 S. Main St., 760/876-5796) is another family-owned restaurant that serves breakfast anytime, beer and wine later on, and entrées include American favorites like chicken-fried steak and chopped sirloin with mushrooms and grilled onions.

Open for dinner only, the **Merry-Go-Round** (212 S. Main St., 760/876-4115) is a quirky, cozy hole-in-the-wall place that specializes in steaks and seafood and gets marks for good service.

Watering Holes

One of the most enjoyable bars you'll find in America, **Jake's Saloon** (119 N. Main St., 760/876-5765) is open daily 'til midnight. The bar is a perfect place to settle down after your Death Valley run and crack your thirst with a cold beer.

Shut-Eye
Motels and Motor Courts

For a small town, Lone Pine offers more than adequate lodging choices. In the middle of town, the 50's-era **Dow Villa Motel** (310 S. Main St., 760/876-5521 or 800/824-9317, www.dowvillamotel.com, $95–145) features clean rooms, a pool, outdoor spa, and rooms with TVs, VCRs, king and queen beds, and mini-fridges. Be sure to check out the John Wayne exhibit in the den that includes a poker table from a movie he shot here (he'd stay in Room 20). They also run the historic Dow Hotel where rooms without a shared bath start at $50. At the south end of town, the **Comfort Inn** (1920 S. Main St. at the junction of U.S. 395 and Hwy. 136, 760/876-8700, www.comfortinn.com, off-season $80 and up) is as clean as can be, with larger than normal rooms and a nice view of Mount Whitney (in back) and the Alabama Hills (in front). Rooms feature two queen beds, bathtubs, mini-fridges, and microwaves. Note that in high season rates can double.

Chain Drive

These chain hotels are in town, or within 10 miles of the city center:
Best Western, Comfort Inn
For more information, including phone numbers and websites, see page 151.

ON THE ROAD: LONE PINE TO YOSEMITE

Aside from facing a monumental wall of wind due to the absence of anything to stop it, the ride north is easy—at least until you turn onto Highway 120 to reach Yosemite. That's when you may want to call your stunt double.

For now, the road out of Lone Pine stays true to form: impressive mountains and straight runs. Fourteen miles later, bypass Independence, and then slow down through well-patrolled Big Pine. Forty miles from here, Bishop's oasis of green lawns, trees, golf courses, and restaurants may entice you to stop.

Taking a left on U.S. 395 you'll continue north with the ride becoming fairly comfortable as you blaze down the road: the Sierra Nevada on your left and the Inyo Mountains on your right. You'll be thankful you've been freed from the confines of a car as the spicy fragrance of the desert is just as bracing as the chill of the mountain air. You're in the groove now, and can look forward to another 120 miles of motorcycle-friendly roads ahead. Forget the canopy lanes of New England; here in the American west the wide-open road has placed you in God's country.

After passing sprawling Lake Crowley on your right, the road rises forever, ascending to 7,000 feet at Sherwin Summit, and then, miles later, Deadman's Pass at 8,036 feet. The change has been so gradual that you may not have noticed that the desert has been replaced by rich, green California forest. If you have time to prolong your ride and acquire other indelible images, watch for Highway 158, which introduces you to the June Lake Loop. Most motorists bypass it, but it's worth the detour for motorcycle travelers. If you follow this road, a small creek running on your right soon spills into one of the most beautiful mountain lakes you'll encounter, and the combination of road, forest, lake, and sky is as picturesque as Switzerland's Lake Lausanne. The road skirts through a ski resort town, so the off-season traffic is lighter and makes it easy to stop for coffee in the small lakefront village. You'll continue the ride for several more miles, rolling quietly past snowcapped mountains, log cabins, and waterfalls until, suddenly, you'll notice an eerie silence. There is a striking absence of movement and people and the landscape has an unusual science fiction look. It's a weird feeling, a remote feeling.

I look back at Highway 158 like taking an extra helping of dessert. With all of the fantastic riding you've done so far you don't really need it, but it's good to have a little more. When the loop connects back with U.S. 395, turn left and ride to Lee Vining, a nice town with a few motels and restaurants. If you're scared of heights or aren't prepared for the demanding two-hour, 74-mile push to Yosemite Village, you should stop here and look for a room. Seriously. Since there's an abundance of incredible sights on the road ahead, racing the sun just to get a room inside Yosemite isn't worth it. You may also be stopped in Lee Vining when Highway 120 closes following the first big snowstorm after November 1.

But if the sun is high and the roads are clear, turn left onto Highway 120 and, after about a quarter mile, you'll see on your left the **Tioga Gas Mart** (22 Vista Point Dr., 760/647-1088). The supermarket-size station gives you a place to stock up on food and supplies for Yosemite. If the weather's nippy, now's the time to get comfortable in a survival suit before heading for the mountains.

Already at 8,000 feet, you'll head up a steep grade on your way to the even higher Tioga Pass (elevation 9,941 feet). Muscle-flexing turns are rampant for the first several miles, and the road demands attention. At the ranger station, pay $10 per motorcycle ($20 for other vehicles) and $10 per passenger (unless you've purchased the $80 America the Beautiful Pass) and enter the mother of the mother

of all national parks. The simple and helpful park pamphlet will be tempting to look at, but chances are you'll be focused on wilderness scenery that'll drop your jaw onto your gas tank.

The two-lane road is fairly wide, and a collection of slow curves and pine forests soon gives way to boulders and cliffs. Guardrails are few and drops precipitous, so be on your best biking behavior. You'll be sucked into several tunnels and spat out to glimpse coming attractions in the distance, and unusually noticeable are the textures you can distinguish. Wood, rock, water, or light, everything appears—if this makes any sense—to be better than nature.

Speeds can reach 60 mph on straights and drop to 20 mph on tight curves, and even though you could make the trip from Lee Vining in two hours, allow an extra hour just to stop at turnouts, shoot pictures, or savor the visual feast of twisting roads and the golden glow of nature.

About 55 miles into this leg, you'll reach Highway 41. Turn left and follow the signs to Yosemite Village. It is bigger and better than anything you can imagine.

YOSEMITE PRIMER

Yosemite conjures thousands of images and raises expectations to dizzying heights. You'd think it would fail to deliver, but it doesn't. It is just as beautiful, wild, tame, rich, and sublime as you'd expect.

While it's tempting to think the rest of America would look like this if we hadn't beat Mother Nature into submission, there is only one Yosemite. Initially set aside by President Lincoln in 1864, Yosemite Valley and the Mariposa Grove of giant sequoias were to be "held for public use, resort, and recreation…inalienable for all time."

In 1890, an act of Congress preserved 1,170 square miles of forests, fields, valleys, and streams equal in size to Rhode

The Bear Facts

Although lead poisoning killed off California grizzlies in the 1920s (they were shot), other bears are still sniffing out food in Yosemite Village. They can easily tear a car to shreds when searching out uncovered food, so when you leave your bike, take anything perishable with you. Better yet, leave items in your room. If you're camping, invest in bear-proof containers. Maybe buy one large enough to sleep in.

Island. Today, it is traversed by nearly 200 miles of paved road, about 70 miles of graded road, and 800 miles of hiking trails. Yosemite is home to 150 species of birds, 85 species of mammals, and close to 1,500 species of flowering plants.

The park is as bold and as beautiful as America. Enjoy it.

ON THE ROAD: YOSEMITE

While you could take your bike and explore the park on your own, you may be better off by putting yourself in the hands of Yosemite's park rangers. They are knowledgeable and courteous and will likely be able to answer every question you have.

Although it sounds like high cheese, the tram tour (or bus tour in cold weather) is the best way to see Yosemite Valley, the most visited section of the park. The tour also stops at Bridalveil Fall and offers great views of Half Dome, and monumental El Capitan. If you've only seen it in a book, wait until you see it here.

Although the size of the high granite edifice may not impress you at first, take a few moments and look at it closely. When you spot a pinpoint dabbed on the mountain you'll get an instant education in proportion. *That* is a mountain climber. And those parsley sprigs tucked in slivers of rock? Those are pine trees you are looking at, and they are at least 80 feet tall. Soak

this in, and respect for those pin-headed climbers increases.

The tour takes you by lush meadows that make up only 20 percent of the park but support 80 percent of its flowers. How do I know this? Because just about every guide thinks they're at a *Jeopardy!* audition and freely fling out data on botany, geology, and forestry throughout the two-hour tour. When it's over, you'll be armed with plenty of information, a good sense of direction, and an understanding of what you'd like to revisit.

After a tour, exploring on your own may be the most rewarding experience of Yosemite. At Curry Village and Yosemite Village, you can fill up a backpack with water, snacks, camera, and film, and the park is yours. Hiking trails, which range from easy to very strenuous, deliver you to impressive sights, such as giant boulders and trees as wide as Cadillacs. The woods are welcoming in their solitude and open your senses to every movement, sound, and fragrance. Rustling leaves recall a rushing stream, flaked bark peels off the gnarled trunks of cedar trees, acorns drop, and pine cones fall with a soft splat.

Stopping to feel the environment is akin to slowing down on a great ride and at times it feels far more satisfying. When you take time to rest when you want and where you want, there's immense pleasure in knowing that the "real world" is hundreds of miles away and your office even farther. If you absolutely have to do something, check the lodges for listings of daily events, such as fishing, photography classes, and nature talks.

When night falls, the sky looks more white than black, since stars can be counted by the millions. It's been only two days since leaving Las Vegas. There, the city demanded you stay up late. Here, the rewards of Yosemite are offered when you rise early and take advantage of another day in paradise.

PULL IT OVER: YOSEMITE HIGHLIGHTS
Attractions and Adventures

As mentioned, sightseeing tours are a good way to get acquainted with the park and several different types are available; call 209/372-1240 for details on each. Led by park rangers or tour guides, the most popular is the introductory **Valley Floor Tour** ($25), which lasts two hours and travels 26 miles through the heart of Yosemite. A full day's adventure, the **Grand Tour** ($82) winds through Glacier Point and Mariposa Grove, site of the famous giant sequoias. The **Glacier Point Tour** costs $41 round-trip, $25 one way.

When you're not in a bus or on your bike, you may be in Yosemite Village in the heart of Yosemite Valley. Like a small downtown, it's complete with post office, groceteria, pizza parlor, deli, auditorium, museum, cemetery, and the Ansel Adams Gallery that features works for sale by Adams and other wildlife photographers. At the visitor center, you can sign up for photo courses or ranger-led activities, check road conditions, or buy some books. Over at Curry Village, there are gift shops, a tour center, bike rentals, and snack shops.

If you plan to fish at Yosemite, you need

a fishing license, available at the Sport Shop in Yosemite Valley, the Wawona Store, and the Tuolumne Meadows Store. But if your thirst for adventure is higher and you were inspired by the climbers you saw earlier, take the first step toward tackling El Capitan and sign up for climbing lessons by calling the **Mountaineering School** (209/372-8344).

Blue-Plate Specials

After a day of grazing on picnic grub or at concession stands, experience lunch or dinner at the **Ahwahnee** hotel (209/372-1489, www.yosemitepark.com). At this four-star hotel the setting is extraordinary, the meals perfect, and the service flawless. The entire experience is enhanced by the architectural style called National Park Service Rustic that characterizes this massive room. Call me, and I'll join you.

Shut-Eye

Yosemite used to reach peak popularity between Memorial Day and Labor Day; today, stretch that from April to the end of November. Make reservations as far in advance as possible. For **hotel reservations** within the park, call 801/559-5000 or visit www.yosemitepark.com. For **campground reservations,** call 877/444-6777 or visit www.recreation.gov.

The park boasts a range of facilities, from dirt-cheap rustic to over-the-top indulgent. In the heart of the park, Yosemite's fabled **Ahwahnee** (209/372-1407, $439 and up) tops the price list. One of the most beautiful inns in America, it was built in 1927 and is breathtaking in design, superb in service. You'll find character and tradition in the grand fireplace, massive timbers, Great Room, and baronial dining room. Reserve one of 123 rooms, at eyebrow-arching prices, as far in advance as possible. Other choices offer greater variety at a wider price range, the difference depending on whether they are actual buildings, cabins, canvas tents, or have private baths. Choose from the motel-style **Yosemite Lodge** ($153–185), **Wawona Hotel** ($128–199), or **Curry Village tents and cabins** ($85–152).

SIDE TRIP: YOSEMITE TO LAKE TAHOE

The road so far has been rich in both kindness and treachery. If you think it's been more of the latter, leave Yosemite Village on Highway 120 West and head for home. Otherwise, get ready for another adventurous 200-mile run, returning via Highway 120 East to U.S. 395 and on to Lake Tahoe. Warning: Make this a daytime ride, since the tight curves can be dangerous after dark.

Even if you never ride another mile, you'll have experienced the most complicated blend of riding in terms of terrain, scenery, sociology, psychology, and climate. And there's more to come.

About three miles north of Lee Vining, Mono Lake reveals itself from a highway vista. Now drying out like a Miami retiree as folks in Los Angeles drain the lake for their lawns and bathwater, the exposed white sands are a curiously surreal landscape.

Six miles later, you're at 7,000 feet and climbing, with the vast Mono Basin in the distance on your right. This run soon places you back in a desert landscape, a curious fact when you cruise past 7,700 feet and look back to see Yosemite's Tioga Pass. The rise in altitude also introduces winds that can kick your tires out from under you. Keep a low profile.

It's difficult to fathom that these changes are occurring during one incredible journey. And to prove its power, nature will once again change environments on

you. After you cross the Conway Summit at 8,138 feet, the desert leaves the stage and you enter California ranch country where small cow towns come into view. Scan the horizons and you may spy snow falling in one section, clear blue skies in another, rain in a third. It is altogether impossible to absorb the varying expressions of nature that surround you, but you don't really need to. Just file this information away under Memorable Motorcycle Run.

Past Bridgeport, the slow winding roads get their act straightened out and whisk you into Devil Gate's Summit at 7,500 feet, sharpening your senses for the impending pinball run. But for now, the hills are low and rolling and fun.

Although you've already defeated the toughest terrain, you now face Walker Creek Canyon. After 10 miles of tranquility, the winding roads snatch you back into the challenge of rushing water, boulders, pine needles, and fallen trees. As you catch fleeting glimpses of red rocks and black rocks and sand, you'll be making mental notes to thank the highway engineers and sign up for the Sierra Club.

When the canyon breathes its last, you'll enter the tiny town of Walker, where nothing seems to be living, and then Coleville (pop. 43), which makes Walker look like Chicago. The next town, Topaz, is your cue to look for Highway 89; if it's open, it will be on your left.

For a minor road, Highway 89 is amazingly beautiful. Three miles into it, you climb to 6,000 feet and enter a fertile valley rich with fields of pines and sagebrush. You have no choice but to keep riding, and you won't be disappointed. The higher you ride—and you will—the more spectacular the view. As your attorney, I advise you to stop at the peak and look back over the valley. It is an image that will stay with you for a long, long time. You can look for miles down the valley's breadth, and with keen eyesight you may make out stacks of logs that are, in fact, remote cabins locked within the breeches of behemoth mountain walls. I don't know what type of people live out in this wilderness, but I admire the fact that they do.

No picture can do justice to this image; only your memory will capture the scope of this incredible vista. Desert, snow, mountains, valleys...It's a view that is as inspiring as it is humbling.

You are nearing Monitor Pass at a mighty 8,300 feet which guarantees that the imminent descent will be a gift to enjoy. Drop it into neutral and rest your engine for several miles as you glide your bike into easy curves and experience the decline of western mountain ranges.

Continue on Highway 89 toward Markleeville, 32 miles south of Lake Tahoe. You may decide to stop here for several reasons. If the sun is setting, the mountains you just crossed will look like a Maxfield Parrish landscape painted with pinks, violets, blues, and crimson, and you should certainly avoid the upcoming roads at night. Another good reason is the **Cutthroat Saloon** (14830 Hwy. 89, 530/694-2150). It's quite popular with riders because of the Western Victorian decor, the adjoining Wolf Creek restaurant, and the ladies'

underwear pinned on the ceiling. Maybe you'll find something in your size. With 11 units, the **Creekside Lodge** (530/694-2511) is the lodging option here.

From here, the road is pleasing and predictable and leads to South Lake Tahoe. Although you'll find motels, hotels, and cabins here, the city's large population is why you may prefer to ride to the less populated northern shore.

To wrap up the ride with a final burst of excitement is Highway 28 along the west shore. Unlike most lakefront roads that blend into the shoreline, this one has dangerously high cliffs, skin-tight switchbacks, and eye-popping glimpses of Lake Tahoe from inlets and Alpine vistas. In a way, this heart-throbbing run is the natural counterpoint to the artificial fun of Las Vegas.

Shut-Eye
Chain Drive
These chain hotels are in South Lake Tahoe, or within 10 miles of the city center:

Best Western, Days Inn, Embassy Suites, Holiday Inn, Howard Johnson, Motel 6, Quality Inn, Rodeway, Super 8, Travelodge

For more information, including phone numbers and websites, see page 151.

Resources for Riders

Las Vegas–Yosemite Run

Nevada Travel Information
Nevada Road Conditions—877/687-6237, www.safetravelusa.com/nv
Nevada State Parks—775/684-2770, www.parks.nv.gov/
Nevada Tourism—800/638-2328, www.travelnevada.com

California Travel Information
California Association of Bed & Breakfast Inns—800/373-9251, www.cabbi.com
California Division of Tourism—916/444-4429 or 800/862-2543,
   www.visitcalifornia.com
California Road Conditions—800/427-7623
California State Parks—916/653-6995, www.parks.ca.gov
California Weather Information—916/979-3051

Local and Regional Information
Lake Tahoe Forecast and Road Conditions—530/542-4636, ext. 3
Las Vegas Chamber of Commerce—702/641-5822 or 702/735-1616 (info center),
   www.lvchamber.com
Las Vegas Visitors Information Center—702/892-7575 or 877/847-4858,
   www.visitlasvegas.com
Lone Pine Chamber of Commerce—760/876-4444 or 877/253-8981,
   www.lonepinechamber.org
North Lake Tahoe Resort Association—530/583-3494 or 888/434-1262,
   www.gotahoenorth.com
Yosemite Information—209/372-0200, www.yosemite.com or www.nps.gov/yose
Yosemite Road Service—209/372-0200, ext. 1

Nevada Motorcycle Shops
Carter Powersports—6275 S. Decatur Blvd., Las Vegas, 702/727-6365,
   www.carterpowersports.com
Las Vegas Harley-Davidson—2605 S. Eastern Ave., Las Vegas, 702/302-4936 or
   888/218-0744, www.lasvegasharleydavidson.com
Motorcycles 702—2010 Western Ave., Las Vegas, 702/645-1500,
   www.motorcycles702.com
Red Rock Harley-Davidson—2260 S. Rainbow Rd., Las Vegas, 702/876-2884 or
   866/965-8224, www.redrockharley.com

California Motorcycle Shop
Golden State Cycle—174 S. Main St., Bishop, 760/872-1570,
   www.goldenstatecycle.com

Pacific Coast Run

Calistoga, California to Carmel, California

As evidenced by the ride through Death Valley, Lone Pine, and Yosemite, eastern California was designed by God specifically for motorcyclists. Apparently that must have given God a lot of confidence since he managed to repeat his success on the West Coast as well. Get to Napa Valley and it's the closest you'll come to riding along Mediterranean roads, unless you ship your bike to Athens. And although the region is marked by affluence, you don't need deep pockets since the roads are free.

From the luxury of Calistoga's spas to the pure beauty of the San Francisco skyline, from Carmel's fantasy architecture to the dream world of Hearst Castle, this run features short rides on roads that are just right. What's more, the journey from valley to hill to coastal highway creates a satisfying blend of environments.

CALISTOGA PRIMER

Some motorcycle travelers make an unfortunate error when visiting Napa Valley—and that's deciding to stay in the valley's namesake, Napa. Far more appealing is the town of Calistoga. As your advance team, let me tell you why you need to stay here.

Several thousand years ago, a volcano named Mt. Konocti erupted 20 miles away and plopped about five feet of ash on the valley floor. Around the 1500s, the Wappo Indians realized the ash had mixed with the naturally heated mineral water and started bathing in the mud and water. They finished up with a sweat wrap, and they felt good. Damn good. The Wappos called the valley Tu-la-ha-lu-si ("Oven Place").

When Sam Brannan, California's first Gold Rush millionaire, arrived here in the 1860s, he saw the potential for a resort spa town. At a promotional supper, he proclaimed that this would be the "Calistoga of Sarafornia!" The slip became a marketing ploy, and Calistoga was born. Farewell, Wappos. Riding the wealth of the mines and the natural hot springs, Brannan's

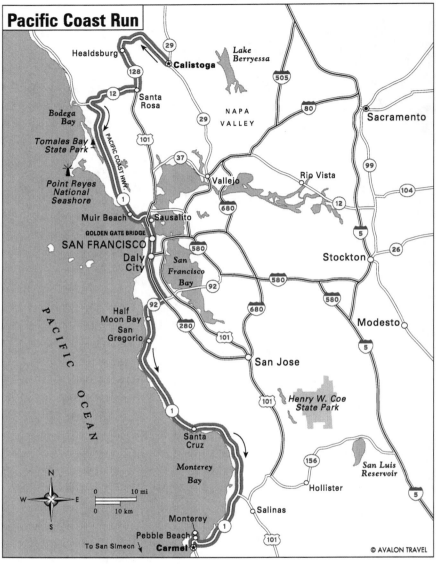

Route: Calistoga to Carmel via Sausalito, Monterey, Big Sur, Pacific Coast Highway

Distance: Approximately 310 miles

First Leg: Calistoga to Sausalito (80 miles)

Second Leg: Sausalito to Carmel (120 miles)

Optional Third Leg: Carmel to San Simeon (112 miles)

Helmet Laws: California requires helmets.

What's in a Mud Bath?

You know how you can get achy after too many hours in the saddle? A mud bath will loosen you up faster than an Ex-Lax smoothie. How does it work? A mud bath is a mixture of heated mineral water and volcanic ash and/or peat moss. After you settle into this gloop, the thick mixture heats up to penetrate your body, relax your muscles, and alleviate stress, tensions, aches, and pains. Ten–twelve minutes should be enough, or stay muddy longer if you're really keyed up.

community became the central point for a railroad serving the upper valley, and it sustained itself through the turn of century, past World War II, and into a new millennium and never lost its appeal.

As in Brannan's day, Calistoga appears to be riding the crest of a prosperous wave. Spas and businesses are thriving now and the film *Sideways* impressed an already intense subculture of San Francisco wine sippers, who continue to flock to town for vineyard runs and body wraps. But if you see 'em, don't even mention merlot. The most telling sign that this is a good place for a base are the motorcycles parked up and down Lincoln Avenue, their riders frequenting small saloons and planning sorties into the surrounding mountain roads. One of the state's more pleasing towns, it is the perfect starting point for this journey.

ON THE ROAD: CALISTOGA

I've come to believe that the best towns to visit are those where you can ride in, park for free, and check out the town on foot. Calistoga is just such a place and one of the best motorcycle towns you'll ever find—especially if you like drinking wine and having someone upgrade the condition of your muscles to happy. From Dr. Wilkinson's Hot Springs and Mud Baths to the fine restaurants, this is the Old

West with a 21st-century facelift. Unfortunately, you'll have to wait to see all that it offers, because the roads of this region are so damn tempting you'll be hard-pressed to sit still.

Open a map and you'll see that the number of riding options rivals that of vineyards. Even better, these are not ordinary roads; they seem to offer the same sort of riding that you'd find in the Greek Peloponnese, Swiss Alps, and Italian Dolomites. Within minutes, you can take comfort in roads as curvaceous as Marilyn Monroe, traverse hills that are soft and low, ride over green creeks and past drooping brown trees and pumpkin patches and groves bursting with almonds, avocadoes, and black walnuts. Not only will your ride be visually exciting, it will be redolent with the fresh, fragrant aroma of nut trees, strawberries, grapes, and flowering plants.

It is a thrilling experience to be here, where the outdoors are treasured, not tamed. You should see all of this and travel beyond the hills, but also consider a manageable trip to the region north of Napa Valley.

Although the larger wineries are in the southern Napa Valley, head north on Highway 29 (aka Silverado Trail), on the east side of the valley. Turn left on Tubbs Lane, and then right at Highway 128. Soon you're on twisting canopy roads that offer some of the finest motorcycle riding in the country. Motorcycles springing up and over the hills look like ants on a mound; but be careful when the afternoon sun and shadows play tricks on the pavement.

Head north, and you'll ride into Alexander Valley. Although there are no major towns, you must stop in Healdsburg at the strangely well-stocked **Jimtown General Store** (6706 Hwy. 128, 707/433-1212, www.jimtown.com). Think back a few decades and then discover that they've recovered part of your childhood with Mary Jane candies, bubble-gum cigars, Chinese finger traps, whoopee cushions, old toys from the '40s and '50s, a convenient deli, and, if your name is Jim, a chance at immortality by signing the autograph hound.

From here, you can head farther north, south, east, or west to explore other valley back roads. Like those around New Hope, Pennsylvania, all roads lead to a great ride.

PULL IT OVER: CALISTOGA HIGHLIGHTS
Attractions and Adventures

If you want a spa treatment without feeling obligated to stay at a resort, you have two options and each of these have stood the test of time. Established by town founder Sam Brannan in 1871, **Indian Springs** (1712 Lincoln Ave., 707/942-4913, www.indianspringscalistoga.com) is the oldest continuously operating thermal pool and spa in California. Mud baths, thermal geysers, massages, and a mineral pool are spread across 16 acres of volcanic ash. **Dr. Wilkinson's Hot Springs** (1507 Lincoln Ave., 707/942-4102, www.drwilkinson.com) was founded in 1951 by Doc Wilkinson. Aside from a great name and continuous family ownership, the spa

features mud baths, mineral whirlpools, steam rooms, facials, and an indoor mineral pool.

Of course one of the main reasons you're here is because of the more than 150 wineries in this region. You can get information and directions to all of them by making a few calls, doing a little pre-trip online research, or stopping at the **Chamber of Commerce and Visitors Center** (1133 Washington St., 707/942-6333, www.calistogavisitors.com) for maps and discount coupons to wineries and spas. The hunt is well worth it since the roads to the vineyards are unusually seductive. For more information contact the **Napa Valley Vintners Association** (707/963-3388, www.napavintners.com), the **Sonoma County Wineries Association** (707/522-5840, www.sonomawine.com), or **Alexander Valley Wine Growers** (888/289-4637, www.alexandervalley.org).

As you may have gathered, the terrain throughout these valleys is beautiful and found nowhere else in America. It's great to ride it, but there's also a way to soar above it with **Napa Valley Balloons** (707/944-0228 or 800/253-2224, www.napavalleyballoons.com). The experience is as extraordinary as the price ($220); although the steep fee includes breakfast before the launch from the Domaine Chandon Winery and flights of up to two hours. Another choice is right in Calistoga: the appropriately named **Calistoga Balloons** (707/942-5758 or 888/995-7700, www.calistogaballons.com). Their sailings also include breakfast and a flight lasting around an hour. Check online for discounts that drop the price just south of $200. The **Bonaventura Balloon Company** (133 Wall Rd., Napa, 707/944-2822 or 800/359-6272, www.bonaventuraballoons.com) is another option with similar rates (around $235). Each operation includes add-ons for breakfasts, picnics, or champagne brunches. Before deciding on any flight, ask how many passengers share your basket, whether or not you'll be able to help (if you'd like) as part of the crew, and if you can suck in some helium to change your voice.

For a visual representation of Calistoga's history, see how it was portrayed by a gifted artist. Ben Sharpsteen made good by becoming an Academy Award–winning animator, producer, and director for Walt Disney. His love for his adopted hometown led to the creation of the surprisingly fascinating **Sharpsteen Museum** (1311 Washington St., 707/942-5911, www.sharpsteen-museum.org). The downtown museum provides a great introduction to Calistoga and the history of upper Napa Valley. With careful detail, its 32-foot diorama depicts 1860s life at the opulent resort. Sam Brannan's cottage is connected to the main museum, which is open 11 A.M.–4 P.M. year-round. Admission is free—but they'd appreciate it if you slipped 'em a few bucks.

Who knows if you'll take advantage of this next one? But the type of spa treatment here is so unusual you'll remember it for years. West of Calistoga is **Osmosis** (209 Bohemian Hwy., Freestone, 707/823-8231, www.osmosis.com), where, after a Japanese tea ceremony, you strip down until you're absolutely bare naked and recline within a wooden tub filled with antiseptic cedar fiber, rice bran, and 600 active enzymes. An attendant takes a shovel and covers you up with the sawdust and then you spend the next 20 minutes in this compost heap throwing off more sweat than Secretariat. After you're dug up, you're hosed down and then invited upstairs for the pièce de résistance—a massage. Surreal, relaxing, and it'll do a number on your muscles. The enzyme bath is $85; add the tea ceremony and a massage and the 2.5-hour experience costs $180.

Blue-Plate Specials

Locals agree that one of the best breakfast spots is the **Café Sarafornia** (1413 Lincoln Ave., 707/942-0555), the "last old-fashioned diner in the Valley." A casual start to an extraordinary day's ride, the breakfasts—scrambles, omelettes, blintzes, crepes, and oat bran pancakes—range between a modest $4–12. There are also hamburgers, sandwiches, and salads for lunch.

Perhaps the nicest restaurant in town, **Brannan's Grill** (1374 Lincoln Ave., 707/942-2233, www.brannansgrill.com), serves lunches and dinners that are elegant, simple, and creative. The wide-open dining room and fireplace are settling, and the pace never seems rushed, even when it's packed. The menu changes seasonally, so check its website for current appetizers and entrées.

A low-key local favorite, **Pacifico Restaurante Mexicano** (1237 Lincoln Ave., 707/942-4400, www.pacificorestaurante-mexicano.com) uses only fresh ingredients ("no cans, no way") to create traditional Mexican food for lunch and dinner. It wins high marks for its chips, salsa, guacamole, and hand-shaken margaritas. The full bar is a rarity in Napa Valley.

Watering Holes

Open daily 'til 2 A.M., **Susie's** (1365 Lincoln Ave., 707/942-6710) is literally a hole in the wall. Head down a narrow hallway and you end up here, at a cool, dark refuge in the netherworld between "dive" and "joint." Regulars are quick to befriend strangers, and you'll soon settle in at the only pool tables in town. You're also welcome to try your hand at the piano (provided you can play). Happy hour? All day long. The Redwood Empire HOG Chapter dubbed Susie's a biker-friendly bar.

You'll find a microbrewery and full bar at the **Calistoga Inn** (1250 Lincoln Ave., 707/942-4101); the type of Napa wine bar you visualize at **Bar Vino** (1457 Lincoln Ave., 707/942-9900, www.bar-vino.com) inside the Mount View Hotel; and a full bar all by its lonesome at the **Hydro Bar and Grill** (1403 Lincoln Ave., 707/942-9777), where there's live music and 20 microbrews on tap.

Shut-Eye

Calistoga is so perfect, you may want to extend your stay by a year or two. Most lodging options include a spa, so plan on at least one massage to complement your visit. You can search for these yourself or save yourself some time by contacting the **Calistoga Visitors Center** (707/942-6333, www.calistogavisitors.com) for recommendations and reservations for lodging, spas, winery tours, etc.

Motels and Motor Courts

The **Roman Spa** (1300 Washington St., 707/942-4441, www.romanspahotsprings. com, $135 and up) has ordinary rooms but lush landscaping and a laid-back atmosphere. After a ride, you can rest outside in a mineral pool, jet spa pool, or sauna. Its spa services include the standard lineup of mud baths, mineral baths, and massages. Rates here run about 20 percent less off-season.

Inn-dependence

One of the most pleasing places you can stay is the **Cottage Grove Inn** (1711 Lincoln Ave., 707/942-8400 or 800/799-2284, www.cottagegrove.com, $250 and up). These luxurious Napa Valley cottages

are shaded by towering trees and feature whirlpool tubs, fireplaces, private porches, and distinct themes (fly-fishing, equestrian, Audubon, musical, etc.). The price may induce panic in most riders, but the cottages sleep three and they *do* include breakfast.... Check them out; you may think it's worth it just to be able to park your bike out front and walk downtown. No loud pipes, please.

Chain Drive

These chain hotels are in town, or within 10 miles of the city center:
Best Western, Clarion, Comfort Inn, Motel 6

For more information, including phone numbers and websites, see page 151.

ON THE ROAD: CALISTOGA TO SAUSALITO

There are several ways to get out of Calistoga, two of which are quite different. For a fast, ordinary, straight shot, ride west to U.S. 101 and then drive south until you reach Sausalito. But there's an alternative for experienced riders ready for a challenge.

Route 12 South (also called Calistoga Rd.) heads about 30 miles due west to the coast, passing through the congestion in Santa Rosa and then past some less than spectacular scenery. A slight detour on the Bodega Highway will introduce you to Highway 1 and take you north towards Bodega Bay, the setting for Alfred Hitchcock's *The Birds*. If you like the movie or cool harbor towns, stop over and take a look. From here, fabled Highway 1 (aka the Pacific Coast Highway, or PCH) is about to prove to you why it's a legend. The wild stretch from Bodega Bay south to Sausalito can be pretty spooky, unless you've replaced your tires with mountain goats. Seriously. Curves are very sharp and safety rails nonexistent, the twists can be hypnotic, and sometimes the road's lay-out can range from impassable to impos-sible. But if you're ready, here's what you'll experience.

After you get on Highway 1 near Bo-dega Bay, the road sweeps east and far beyond the view of the coast. To com-pensate, there are great straightaways, and your path follows the rise and fall of the mountains. You'll ride toward Tomales Bay, which is a long drink of water that'll ride with you for about 15 miles. It's a lonely stretch where the rustic cabins of anglers crop up every few miles.

The scenery remains a constant quiet; there are simple villages that appear, the road sometimes leads into a forest, and then there are a brief but enjoyable series of 20-mph turns and shady, slow twists. Miles later, you're still rumbling along the mighty low road beside this smooth and graceful inlet.

When you reach Point Reyes Station, glance at the map and then at your watch and see if you have time to follow the path blazed by other bikers and head out to the Point Reyes Lighthouse. If you pass it by, the next really big show is waiting for you south of Stinson Beach.

The ability to ride from here for about 12 miles past Muir Beach and Tamalpais Valley to reach U.S. 101 is what separates humans from animals. Throw back a few Maalox tablets and get ready to meet a road that's a paved funhouse of gravel, dangerously sharp turns, and very steep drops. Maybe it was because I was riding a monster bike, but I often tapped it into first to navigate turns at a speed exceeded only by tree sloths. While you may get an adrenaline rush out of this, as I was work-ing it out my mood alternated between excitement and sheer panic. Just about the time I was wondering how I got mixed up

with a mess of blacktop like this, I was dumped out into level-headed Tamalpais Valley which gave my nerves time to settle as I rolled onto U.S. 101 for a short, citi-fied ride in Sausalito.

About time.

SAUSALITO PRIMER

It's almost a cliché to find that a quaint seaside town was once a hotspot for drunken sailors, bawdy saloons, and come one, come all bordellos—but I still get a kick knowing that all this happened in Sausalito. It has the essence of the Cote d'Azur in France, and this European style is no accident. The town was discovered by Juan Manual de Ayala in 1575 and later became a favored shelter for full-rigged sailing ships from around the world. Today, those ships have been replaced by private yachts.

During World War II, Sausalito was a major shipbuilding site, with Liberty ships, landing craft, and tankers taking shape here. Afterward, the area became a haven for writers and artists—as evidenced by the galleries along Bridgeway Street. It's an uncommonly exotic town, and I guar-antee you'll enjoy it.

ON THE ROAD: SAUSALITO

You've already enjoyed a ride from the northeast, and later you'll embark on a great ride south. For now, just park your bike and enjoy the town. You'll never tire of the view, which is even more impressive than that of Camden, Maine, where the Appalachians dissolve into the Atlantic.

Sausalito also has plenty of restaurants and galleries and pubs, and if you need even more, simply head over to San Fran-cisco via ferry or the mighty Golden Gate Bridge.

I chose to continue the low-key theme I'd grown accustomed to in Calistoga and decided to stay in town. Not a bad choice. The heart of Sausalito is as foreign as any village along the Mediterranean and evokes the loveliness of the Riviera.

Besides, the views from here rival any in the world, from the San Francisco skyline to the fogbanks rolling over the bay. The only thing missing is the Golden Gate Bridge, hidden from view behind some ill-placed hills.

In town, the Plaza de Vina Del Mar Park has a visitors center and, more prominently, two 14-foot-tall elephant statues created for the Panama-Pacific Exposition of 1915. The architecture defies generic business district, instead blending Victorian, French, Spanish, and Irish accents. Not only are the people friendly and the setting perfect, you'll find the town to be as cosmopolitan and as relaxed as any you'll find as you explore the central district.

This is clearly a town of affluence. I deduced this from the forest of yachts I saw at the marina, which is just a short and pleasant walk from the park. As you roam the town, a few shops are worth exploring in greater detail. The **Venice Gourmet Delicatessen** (625 Bridgeway St., 415/332-3544, www.venicegourmet.com) has been here since 1969 and continues to be the local favorite. The shop is cluttered with copper kettles, baklava, dried sausage, soft drinks, and premium wines.

If you finish making the rounds early, you may opt to visit San Francisco, or head north on Bridgeway to reach Caledonia Street, which is an authentic Sausalito neighborhood.

Then, in the evening, as ferryboats start knocking across the waters to shuttle workers back from San Francisco, you can relax on the promenade or inside a waterfront restaurant and watch the most spectacular city skyline in America come to light.

PULL IT OVER: SAUSALITO HIGHLIGHTS
Attractions and Adventures

While an inmate on Alcatraz, I was only able to cruise the bay on my inner tube. Now released, I can cruise to SF cheaply aboard the **Blue and Gold Ferry** (415/773-1188, www.blueandgoldfleet. com). The ships depart Sausalito several times daily ($9.50 one way, $19 round-trip) for Fisherman's Wharf. From the Wharf, **Alcatraz Cruises** (415/981-7625, www.alcatrazcruises.com, $26) has boats that'll take you to and from the shuttered prison, which includes a cell house audio tour. Make reservations in advance, tours can sell out. **Golden Gate Ferry** (415/923-2000, www.goldengate-ferry.org) avoids Fisherman's Wharf and goes to the foot of Market Street; fares are $7.85 one way. Sorry, no room for motorcycles.

Mark Reuben Vintage Gallery (34 Princess St., 415/332-8815 or 877/444-3767, www.markreubengallery.com) displays thousands of vintage photographs, many taken from the original negatives. Matted and framed original pictures include those of Harley and Davidson, the Beatles, and Marlon Brando in *The Wild One*. You could spend days in here. Topics cover sports, history, entertainers, political figures, and other photos perfect for the office and home. Shipping's available.

Blue-Plate Specials

Neighboring San Francisco has more restaurants and variety than you could experience in a lifetime, but if you prefer to dine in Sausalito, here are two choices that may satisfy. A great way to start the day is at the **Bridgeway Cafe** (633 Bridgeway St., 415/332-3426). With a great view of the city and the bay, this friendly little diner serves all-day breakfasts, lunches, and dinners, and the waitstaff is kind and considerate.

When the evening falls, consider **Horizons** (558 Bridgeway St., 415/331-3232, www.horizonssausalito.com). In addition to its rich woods and high ceilings, the wide bay windows and patio dining reveal a breathtaking view of San Francisco. Serving lunch and dinner, the waterfront restaurant features fettuccini jambalaya, five-cheese spinach cannelloni, and lobster tails.

Watering Holes

At the **No-Name Bar** (757 Bridgeway St., 415/332-1392), there's character in abundance, a fireplace inside, and a garden patio outside. Owner Al Stanfield rides and often makes the 2,000-mile jaunt to Sturgis. His place delivers live jazz on weekends, blues on weekdays, and pub food in the afternoon. Beers and spirits abound in this mighty beautiful bar. **Smitty's** (214 Caledonia St., 415/332-2637, www.smittysbar.com) is a "friendly neighborhood bar" that's been around since 1938. To this day, it remains a favorite of locals who appreciate the casual feel, the easy camaraderie, and the truth in advertising of "damn fine drinks."

Shut-Eye

I'd suggest making every effort to stay the night in Sausalito, but across the bridge in San Francisco exists every chain hotel known to man.

Inn-dependence

There are three unique and (thankfully) non-generic hotels in Sausalito and, for what they offer, they seem affordable. The **Casa Madrona Hotel** (801 Bridgeway St., 415/332-0502 or 800/288-0502, www.casamadrona.com, $149 and up high season) opened in 1885. It features single cottages and elevated rooms with perfect bay views. The staff is friendly; the rooms are plush; the gardenlike atmosphere is soothing; and it's all within sight of one of America's largest and loudest cities. Room 315 lets you soak in the tub while watching the city lights. Included in the rate is an evening social hour that affords the opportunity to get looped on some free wine.

On the park, **Hotel Sausalito** (16 El Portal, 415/332-0700 or 888/442-0700, www.hotelsausalito.com, $155 and up) is the most European of them all. The rich, warm, gold tones of this hotel perfectly mirror the sunrise over the bay. The hotel offers 16 1920s-style rooms and suites with modern amenities and views of the park or harbor.

The priciest option is the **Inn Above Tide** (30 El Portal, 415/332-9535 or 800/893-8433, www.innabovetide.com, $325 and up) which, as the name implies, is on the waterfront. All 30 rooms face the hillside city, although they are more modern than I prefer. You may be lured by the free breakfast and sunset wine and cheese receptions.

Chain Drive

These chain hotels are in town, or within 10 miles of the city center:

Best Western, Clarion, Comfort Inn, Courtyard by Marriott, Days Inn, Econo Lodge, Hilton, Holiday Inn, Howard Johnson, Hyatt, Motel 6, Omni Hotels, Quality Inn, Radisson, Ramada, Rodeway, Sheraton, Super 8, Travelodge

For more information, including phone numbers and websites, see page 151.

ON THE ROAD: SAUSALITO TO CARMEL

The next leg of the journey revs you up for some spectacular scenery and also offers the unforgettable experience of riding across the Pacific Ocean in less than five minutes.

When you leave Sausalito, take Bridgeway Street and follow it south. Three minutes from the center of town, you'll round the bend and see the twin towers of the Golden Gate Bridge straight ahead. Before you cross the bridge, get in the right lane and watch for a lightly trafficked access loop road that leads to Point Bonita at the Marin Highlands. Taking this road will afford one of the best souvenir photos you'll ever take. Turn right, and a few hundred yards ahead, pull off and pose with your bike. With the Golden Gate Bridge, the bay, and city behind you, you've got a photo suitable for framing. To your left, on the northeast corner of the bridge, there's another pullout called Vista Point.

When you get back on the road, you'll pay five bucks to cross the bridge and even though you'd think it would be paid off by now, it's worth it. To your left is the bay and to your right is the Pacific Ocean, which will be your traveling companion for the next 100-plus miles.

Navigating through town to reach PCH is a little tricky and trying to explain how to do it can drive a man to drink. The abridged version is this: After crossing the bridge, veer to the right to reach 14th Avenue—which is also Highway 1—which soon jogs further to the west over to 19th Avenue to take you through residential neighborhoods toward Daly City. At some point Highway 1 joins up with I-280 until, just beyond Exit 48, the road splits again to give you the opportunity to follow Highway 1 over to the coast for a waterside ride.

But after suffering through slow city traffic I wanted to blow out the cobwebs, so I stuck with I-280 and rode farther south to reach Route 92 which leads west toward Half Moon Bay. Surprisingly, it wasn't bad. The farther from the city you get, the greater the pleasure as you see buildings and urban sprawl wither away into the natural landscape. Another surprise was Route 92 West itself, which took me back to the land of curvy roads and nice lakes. There were also miles and miles of flower farms which emitted a far sweeter aroma than what I sniffed in Amish country.

The road ends at PCH, and from here, it's 100 miles south to the Monterey Peninsula. Unlike Highway 1 north of San Francisco, the road here is fairly flat, straight, and ordinary. It is less mountainous and more fertile, which explained the wealth of roadside produce stands. I deduced from the handmade signs that the farmers of this fertile region raise artichokes, pumpkins, carrots, hot dogs, and soft drinks.

It's impossible to explain how easy this road is. Flat and smooth, the pleasure is in the tranquility of the environment that lasts for about 60 coastal miles until you reach the Santa Cruz county line. Then, almost in an instant, the scenic ride ends.

Unfortunately, you have to run a gauntlet of urban ugliness to reach your final destination. For more than 10 miles comes a crappy highway with fast food joints, gas stations, and bike shops. It's also a shame that the ocean remains hidden behind miles of land and there's not a thing you can do about it. The one remedy is to look forward to reaching one of the most enchanting towns in California. After passing Monterey, look for Ocean Avenue, turn right, and head straight into a dreamscape called Carmel.

Most extraordinary Carmel.

CARMEL PRIMER

Carmel may be the crown jewel in the Monterey Peninsula, one of California's more naturally beautiful regions. The

Esselen Indians knew it when they made it their home in A.D. 3,000–500. Next the Ohlone Indians showed up, and they were doing just fine until their time started running out in 1542, when Spanish explorer Juan Rodriguez Cabrillo sighted the white sand beach and pine forest. Even though Cabrillo couldn't land because of rough waters, he decided he could claim it for Spain anyway.

Yes, he did. And I've decided that I own the Bahamas.

Several explorers later, in June 1770, Father Junipero Serra, a Spanish governor and a Franciscan priest, proclaimed the area the military and ecclesiastical capital of Alta, California.

With natural beauty and easy access to the ocean, it was obvious why people have coveted the Monterey Peninsula. Mexico owned it but later surrendered it to the U.S. Navy without a fight. In 1906, refugees from the San Francisco earthquake headed south and made it their new home. And in 1916, bohemian artists with no architectural training showed up and formed the village of Carmel on Halloween. Maybe it was their lack of training and artistic gifts that made it what it is.

From the town's earliest days, art was in the forefront. When Hugh Comstock's wife asked him to build a separate house for her doll collection, he did and then got busy building 20 more whimsical cottages that are still highly prized (and livable) today. While best known as Clint Eastwood's domain (he served as mayor from 1986 to 1988), the town of 4,500 remains true to the original vision of its founding artists and preserves an oasis of art and extraordinary beauty.

ON THE ROAD: CARMEL

Before you start wandering around the village, you may want to stock up on a few dozen digital cameras and memory cards, since you could easily use them up shooting every picturesque building, alcove, courtyard, and garden in town.

On one street, you may photograph a Swiss village, turn the corner and enter a Spanish *mercado,* and then spy the rounded archways and thatched roof of an English cottage. It has the feel of a village and it will always be that way since restrictions prohibit neon signs, street numbers, parking meters, high-rises, plastic plants, and high heels. Really.

One other thing to love about Carmel is that it embodies the freedom you seek on a motorcycle tour. You can walk a few blocks to the beach, take it easy at a sidewalk café, or just hang out. A great way to understand the essence of the village and appreciate its history is with **Carmel Walks** (831/642-2700, www.carmelwalks. com), which offers two-hour guided tours through secret pathways, courtyards, and side streets and is filled with some insider information. Tours ($25) are given at 10 A.M. and 2 P.M. on Saturday, 10 A.M. Tuesday–Friday. Alternatively, you can take a free walking tour with a map provided by the visitors center, which is upstairs on San Carlos between 5th and 6th.

Touring downtown is only the beginning. Off Ocean Drive, for $9.25 you can gain access to the Carmel Gate of legendary 17-Mile Drive, which rolls out and around Pebble Beach. But there's a catch: motorcycles aren't allowed. If you're determined (and you should be, since this is a hyperfun run), maybe it's worth renting a car—a convertible perhaps? With the top down and sea winds blowing, it's the next best thing to being on a bike.

If you can swing it, after paying the toll you'll get a map listing points of interest along 17-Mile Drive, and you can drive in and out from various gates around the loop. Theoretically, road signs should direct you on the tour, but they're often hard to follow. Just follow the map's red dashed line that signifies the route. Soon it'll take you close to the coastline where you should have your camera ready.

Several points jut into the Pacific, each with turnouts that reveal the sheer beauty of this rugged coastline. At Pescadero Point, white foam wraps around rocks, and at Cypress Point, a lone tree estimated at 250 years old sits alone on a rocky point, the inspiration for one of California's signature icons. A little farther, at Bird Rock, the seals and birds bark and caw without pause.

Although you may not have your favorite clubs with you, it'd be a shame to miss **Pebble Beach** (800/654-9300, www.pebblebeach.com). Golfers consider this America's St. Andrews and are charged accordingly: Non-residents pay a whopping $495(!) for 18 holes. Personally, I'd invest that kind of cash in an income-producing troupe of skating monkeys. Even if you don't golf, it's worth driving through just to see the dynamic shoreline.

You can exit at the gate at Pacific Grove, a wonderfully cool village that's home to rows of bungalows, Victorian homes, and a neat main street. There's something else about this village: Each October, swarms of monarch butterflies return here, just as sure as vultures return to roost in Washington, D.C.

Eventually, the roads and advice of well-intentioned friends will guide you to Monterey and Cannery Row. According to brilliant American writer and native son John Steinbeck, Cannery Row was "a poem, a stink, a grating noise, a quality of light, a tone, a habit, a nostalgia, a dream." Now it's all this, plus some tacky tourist shops. Fisherman's Wharf is part carnival midway, where merchants seem to believe that the world's problems could be solved if everyone ate "chowder in a bun," a concoction that looks suspiciously like a bread bowl full of vomit. To be fair, the vibe is changing as new luxury hotels and spas move in, and if you're in town during July's Red Bull U.S. Grand Prix at the Mazda Raceway Laguna Seca, the entire street is closed for all but motorcycles who get front and center parking at all Cannery Row locations.

Above all, the definitive attraction is the **Monterey Bay Aquarium** (886 Cannery Row, 831/648-4888, www.montereybayaquarium.org, $29.95). More than 100 galleries and exhibits highlight the diverse habitats of the bay, and most are larger than life. In addition to the million-gallon outer bay exhibit, there are whale skeletons, a stingray petting pool, and an otter exhibit (did you know otters have pockets?). If you don't scuba dive, the aquarium is a good substitute, and the outdoor promenade puts you on the 50-yard line of the pounding waves.

From here, you can return to Carmel via 17-Mile Drive or work your way over to PCH and take the Ocean Avenue exit back.

PULL IT OVER: CARMEL AREA HIGHLIGHTS
Attractions and Adventures

John Steinbeck was one of our greatest writers, and his favorite topic, America, places his works among the best road-reading material you'll find. The **Steinbeck Center** (1 Main St., Salinas, 831/796-3833, www.steinbeck.org, $11) celebrates his life and work. Open 10 A.M.–5 P.M. daily, the center exhibits items taken from the pages of his books, but the focal point is his GMC camper, Rocinante, from *Travels with Charley*—the inspiring cross-country journey he made with his poodle. If you love Steinbeck, you'll love the 30,000-piece archives that include original manuscripts, oral histories, first editions, photographs, and gifts in the museum store

Hey, Nanook! Wanna see a seal up close? Kayaks are big in this area, and you can rent them from **Adventures by the Sea** (299 Cannery Row, 831/372-1807, www.adventuresbythesea.com) as well as **Monterey Bay Kayaks** (693 Del Monte Ave., 831/373-5357 or 800/649-5357, www.montereybaykayaks.com). Each charges $30 per day, $50 for a docent-led guided tour that explains the bay's natural history as you paddle among the harbor seals, kelp forests, sea lions, otters, snowy egrets, and tourists. The bay is protected from large swells, so it should be smooth sailing.

Besides the sea, there are ranch lands inland to explore. You can ride trails in Carmel Valley at **Molera Horseback Tours** (831/625-5486 or 800/942-5486, www.molerahorsebacktours.com), which depart from and ride through a 4,800-acre state park and onto the adjacent beach. Rates range from $50–70 for 1.5–2.5-hour rides that wind through groves of sycamore and ancient redwood trees, beds of clover and fern, across the Big Sur River, and along the sandy Pacific shore. Rides depart at various times, with a special sunset ride that's magical.

Okey-doke, Icarus, here are a few aerial adventures for you. Forty-five minutes away in Hollister (where a biker's bacchanal inspired *The Wild One*), **Bay Area Glider Rides** (Hollister Airport, 831/636-3799 or 888/467-6276, www.bayareagliderrides.com) features introductory sailplane rides and lessons from $139, thrill-seeker rides from $299, and a pricy but unforgettable one-hour $400 soaring adventure that will glide back to Monterey and out over the Pacific. If you've never flown in a sailplane before, it's akin to riding a bike in the sky.

People who call you crazy for riding a motorcycle would bust a vessel if they saw you cavorting with the folks at **Skydive Monterey Bay** (721 Neeson Rd., Marina, 888/229-5867, www.skydivemontereybay.com). After just 15–20 minutes of training, you can take the world's highest tandem fall—from 18,000 feet! If you're motivated, it offers accelerated free-fall and static-line training programs. Reservations are suggested for the $159 first jump. Naturally you'll pay in advance.

The draw at Laguna Seca, an unusual county park and campground hybrid about 20 minutes northeast of Carmel, is the **Mazda Raceway Laguna Seca** (Hwy. 68, 831/242-8201 or 800/327-7322, www.mazdaraceway.com). Only one motorcycle race is held here each year, but that may be enough to make it worth a visit. In July, the Red Bull US Grand Prix Moto GP World Championship draws SBK and AMA riders to a super showdown.

Shopping

Even though there are stores upon stores upon stores in Carmel, you can have a good time just window-shopping and then dropping into at least two must-sees. **Wings America** (Dolores St. and 7th Ave., 831/626-9464, www.wingsamerica.com) presents aviation accent pieces, flight jackets, signed pictures, tropical shirts, aviation scarves, nearly full-size models, and aerodynamically dynamic accessories designed with an aviation theme. A revolving line of unique memorabilia has included a prop from a DC-6 and a tile from space shuttle *Columbia*. Buy several thousand and build your own spacecraft. The same person owns **Boatworks** (Ocean Ave. at Lincoln St., 831/626-1870, www.boatworkscarmel.com), which is nautical and nice. Like its high-flying counterpart, this shop sells cool clothes, nautical instruments, great steamship posters, ship models, and unusual items like a WWII Japanese sextant. If you made the mistake of ordering the optional boat rack from your bike dealer, you can put it to use with a sleek $28,000 wooden canoe. Both are open 9:30 A.M.–6 P.M. daily.

Blue-Plate Specials

Katy's Place (Mission St. between 5th and 6th Aves., 831/624-0199, www.katysplace-carmel.com) has one of the largest breakfast and lunch menus in Californi-yi-yay, even offering 10 varieties of eggs Benedict alone. Joining the lineup: blintzes, pancakes, hash, burritos, omelettes, French toast, buckwheat cakes, bacon, sausage, steak, eggs, cereal, bagels, and muffins.

In a cozy cottage with a fireplace, **Em Le's** (Pantiles Court Delores between 5th and 6th Aves., 831/625-6780) is hot at breakfast with French toast, omelettes, pancakes, and fresh orange juice. At lunch, the menu switches to burgers, sandwiches, soups, and salads. In addition to having a soda fountain, it serves beer and wine.

There's a fine Italian restaurant at **Il Fornaio** (Ocean Ave. at Monte Verde St., 831/622-5115), but I recommend trying its adjacent bakery for a casual breakfast. This is where the locals go for conversation, coffee, and quiet. It's not fancy, but it smells great and the rounded, draped room features a fireplace and newspapers.

You'll look like a local if you drop in for breakfast or lunch at the **Tuck Box** (Dolores St. between Ocean and 7th Aves., 831/624-6365, www.tuckbox.com), a nonlinear fairytale cottage/breakfast nook. Even if you don't eat breakfast, you need to see this place. One of Comstock's original cottages, it seems it's somewhere beyond the looking glass. Here since 1940, it opens at 7 A.M.

Watering Holes

It's hard, but not impossible, while in Carmel to find a place to have a quiet brew and talk with friends. If there's a designated rider, nightspots on Monterey's Cannery Row have replaced sardines as the main source of commerce.

A local tradition for food and drink since the 1970s, the setting at **Jack London's Bar & Grill** (Dolores St. between 5th and 6th Aves., 831/624-2336, www.jacklondons.com) will seduce you. Tucked inside Su Vecino Courtyard, it's a quiet and secluded place to relax. The menu here offers burgers, calamari, steaks, and Mexican dishes that are all just precursors to a pint in the outdoor setting. Kick back for a while and take advantage of the full bar, seven TVs, and 10 beers on tap.

Forge in the Forest (5th Ave. and Junipero St., 831/624-2233, www.forgeintheforest.com) also has a cool outdoor dining area and an even cooler saloon. If you travel in a pack (like the animal you are), set up your summit meeting at the brick-thick 15-foot table. The place is cluttered with antlers, skates, maps, and dozens of restroom signs, which you'll give thanks for after polishing off a Bass or Spaten Pils.

Shut-Eye

About 50 bed-and-breakfasts and hotels dot the peninsula. And even though Carmel reeks of wealth, rates are remarkably reasonable. If everything's booked in town, numerous chain hotels can be found in nearby Monterey.

Inn-dependence

Tops in my book (and it *is* my book) is **La Playa** (Camino Real and 8th Ave., 831/624-6476 or 800/582-8900, www.laplayahotel.com, $190 and up), a large and gorgeous Mediterranean hotel a few blocks from the ocean. The building's design, character, gardens, pool, and flowers all combine to make this a spectacular choice. A second-floor terrace restaurant and five cottages make it even nicer. Much more affordable, in the heart of the village is the **Normandy Inn** (Ocean Ave. and Monte Verde St., 831/624-3825 or 800/343-3825, www.normandyinncarmel.com, $98 and up). This is an excellent choice, with a collection of buildings and cottages connected by shaded courtyards. Large rooms that feature featherbeds and mini-fridges are pricier; some have fireplaces, and all include a continental breakfast. There's also a pool. Carmel offers more than enough choices, but the **Seven Gables Inn** (555 Ocean View Blvd., 831/372-4341, www. pginns.com, $175–385), in appealing Pacific Grove, is another option. The classic Victorian may seem a far cry from what motorcycle travelers are looking for, but the view from the bay window may be enough to compensate. A full breakfast, four o'clock tea, and a park across the street round out the amenities.

Chain Drive

These chain hotels are in town, or within 10 miles of the city center:

Best Western, Clarion, Comfort Inn, Days Inn, Doubletree, Econo Lodge, Embassy Suites, Hilton, Holiday Inn, Howard Johnson, Hyatt, Knights Inn, La Quinta, Motel 6, Quality Inn, Ramada, Rodeway, Super 8, Travelodge

For more information, including phone numbers and websites, see page 151.

SIDE TRIP: CARMEL TO SAN SIMEON

If you have a fear of heights, consider this ride a pleasant form of aversion therapy. As natural forces continue to pound boulders into pebbles on the shoreline, you'll rise above it all on this 112-mile route that scribbles along the Pacific Ocean. There's a reason why this is one of motorcycle travelers' most favored rides. It combines slow curves, sharp turns, and elevations magnified by the view of mountains and sea.

Watch for the sign south of Carmel: Curves ahead next 74 miles. But unlike the psychologically brutal Stinson Beach/ Muir Beach/Tamalpais Valley ride, you can experience these slow curves and broad vistas without fear of death. In other words, this ride doesn't challenge your mortality; it affirms your vitality.

As you ride south, get used to miles of weaving curves that foreshadow upcoming jolts of adrenaline. You'll want to keep an eye open for loose gravel and unpaved shoulders that mark these roads. You'll also want to make sure your brakes are in working order, because you'll stop often to photograph the handsome cliffs and endless ocean. This is a sustained pleasure that spikes about 30 miles into the run, when you take your bike across the fabled Bixby Creek Bridge. Get those cameras ready, folks.

Construction on the "Rainbow" started in 1919 and took until 1937 to complete, but it was worth the wait. Thanks to some anonymous engineers and the fact that you wanted to get out of the house, you're riding 260 feet above sea level on a 718-foot race to the other side of the mountain.

After this jolt, the road is like a Chesterfield—it satisfies for the next 20 miles. When you arrive in Big Sur, you may start looking for the commercial district but you won't find it here. Big Sur is a decentralized region where residents enjoy the solitude and don't feel compelled to build city halls and shopping malls. That's the reason why writers and artists come here, and where Henry Miller rediscovered his creative spark while living in an abandoned convict labor camp.

Hearst Castle

Hearst Castle (Hwy. 1, 805/927-2020 for recorded information or 800/444-4445 for reservations, www.hearstcastle.org, $24) reminds me of my first apartment—except this place has 165 rooms, 30 fireplaces, and 127 acres of gardens. If not for Hearst Castle, San Simeon (pop. 18) would be nothing surrounded by nothing else. But after losing three runs for political office, William Randolph Hearst decided that his bid for immortality would come not through ballots, but through building.

Everything begins at the visitors center, where you buy a ticket for the mansion that includes the National Geographic IMAX movie *Hearst Castle, Building the Dream,* which describes how the castle was designed, built, and decorated. Then you'll board a bus for a long and winding ride to the mansion.

The scale here is off the scale: Guesthouses are the size of overwhelming mansions; the gardens are Edenic; the dining room is royal. A seductive and sensual outdoor pool holds 345,000 gallons of spring water, and a smaller indoor Roman pool contains a paltry 205,000 gallons. Furnishings are equally dazzling, and it's worth noting that Hearst had so much extra stuff stashed in a warehouse that he could have built five more castles. At least, that's what Bob the Tour Guide said.

The home is now owned by the citizens of California. Don't be jealous. They also own San Quentin.

The most active address on this stretch of road is **Nepenthe** (48510 Hwy. 1, 831/667-2345, www.nepenthebigsur.com), a stop as necessary for motorcyclists as breathing. Constructed around land and a log cabin once owned by Orson Welles and Rita Hayworth, Nepenthe (Greek for "sorrow banisher") was purchased by Lolly and Bill Fassett and expanded by Rowan Maiden, a disciple of Frank Lloyd Wright. Today, it is a restaurant/overlook where lunch includes such fare as broiled swordfish sandwiches and the famous Ambrosia Burger; sunset dinners focus on steaks and fresh fish. Even if you're not hungry, stop here and feast on the view from the terrace, 800 feet above the shoreline. From this height, the surf below sounds like muffled cannons and adds another memorable experience to your journey.

A quarter mile south of Nepenthe, the **Henry Miller Library** (Hwy. 1, 831/667-2574, www.henrymiller.org) is more of an artists' village than a library, but people still stop. It's open Wednesday–Monday (closed Tuesday) 11 A.M.–6 P.M. Beyond this, PCH gets back into the rugged and exhilarating coastline you've come to love. Within miles, you'll be riding past different environments—ocean, desert, pine forests—each constantly interchanging. One other thing you should be on the lookout for are riders and drivers who've granted Highway 1 status as a test track. It's tempting to race, but it's better to live.

There are few places in the nation more

suited to your purpose. Take advantage of turnouts, where you can just park it and watch the water swallowing rocks the size of mountains and pounding the hell out of monoliths. In some spots, the water seems as clear as the Caribbean, and a few miles later, the coastline disappears into fog.

As you ride south, you'll experience the satisfaction that comes with knowing you're six feet closer to the ocean than those poor bastards in the oncoming lane. When you reach the small town of Gorda there's a convenient service station and general store. From here, the rises are subtle and surprises appear, like views of the ocean that open up and show you 200-foot cliffs that reach down to the sea.

The final miles to **Hearst Castle** (Hwy. 1, 805/927-2020 for recorded information or 800/444-4445 for reservations, www. hearstcastle.org, $24) lose their scenic punch, but I promise that you will look back on this run and agree that this—like your ride across America—was everything you expected it to be. It was dangerous within limits, vast beyond measure, and beautiful beyond description.

Resources for Riders

Pacific Coast Run

California Travel Information
California Association of Bed & Breakfast Inns—800/373-9251, www.cabbi.com
California Division of Tourism—916/444-4429 or 800/862-2543,
   www.visitcalifornia.com
California Road Conditions—800/427-7623
California State Parks—916/653-6995, www.parks.ca.gov
California Weather Information—916/979-3051

Local and Regional Information
Calistoga Chamber of Commerce—707/942-6333 or 866/306-5588,
   www.calistogachamber.com
Carmel Visitors Center—831/624-2522 or 800/550-4333, www.carmelcalifornia.org
Monterey Peninsula Visitors Bureau—888/221-1010 or 877/666-8373,
   www.montereyinfo.org
Napa Valley Visitors Bureau—707/226-5813, www.legendarynapavalley.org
Pacific Grove Chamber of Commerce—831/373-3304 or 800/656-6650,
   www.pacificgrove.org
Sausalito Chamber of Commerce—415/331-7262, www.sausalito.org
Sonoma County Visitors Bureau—707/522-5800 or 800/576-6662,
   www.sonomacounty.com

California Motorcycle Shops
BMW Motorcycles of San Francisco—790 Bryant St., San Francisco,
   415/503-9988, www.bmwmotorcycle.com
California Choppers—1490 Howard St., San Francisco, 415/431-8181,
   www.californiachoppers.com
Dudley Perkins Harley-Davidson—333 Corey Way, So. South Francisco,
   650/737-5467, www.dpchd.com
Golden Gate Cycles—1540 Pine St., San Francisco, 415/771-4535,
   www.goldengatecycles.com
Golden Gate Harley-Davidson/Buell—7077 Redwood Blvd., Novato,
   415/878-4988, www.gghd.com
Monterey County Harley-Davidson—333 N. Main St., Salinas, 831/424-1909,
   www.montereycountyhd.com
Monterey Peninsula Powersports—1020 Auto Center Pkwy., Seaside,
   831/899-7433, www.sports-center.com
North Bay Motorsports—2875 Santa Rosa Ave., Santa Rosa, 707/542-5355,
   www.northbaymotorsport.com
Salinas Motorcycle Center—1286 N. Main St., Salinas, 831/442-3511 or
   800/750- 2953, www.salinasmc.com
Santa Rosa BMW—800 American Way, Windsor, 707/838-9100,
   www.santarosabmw.com
Santa Rosa Powersports—910 Santa Rosa Ave., Santa Rosa, 707/545-1672,
   www.santarosapowersports.com
Santa Rosa Vee Twin—1240 Petaluma Hill Rd., Santa Rosa, 707/523-9696,
   www.santarosaveetwin.com

Resources

MOTORCYCLE WEBSITES

Great American Motorcycle Tours
www.motorcycleamerica.com
Partner site for this book, with abridged ride descriptions, photographs, and links.

Moto-Directory
www.moto-directory.com
Perhaps the best bike site, with roughly 10,000 links to events, rallies, magazines, videos, tours, stolen bike reports, riding clubs, rental operators, dealers, and salvage yards.

Motorcycle Roads—1
www.motorcycleroads.us
Super site with recommendations from riders on popular and seldom traveled roads across America, viewable state-by-state. Links for submitting your favorites and finding travel resources.

Motorcycle Roads—2
www.motorcycleroads.com
Nationwide guide with recommended rides and tours listed state-by-state, graded by scenery, road quality, and roadside amenities, activities, and attractions.

Motorcycle-USA
www.motorcycle-usa.com
News, product reviews, bike tests, photo galleries, classifieds, message boards, and ride ratings.

Trader Online
www.cycletrader.com
The online version of the popular *Trader* magazines. Search by model, size, year, price, location, etc.

Harley-Davidson Links
www.hdlinks.com
Connections to H-D and other American motorcycle related sites.

Motorcycle Accessories Warehouse
800/241-2222
www.accwhse.com
Parts, supplies, and thousands of links to clothes and closeouts, from goggles to tank covers.

Motorcycle Online
www.motorcycle.com
Digital motorcycle magazine with bikes, products, reviews, videos, clubs, events, how-tos, rides, classifieds, financing, and chats.

Rider Magazine
www.ridermagazine.com
Links to *Rider* and *American Rider* magazines, archives, and ride maps.

Sport-Touring
www.sport-touring.net
Extensive discussion forum for tour, tech, and sales information.

SELECTED MANUFACTURERS

Most manufacturers' sites will lead to showrooms, accessories, clothing, riders clubs, FAQs, dealers, and riding products.

BMW
800/831-1117
www.bmwmotorcycles.com

Buell
www.buell.com

Ducati
www.ducati.com

Harley-Davidson
800/258-2464
www.harley-davidson.com

Honda
310/532-9811 or 866/784-1870
www.hondamotorcycle.com

Kawasaki
800/661-7433
www.kawasaki.com

Moto Guzzi
www.motoguzzi.it

Suzuki
www.suzukicycles.com

Triumph
678/854-2010
www.triumph.co.uk

Victory
www.victory-usa.com

Yamaha
800/889-2624
www.yamaha-motor.com

SELECTED MOTORCYCLE ORGANIZATIONS

American Motorcyclist Association
800/262-5646
www.ama-cycle.org
If you belong to one motorcycling organization, make it the AMA. The association sponsors thousands of sanctioned events and provides a monthly magazine, trip routing, hotel discounts, and club information for approximately 250,000 members.

Motorcycle Events Association
727/343-1049 or 866/203-4485
www.motorcycleevents.com
Provides information on Daytona, Sturgis, Laconia, and other major rallies as well as charity rides and motorcycle shows across America.

Motorcycle Product News
800/722-8764
www.mpnmag.com
Lists products, distributors, manufacturers, parts, and accessories; primarily used by dealers and rental operators.

Motorcycle Riders Foundation
202/546-0983 or
800/673-5646
www.mrf.org
Lobbying group for riders' rights, with links.

Motorcycle Safety Foundation
800/446-9227
www.msf-usa.org
Offers safe riding courses throughout the United States; participation can lower your insurance rates. Also features information on rider training and industry contacts.

SELECTED RIDING CLUBS
American Gold Wing Association
www.agwa.com

Blue Knights
207/947-4600 or 877/254-5362
www.blueknights.org

BMW Motorcycle Owners of America
636/394-7277
www.bmwmoa.org

Christian Motorcyclists Association
870/389-6196
www.cmausa.org

Gold Wing Road Riders Association
623/581-2500 or 800/843-9460
www.gwrra.org

Harley Owners Group
800/258-2464
www.hog.com

Honda Riders Club of America
800/847-4722
www.hrca.honda.com

Motorcycle Clubs & Associations
www.moto-directory.com/clubs.asp

Riders of Kawasaki
877/765-2582
www.kawasaki.com/rok

Women on Wheels
800/322-1969
www.womenonwheels.org

SELECTED RALLIES
Each year across the country, there are thousands of rallies of all shapes and sizes. Here are links to some of the largest—visit their websites for upcoming dates. Most rally sites include information on registration, rides, vendors, lodging, histories, and entertainment.

Americade Motorcycle Rally
518/798-7888
www.tourexpo.com
Lake George, New York

Bikes, Blues & BBQ Motorcycle Rally
479/527-9993
www.bikesbluesandbbq.org
Fayetteville, Arkansas

Bike Week and Biketoberfest
386/255-0981 (Bike Week)
www.officialbikeweek.com
386/255-0415 or 800/854-1234
(Biketoberfest)
www.biketoberfest.org
Daytona Beach, Florida

Laconia Rally
603/366-2000
www.laconiamcweek.com
Laconia, New Hampshire

Sturgis Rally and Races
605/720-0800
www.sturgismotorcyclerally.com
Sturgis, South Dakota

SELECTED MOTORCYCLE RENTAL COMPANIES

California Motorcycle Rentals
858/456-9577
www.calif-motorcyclerental.com

EagleRider Motorcycle Rental
310/536-6777 or 888/900-9901
www.eaglerider.com
Nationwide service, renting fully equipped Road Kings, Softails, Fat Boys, and Electra Glides. Locations in America, Mexico, and Europe. Also conducts tours.

Harley Motorcycle Rental
415/456-9910 or 888/812-9253
www.motohaven.net
Novato, California

Motorcycle Rental Resource Page
www.harleys.com/mrrp.html
Rental operators listed by state.

Route 66 Riders Motorcycle Rentals
310/578-0112 or 888/434-4473
www.route66riders.com
Marina Del Ray, California

GENERAL TRAVEL INFORMATION

Historic Hotels of America
800/678-8946
www.historichotels.org
Affiliated with the National Trust for Historic Preservation, HHA is a diverse collection of uniquely American lodgings, from rustic inns to elegant hotels. Rates at these member properties may be on the high end, but if you split the costs, you may do all right.

Kampgrounds of America (KOA)
www.koa.com
Information on more than 500 campgrounds nationwide.

Mad Maps
www.madmaps.com
Superb, informative motorcycle maps custom-designed to highlight scenic roads and popular routes across the country.

MapQuest
www.mapquest.com
Trip planning, route, and mileage information.

National Forest Service
www.fs.fed.us
Links to national forests and campgrounds.

National Parks Camping Reservations
800/436-7275 or 877/444-6777
www.recreation.gov
A one-call-books-all national company that handles reservations for 45,000 campsites at 1,700 national forest campgrounds across America. Books for most national parks, but does not include state parks.

National Park Foundation
202/354-6460 or 888/467-2757
www.nationalparks.org
Partner site of America's national parks, designed to introduce you to the parks and assist in trip-planning.

National Park Service

www.nps.gov
Central point for links to parks and recreation, history and culture, nature, science, interpretation, and education.

Road Conditions

www.usroadconditions.com
Links to information on road conditions in every state.

Road Trip USA

www.roadtripusa.com
Eleven cross-country riding routes to get you off the beaten path and onto pre-interstate roads.

Scenic Byways

www.byways.org
An excellent site detailing thousands of miles of scenic byways and back roads across the nation. Also offers links for trip-planning and personal journals.

State Motorcycle and Helmet Laws

www.amadirectlink.com/legisltn/laws.asp

State and National Park Links

www.llbean.com/parksearch

State Parks

www.stateparks.com
Comprehensive state-by-state listing with contact information, links, and information on hundreds of state parks.

State Park Reservations

www.reserveamerica.com
Facilitates campsite reservations for many state and private parks and campgrounds in North America.

Weather Channel

www.weather.com

ROAD TIPS

America the Beautiful Pass

Each year, America's National Parks are visited more than 265 million times, a figure totaling more fans and guests than visit NFL games, Disney parks, and Universal Studios attractions combined. If you plan to visit more than one national park, invest in the National Parks pass. For $80, the pass will provide admission to any national park for a full year. You're 62 or older? Even better—the cost drops to $10! How far will your money go? As far as 80.7 million acres of park land at 379 national parks, from Acadia in Maine to Zion in Utah, all cared for and explained by more than 20,000 rangers, archaeologists, historians, biologists, architects, laborers, and gardeners.

Food Faves

One of my favorite vocations while riding is finding great roadside diners along the highway or in a village. Two of my favorite American writers are Jane and Michael Stern, who, in addition to writing the classic *Elvis World*, wrote *Eat Your Way Across the USA: 500 Diners, Lobster Shacks, Buffets, Pie Palaces, and Other All-American Eateries*. While my book can lead you to a handful of restaurants, their book is a buffet of great American greasy spoons, hash houses, doughnut shops, cafeterias, and small-town cafés.

Offbeat USA

If your motivation to ride is partially fueled by the chance discovery of kitsch Americana, check out www.roadsideamerica.com. This site is the online guide to offbeat tourist attractions, and it may provide you with some side-trip ideas when you're in the vicinity of places like the Zippo Lighter Visitors Center in Bradford, PA, or the giant advertising statues that still plug businesses across the United States.

Selecting an Organized Tour

As the popularity of motorcycles grows, so does the proliferation of motorcycle tour operators. If you decide to ride on a prearranged trip, there are two constants you'll encounter: You will need a major credit card and a motorcycle endorsement on your license. There are also several variables. For instance, you may or may not need to bring your own bike, helmet, or rain gear.

With these variances, play it smart by asking the "stupid" questions. Ask who covers specific expenses: lodging, meals, tolls, fuel, laundry, tips, insurance. What type of lodging can you expect? Is it a flophouse, campground, or inn? Private bath? Shared rooms? Carrying a passenger will cost extra—how much? As you sift through these questions, also ask if you'll be allowed to break away from the group and meet them later. Is there a guide? A support vehicle? A trained mechanic? Does the ride include overnights, or do you return to the same city each evening?

Make sure that if your ride is cancelled because of inclement weather, your deposit will be refunded (you may want to safeguard your investment by taking out traveler's cancellation insurance).

CHAIN HOTEL GUIDE

Best Western
800/528-1234
www.bestwestern.com

Clarion
800/252-7466
www.choicehotels.com

Comfort Inn
800/221-2222
www.choicehotels.com

Courtyard by Marriott
800/321-2211
www.marriott.com

Days Inn
800/329-7466
www.daysinn.com

Doubletree
800/222-8733
www.doubletree.com

Econo Lodge
800/553-2666
www.choicehotels.com

Embassy Suites
800/362-2779
www.embassy-suites.com

Fairfield Inn
800/228-2800
www.fairfieldinn.com

Hampton Inn
800/426-7866
www.hampton-inn.com

Hilton
800/445-8667
www.hilton.com

Holiday Inn
800/465-4329
www.holiday-inn.com

Howard Johnson
800/446-4656
www.hojo.com

Hyatt
800/233-1234
www.hyatt.com

Knights Inn
800/843-5644
www.knightsinn.com

La Quinta
800/687-6667
www.laquinta.com

Motel 6
800/466-8356
www.motel6.com

Omni Hotels
800/843-6664
www.omnihotels.com

Quality Inn
800/228-5151
www.qualityinn.com

Radisson
800/333-3333
www.radisson.com

Ramada
800/272-6232
www.ramada.com

Red Carpet Inn
800/251-1962
www.reservahost.com

Red Roof Inn
800/843-7663
www.redroof.com

Residence Inn
800/331-3131
www.mariott.com

Rodeway
800/228-2000
www.rodewayinn.com

Scottish Inns
800/251-1962
www.reservahost.com

Sheraton
800/325-3535
www.sheraton.com

Sleep Inn
800/627-5337
www.sleepinn.com

Super 8
800/800-8000
www.super8.com

Travelodge
800/578-7878
www.travelodge.com

Acknowledgments

It's never far from my mind that an ongoing project like this requires assistance from others—and I've had it. There are hundreds of people across the nation who've pitched in to make this possible. As always, they're listed in order of their favorite Beatle.

John Lennon: John McKechnie, Bud McKechnie, Ian McKechnie, all McKechnies everywhere, Peter Fonda, Kevin McLain, Darren Alessi, Donna Galassi, Peg Goldstein, Cassandra Conyers, Dianna Delling, Robyn McPeters, Mike Zimmerman, Jennifer Gruber, Amanda Lee, Ty van Hooydonk, Michelle Greco, Joel Cliff, Walter Yeldell, Carrie Saldo, Beth Krauss, Ron Dusek, Jennifer Williams, Mary Ann McClain, Matthew Carinhas, Evelynn Bailey, David Lorenz, Amy Seng, Mike Norton, Andy Moon, Mike Houck, Dana Alley, George Milo, Ken Thompson, Jessica Icenhour, Fred Good, Jana Greenbaum, Chuck Haralson, Ken Grimsley, Lisa Richardson, Tracy Brown, Alissa Clark, Bill Seratt, Mary Beth Romig, Carl Whitehill, Anne Barney, Tessy Shirakawa, Bronwyn Patterson, Marci Penner, Kathy Giffin, Cindy Andrus, Chad Sterns, Dan Bookham, Valerie Ryan, Jimmy Sample, Jeff Feldman, Eden Umble, Celeste White, Heather Hermen, Walter Yeldell, Barbara Golden, Jennifer Haz, Erik Skindrud, Lou Ann Nelson, Heather Falk, David Fantle, Jon Jarosh, Jeri Riggs, Lynn Berry, Nick Noyes, Jo Sabel Courtney, John Formichella, Anne Marie Basher, Nancy Arena, Ruth Parsons, Stacey Fox, Philip Magaldi, Charles Hardin, Melody Heltman, Erika Backus, Rich Wittish, Chris Nobles, Melina Martinez, Michelle Revuelta, Josie Gulliksen, Emy Bullard Wilkinson, Beverly Gianna, Jon Jarosh, George Milos, Jezal McNeil, Phil Lampert, Kelly Barbello, Kim Latrielle, Judy Siring, Jay Humphries, Anne Barney, Sandy Smith, Kim Cobb....

Paul McCartney: Jean James, Lin Lee, Susan Albrecht, Patricia Kiderlen, Lynn Dyer, Judith Swain, Suzanne Elder, Phyllis Reller, Karen Baker, Gwen Peterson, Tony Fortier, Ken McNenny, Susan Sullivan, Pepper Massey-Swan, Karen Connelly, Liz Porter, Steve Lewis, Shelly Clark, Susie Haver, Jenny Stacy, Susan Belanski, Jack Dunlavy, Phillip Magdali Jr., Paula Tirrito, Steven Skavroneck, Valerie Parker, Joel Frey, Lenore Barkley, Jan Osterman, Howard

Gray, Christine DeCuir, Sandy Tucker, Don Sparks, DeRoy Jenson, Ed and Minna Williams, Rennie Ross, Didi Bushnell, Jim Pelletier, Stan Corneil, Chris Mackey, Amy Ballenger, Jeff Ehoodin, Jeff Webster, Nina Kelly, Todd Morgan, Dave Blanford, Nancy Borino, Tom Lyons, Krista Elias, Shannon Mackie-Albert, Carolyn Hackney, Rachel Keating, Maureen Oltrogge, Mike Finney, Julia Scott, Sue Bland, Natasha Johnston, Janie McCullough, Laura Simoes, Tessie Shirwakawa, Aimee Grove, Melanie Ryan, Steve Lewis, Jan Mellor, Jennifer Wess, Kathy Lambert, Dwayne Cassidy, Ron Terry, Erika Yowell, Kathleen New, Wyndham Lewis, Dennis Cianci, Marjie Wright, Karen Hamill, Sue Ellen Peck, Tom Hash, Rick Gunn....

George Harrison: Rick Wilder, Ken Crouse, Donna Bonnefin, Pettit Gilwee, Keith Walklet, Amy Herzog, Susan Carvalho, Kathy Langley, Kirk Komick, Jennifer Franklin, Mike Pitel, Jody Bernard, Sarah Pitcher, Nancy Brockman, Paul Schreiner, Bev Owens, Billy Dodd, Heather Deville, Sarah Baker, Joel Howard, Annie Kuehls, Bob and Paula Glass, Troy Duvall, Matt Bolas, Carrie Clark, Trey Hines, Tony Hayden, Chris Jones, Haley Gingles, Greg Lasiewski, Jan Plessner, Tim Buche, Cheryl Smith, Trish Taylor, Hal Williams, Emily Raabe, Cara O'Donnell, Alan Rosenzweig, Barbara Ashley, Janet Dutson, Mary Bennoch, Jeff Lupo, John and Diane Sheiry, Croft Long, Mel Moore, Mark Kayser, Lisa Umiker, Rich Gates, Ray Towells, Julie Smith, Scott Gediman, Mike Dorn, Wendy Haase, Jan Dorfler, Mary Cochran, Traci Varner, Dirk Oldenburg, Mark Reese, Scott Heath, Linda Adams....

Ringo Starr: Trevor and Regina Aldhurst, Rosemary and Fabrizio Chiarello, Frank and Mary Newton, Mary Beth Hutchinson, Anna Maria Dalton, Karen Hedelt, Emily Case, Pauli Galin, Carol Jones, Sue Mauro, Beth Culbertson, Ron Gardner, Ellen Gillespie, Timothy James Trifeletti, Carrie Wilkinson-Tuma, Elmer Thomas, Nancy and Tom Blackford, Karen Suffredini, Mike McGuinn, Susan Williams, Virginia Mure, Ron and Sue Ramage, Leslie Prevish and Joe Hice....

Pete Best: Every engineer, surveyor, road crew, and chain gang that helped build America's beautiful back roads.

About the Author

© NANCY HOWELL

Gary Mckechnie

As an advertising copywriter, Gary McKechnie spent his days writing about how consumers could design a better life. Influenced by his own writing, he decided to design a better life for himself. He started by quitting his job.

The decision was in line with earlier steps Gary took to make sure that his life would be consistently interesting. He put himself through college as a stand-up comedian and skipper on Walt Disney World's Jungle Cruise. The morning after graduating, he didn't report to a new job—he hopped on a flight to Europe instead, the beginning of a seven-month backpacking and hitchhiking excursion across the continent.

Returning to the United States, Gary earned enough money through a series of short-term jobs to enjoy long-term travel. He began exploring America by motorcycle and by car, and eventually decided on a career that would subsidize his vacations: writing travel features for newspapers and magazines. In 2000, he completed the 20,000-mile motorcycle odyssey that resulted in the first edition of *Great American Motorcycle Tours*. It became the first motorcycle guidebook to receive two awards: the Lowell Thomas Travel Journalism Award (recognized as the Pulitzer Prize of travel writing) and the Benjamin Franklin Gold Award, presented by the Publisher's Marketing Association.

In addition to taking lengthy road trips for subsequent editions of *Great American Motorcycle Tours*, Gary conducted an intensive national tour to research the places, events, and festivals that collectively create the American Experience. The result of his efforts was his next book, *USA 101*, published in May 2009. It has been featured in local, regional, and national media, and is one of only two *National Geographic* travel publications recommended by the American Library Association's *Booklist*. In December 2009, Gary became a speaker for Cunard Insights, presenting his views on America aboard the *Queen Mary 2*.

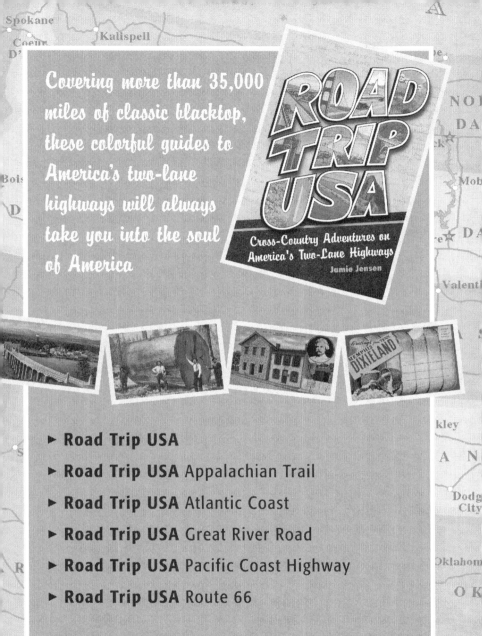

Covering more than 35,000 miles of classic blacktop, these colorful guides to America's two-lane highways will always take you into the soul of America

ROAD TRIP USA

Cross-Country Adventures on America's Two-Lane Highways

Jamie Jensen

- ► **Road Trip USA**
- ► **Road Trip USA** Appalachian Trail
- ► **Road Trip USA** Atlantic Coast
- ► **Road Trip USA** Great River Road
- ► **Road Trip USA** Pacific Coast Highway
- ► **Road Trip USA** Route 66

Road Trip USA guidebooks are published by Avalon Travel and available at bookstores and through online retailers.

Find free audio tours, a driver's almanac, blog, and more at RoadTripUSA.com.

Great American
Motorcycle Tours of the West

Avalon Travel
a member of the Perseus Books Group
1700 Fourth Street
Berkeley, CA 94710, USA

Editor: Kevin McLain
Copy Editor: Naomi Adler Dancis
Graphics and Production Coordinator:
  Darren Alessi
Cover and Interior Designer:
  Darren Alessi
Map Editor: Mike Morgenfeld
Cartographers: Kat Bennett, Brice Ticen

ISBN: 978-1-59880-583-3

Front cover photo:
  © Zuki/istockphoto.com
Title page photo: © Nancy Howell
All interior photos: © Nancy Howell

Printed in the United States

Text © 2010 by Gary McKechnie.
Maps © 2010 by Avalon Travel.
All rights reserved.

Some photos and illustrations are used
by permission and are the property of the
original copyright owners.

Avalon Travel and the Avalon Travel logo
are the property of Avalon Travel. All other
marks and logos depicted are the property
of the original owners. All rights reserved.
No part of this book may be translated
or reproduced in any form, except brief
extracts by a reviewer for the purpose of a
review, without written permission of the
copyright owner.

Although every effort was made to
ensure that the information was correct
at the time of going to press, the author
and publisher do not assume and hereby
disclaim any liability to any party for any
loss or damage caused by errors, omissions,
or any potential travel disruption due to
labor or financial difficulty, whether such
errors or omissions result from negligence,
accident, or any other cause.